TAKING LIFE

TAKING LIFE

Three Theories on the Ethics of Killing

Torbjörn Tännsjö

OXFORD
UNIVERSITY PRESS

OXFORD
UNIVERSITY PRESS

Oxford University Press is a department of the University of Oxford. It furthers the University's objective of excellence in research, scholarship, and education by publishing worldwide.

Oxford New York
Auckland Cape Town Dar es Salaam Hong Kong Karachi
Kuala Lumpur Madrid Melbourne Mexico City Nairobi
New Delhi Shanghai Taipei Toronto

With offices in
Argentina Austria Brazil Chile Czech Republic France Greece
Guatemala Hungary Italy Japan Poland Portugal Singapore
South Korea Switzerland Thailand Turkey Ukraine Vietnam

Oxford is a registered trademark of Oxford University Press in the UK and certain other countries.

Published in the United States of America by
Oxford University Press
198 Madison Avenue, New York, NY 10016

Library of Congress Cataloging-in-Publication Data
Tännsjö, Torbjörn, 1946—
Taking life : three theories on the ethics of killing / Torbjörn Tännsjö.
pages cm
Includes bibliographical references and index.
ISBN 978–0–19–022558–2 (pbk. : alk. paper) — ISBN 978–0–19–022557–5 (cloth : alk. paper) 1. Life and death, Power over. 2. Justification (Ethics) I. Title.
BJ1469.T36 2015
179.7—dc23
2014043781

1 3 5 7 9 8 6 4 2
Printed in the United States of America
on acid-free paper

CONTENTS

PREFACE

When I was in my late teens I was already interested in philosophy. But the interest was theoretical. I wanted to know what it means to know something, whether we can know at all, and, if so, how. However, two simultaneous personal experiences drew me to *moral* philosophy. Like all Swedish men, I was conscripted to military service, and my gut feeling was to refuse to serve. I did not want to kill other people. It seemed to me wrong, if not in principle, so at least in practice. There were no serious military threats facing Sweden, and if the situation would change there was no guarantee that I would turn out to be a just rather than an unjust combatant. Moreover, the kind of values for which I was supposed to kill, such as democracy and national independence, were better served, I thought, through non-violent action. This was during the heyday of the civil rights movement in the American South. My arguments were met with no sympathy from the military authorities. They threatened me with jail if I was not prepared to serve.

At the same time my father became ill. It soon turned out to be serious. He suffered from cancer in his liver with metastases in many places of his body. The prediction was that he should be dead within a few months. This prophecy was borne out by reality. My father reacted with good sense and courage to the prophecy. He was sad to leave in such an untimely manner, he told my mother and me, but he had had more than fifty rich years, so he wasn't resentful. And he swiftly took care of all sorts of practical matters relating to his death. However, something he had not expected happened. His sufferings turned out to be unbearable. The medical doctor who treated my father was his personal friend, and my father was given morphine and all sorts of palliative care. However, his pain could not be controlled. His last weeks were terrible. He sometimes fell asleep. When he woke up he was still in a delirious state caused by the morphine, and he asked me, his only child, and my mother, whether he was dead or alive. We had to inform him that he was not yet dead; he had to struggle on for yet awhile longer. He asked his doctor to assist him in his dying. He begged for euthanasia. His doctor turned down his request with the words that euthanasia was not only illegal, but was 'at variance with the principles of medical ethics'. My father's agony increased and culminated in a state of terminal agitation and ended only with his very last choking breath.

I was much concerned with what had happened. It did more than affect me emotionally. I was intellectually in a state of deep confusion. How could it be that I had a legal obligation to kill people I did not know, and who did certainly not consent to it, while my father's doctor could not help my father to die when my father asked for it? My consternation brought me to moral philosophy and a lifelong search for an answer to the question of when and why we should kill, and when we should not. To kill or not to kill, that was the question that haunted me. I began to study the ethics of killing.

The present study started with a preliminary but in many ways similar book in Swedish, *Du skall understundom dräpa* (*Thou Shalt Sometimes Kill*, 2001), which was also published in German (*Ethik des Tötens*, 2007) and in Norwegian (*Noen ganger skal man drepe*, 2008). I have not attempted to translate the old book into English, however. I have started from scratch, so this is a new book in its own right, and I have developed my argument in many ways since I wrote the earlier book, but I rely, in the present book, as I did then, on surveys of the public opinion about crucial forms of killing, such as murder, suicide, assisted death, abortion, the killing in war, and the killing of animals. It is helpful to learn what other people think about these matters, when you want to make up your own mind. Their views do not constitute what I call *considered* intuitions. One must not think that such findings can serve as evidence for any moral theory in particular. They can help you to a better understanding of your own thinking, however. They can help you transcend your own narrow cultural horizon. More about this in the sequel.

I came to realize, however, when I wanted to first survey public opinion in Sweden about these matters, how sensitive the issues were. I had obtained funding from the Swedish Research Council for the survey and I approached the Swedish state authority for official statistics and asked them to perform my survey, only to receive the following letter from the chief executive officer of the authority, called SCB (Statistics Sweden):

> After careful discussions within the authority SCB has decided not to undertake the proposed survey you describe in your letter of 4 February 1999. The reason is that SCB, like other institutes in the world, has very little experience of the gathering of this kind of highly sensitive data. We do not want to risk that a survey like the proposed one should initiate psychological reactions among the respondents that are difficult to handle. We think here of respondents who have suffered in war, who are suicidal, or who have experienced difficult decisions in relation to abortion ... The final decision was taken by the Chief Executive Officer of SCB after a discussion within the board of the office. (My translation)

I do not deny that the problems I discuss are sensitive. However, since they are also in a sense mundane—they are questions we *have* to face now and then in our lives—I think we had better ponder over them. And it is a good idea to do so before any problem of killing becomes a live issue! So I have not hesitated to discuss them, and I have also managed to find another research institute, the private business SIFO, that has taken on the surveys, which have been conducted this time in China, Russia, and the United States. In each country 1,000 people were randomly sampled for my investigation.

When you and I are confronted with these results of the surveys, this helps us, I hope, to transcend some of our cultural biases that tend to stop us from pondering over these problems in the proper, detached way. This is only possible when you sit down and think about them in the cold light of day.

I will pursue my discussion under the assumption that moral facts exist, independently of our thought and conceptualization (the position known as moral realism). It is possible to be mistaken about them. When two moral assertions contradict one another, at least one of them is false. Moral nihilism, the idea that all positive moral assertions are false, since there is no fact of the matter to be right or wrong about, is grotesquely implausible. There are arguments in defence of moral nihilism, from relativity (with regard to actual moral opinions), from queerness (with regard to moral properties), and so forth, but they are less convincing than is often thought.[1] And since moral nihilism has moral implications (all moral theories are false, all particular moral assertions are false as well, according to moral nihilism), we may safely argue from any firm moral belief against moral nihilism. We know, for example, that it is wrong to inflict pain on a sentient being for no reason whatever (doing so makes the world a worse place, we have not promised to do it, the being doesn't deserve it, and so forth). But if this is so, then moral nihilism is false.

However, even if moral realism is true, even if moral facts exist independently of our thought and conceptualization, and even if we have some moral knowledge, this does not mean that we have any *systematic* moral knowledge. I believe we can approach such systematic moral knowledge, however. This means, though, that we must be careful in our choice of a method of moral investigation. In the

1. I discuss them in chapter 3 of my book *From Reasons to Norms. On the Basic Question in Ethics.*

first chapter of this book I will indicate how I conceive of such a method.

There are several good books on the ethics of killing. Just to mention four excellent examples: Jonathan Glover's *Causing Death and Saving Lives*, Peter Singer's *Practical Ethics*, F. M. Kamm's *Intricate Ethics: Rights, Responsibilities, and Responsible Harm*, and Jeff McMahan's *The Ethics of Killing: Problems at the Margins of Life*. What is special in *this* book, and which distinguishes it from the others, is my methodology. I am sceptical of any attempt to establish moral principles through swift and abstract arguments. In this respect I am more sceptical than Glover and Singer. It is not possible to show that a moral principle is true in the abstract. Moral principles always surprise us in concrete applications. We need therefore a more indirect, and inductive, method. We need to tease out the implications of various *different* moral hypotheses in particular cases and confront them with the content of our considered intuitions. Are the hypotheses intuitively adequate—are their implications compatible with the content of our considered intuitions? Can they explain the content of our considered intuitions? If several hypotheses are intuitively adequate, which one among them gives the *best* explanation of the content of our intuitions? Once we know that, we can make an inference to the best explanation of our intuitions. We have evidence in support of the hypothesis (or, we say more cautiously, that it has been corroborated). In this respect I am *less* sceptical than Kamm and McMahan. I believe it is reasonable to search for a single principle that can explain the content of all our considered moral intuitions.

In Chapter 1 I present and defend my very special methodological approach in more detail. I *tell* you in that chapter about the method I put to use in this book and I *argue* that it is a good method. My 'vindication'[2] of the method is, in the final analysis, pragmatic in nature. We do not know whether a comprehensible true moral

2. In Herbert Feigle's sense of the word. See his 'Validation and Vindication' for a discussion.

theory exists in the first place; however, only if we resort to the method I advocate will we be able to unravel it—if indeed it does exist. In the rest of the book I try to *show* how moral understanding can be obtained, within one narrow field: the ethics of killing.

In a sense this chapter is autobiographic. I present my *own* moral realist (there is a truth out there to be found) and cognitivist (it is within our reach) understanding of my project. I suppose that people who do not share my belief in moral realism and moral cognitivism can understand what I do in *their* favoured terms. My experience is that even some thinkers who are moral irrealists (nihilists) are still willing to do normative ethics. And they are then not just attempting to show that all moral propositions are false, that all putative moral theories are wrong, but they are prepared to search for one of them in particular to cherish. If their project is feasible, it should also be possible to read my book in the light of it. I have my doubts about the feasibility of this project, but I will say no more about these doubts in the present context.

In the simplest terms possible, the book could be described like this, then. I apply three basic moral principles to problems of killing and I discuss whether their various different implications are reasonable or not.

The three basic ideas I discuss are the ones I believe first come to mind. (1) The simple deontological theory that there are certain kinds of actions that are just plain wrong, regardless of their consequences. And if any action is plain wrong in this way, it must be something like the intentional killing of an innocent human being. (2) The idea that we own (at least) ourselves and, hence, are permitted to do as we see fit with ourselves, unless we violate the rights of others. So we are not allowed to kill others against their will but we are allowed to kill ourselves—and we are allowed to kill others at their request. (3) Utilitarianism, the idea that we should maximize the sum total of happiness in the world. On this theory, the end justifies the means and it may sometimes be all right to kill.

With an exception for the concluding chapter, I discuss these theories in their pure forms. My ambition is to be true to the rationales behind them. The theories can, of course, be modified; compromised positions can be sought among them, and so forth. However, my strong impression is that intellectual compromise often comes at too high a price. So at least we should try out the pure forms of the theories before we attempt to find compromises among them.

A strong reason to do so is that each of the three theories has a strong intuitive appeal. If you like good ideas, your initial reaction, when you are at first told about these theories, is probably that you want to hold on to all three of them. However, as we will see, they give conflicting advice in the area I have chosen as my moral laboratory (the ethics of killing). Hence, there is no intellectually and morally acceptable way of accepting them all.

My own considered opinion is that utilitarianism gains the upper hand in the competition I have arranged. It is unique in that it reaches the right conclusions with regard to the different types of killing, and it can explain why these conclusions are the right ones. It can also explain the relative success of the competing theories.

This is a highly controversial claim, of course. Many of my readers will not share it. However, I believe that those who do not share my assessment will yet have *something* to learn from the book. As a matter of fact, the last concluding chapter, where I take stock and sum up the arguments, could have been written in many ways. I have suggested one way, my own preferred one. The reader is invited to re-write—or at least re-think—the concluding chapter for herself!

My hope is that the reading of the book, irrespective of whether it leads the reader to the acceptance of utilitarianism or not, will bear witness to the fact that critical and systematic progress is possible in normative ethics.

ACKNOWLEDGEMENTS

I started to work on this book at Swedish Collegium for Advanced Study (SCAS) in Uppsala in fall of 2008. A first draft of the entire book was finalized in the spring of 2011 at the Centre for Advanced Study in Bioethics in Münster. I thank the centres for kind support.

Work on the book has been rendered possible because of generous support from the Swedish Research Council, Riksbanken Centenary Foundation, and Granholm Foundation. Granholm Foundation subsidized my surveys of opinions on killing in China, Russia, and the United States.

I presented the chapter on the trolley cases (Chapter 3) in a preliminary form in a keynote speech at the Swedish Philosophical Association in the spring of 2011. I gave another keynote presentation of it in Copenhagen in 2013 at an international conference on applied philosophy at the Carlsberg Academy, organized by the Nordic Network on Political Ethics. When I wrote the chapter I received good advice from Joshua Greene and Fiery Cushman. Guy Kahane read a penultimate draft of the chapter and gave valuable criticism. His comments helped me to a much better version of the chapter, but not to any agreement with him.

Some of the chapters in this book draw on material previously published even if they do not appear here in exactly the same form.

Chapter 1 draws on the article 'Applied Ethics. A Defence', *Ethical Theory and Moral Practice*, 2011 as well as on my contribution to John Coggon et al. (eds.), *Festschift for John Harris* (2015). Chapter 5 draws on 'Capital Punishment', in Ben Bradley, Fred Feldman, and Jens Johansson (eds.), *Oxford Handbook of Philosophy and Death* (2012). Chapter 8 draws on material from 'The Ethics of Killing. An Example: Abortion', in Rysiek Sliwinski and Frans Svensson (eds.), *Neither/Nor. Philosophical Papers Dedicated to Erik Carlson on the Occasion of His Fiftieth Birthday* (2011). And Chapter 11 draws on material from my short book, *Animal Ethics* (2010). I thank the publishers for allowing me to use it here.

Many people have read and commented on the manuscript. They are way too many to be mentioned. In particular, however, I want to thank Helen Frowe and Lisa Hecht, who read and commented upon the penultimate draft of the chapter on killing in war (as a matter of fact, Lisa commented on the entire manuscript), and my students who commented on an earlier draft of the entire book when they took an advanced course on the ethics of killing in the spring of 2013: Lise-Lott Karlsson, Hanna Sulkakoski, Theo Nyreröd, Andreas Quak, William Bülow, Daniel Ringdahl, and Thomas Hartvigsson. Their comments were highly valuable. Maria Svedberg gave comments on a short section on free will (in the final chapter). Derek Parfit has commented on the section on population ethics in Chapter 8. His comments were most helpful, but our disagreement remains. Jens Johansson read the penultimate draft of four chapters of the manuscript. His comments were, as always, extremely valuable and he spotted several mistakes in my argument. I wish he had read the entire manuscript! I realize that I must now myself assume responsibility for any remaining mistakes. In addition, two reviewers for OUP have provided me with extremely helpful and constructive comments.

Finally, I want to thank Peter Ohlin at the press for his patience and skill in his handling of the reviewing process of my manuscript—and for suggesting the title of the book.

TAKING LIFE

Chapter 1

Method

1. INTRODUCTION

In this chapter I describe and defend the method I will use in this book. The main thrust of my argument is that in our search of the truth in normative ethics we need to resort to a kind of applied ethics (turned upside down). Applied ethics (turned upside down) provides a unique route to deep moral understanding.

Even if intuitions, as we will see, play a role in the method I advocate and use, the method must be characterized as hypothetical deductive rather than intuitive. This is a distinguishing characteristic of this book, as compared to many other books in the same field (on the ethics of killing). I try out the implications of ethical theories in what I will speak of as crucial experiments. This is how I proceed.

2. APPLIED ETHICS

To get a grasp of the method used we should take our departure in a traditional way of doing applied ethics. In applied (or practical) ethics, we seek answers to practical questions about what to do. These questions are as varied as human life. They range from individual questions (what ought I to do with my life?) to very general political questions (ought we to abolish capital punishment?). In this book, each chapter is devoted to one such question. Practical questions include also, as we shall see, problems raised by thought experiments. In the present context, the questions raised are all questions about killing.

The reasonable way of answering a practical question is as follows. We find a moral principle, which is applicable to the case at hand, we make an account of the relevant non-moral facts, and we deduce the answer to our question:

(1) Moral principle
(2) Relevant non-moral facts

———

(3) Practical conclusion

By so doing, if we take as our point of departure a true moral principle, we get moral guidance; we learn what to do. Moreover, since the argument has the structure of an ordinary covering-law explanation in science, where the practical conclusion plays the role of our *explanandum*, and the moral principle the role of the statement of a law of nature, we also learn *why* we ought to do what we ought to do. It is assumed here that the moral principle has a kind of necessity built into it, quite similar to the one built into a law of nature. We can project it onto unknown cases; it supports counterfactuals, and so forth. The principle is an essential part of the *explanans*. The principle specifies right- and wrong-*making* characteristics. Hence, by referring to it, we can make moral explanations.

The application of the model is sometimes quite straightforward. If we apply a simple deontological principle, such as the one that it is wrong to intentionally kill an innocent human being, to a case where an innocent human being was killed intentionally, we can deduce the conclusion that this was wrong. Moreover, if the principle specifies a wrong-making characteristic, we can claim that we now know *why* the action was wrong. It was wrong *because* it was an example of intentional killing of an innocent human being.

However, more subtle principles, such as utilitarianism, are more demanding of non-moral factual information. Here we need to have recourse to various different auxiliary, 'bridging', hypotheses, and even methods of decision making motivated on utilitarian grounds, in order to reach a tentative conclusion about a particular case. Or, we apply it in a thought experiment, where we have abstracted from all kinds of uncertainties. It then yields definite implications.

2.1. Applied Ethics Can Help Us Clarify Existing Discussions

These are two obvious uses of the model; it can give us moral guidance and moral understanding. But it can also be put to a more mundane use. In many discussions about controversial issues, there is little understanding of the principled aspects of the issues. By putting the model to use, and by tentatively trying out various different putative moral principles, which may seem plausible to different people involved in the controversy, we can shed new light on it. This is something that will be done in passing in this book, sometimes with rather unexpected results. There are at least six possible outcomes of such a study.

(i) Practical disagreement based on fundamental moral disagreement. We can learn that the reason that people disagree, or should disagree, is that the different principles to which they adhere yield different conclusions once the relevant non-moral facts (relevant to each one of the principles involved in the controversy, that is) are on the table.
(ii) Practical agreement based on an overlapping consensus. We can learn that even if people disagree on basic principled moral questions, they should agree on the practical question at hand, since each principle, given its relevant non-moral facts, yields the same practical conclusion.
(iii) Practical disagreement based on non-moral factual disagreement. We can learn that the disagreement that surfaces

in the discussion does not depend on different principled moral stances (since upon closer inspection those involved in the controversy agree about these); rather, the disagreement, if it is recalcitrant, can be traced to different beliefs about the relevant non-moral facts.

(iv) Practical disagreement based on logical mistakes or the use of different systems of logic. Two persons who agree about moral principles and relevant non-moral facts may yet disagree; at least one of them may have made a logical mistake, or they may be relying on different systems of logic. Even in logic, and in particular in deontic logic, there is room for *some* reasonable disagreement.

(v) Practical disagreement that is merely verbal; it is possible that the parties speak at cross-purposes. They employ the same moral terms but use them with different meanings. There could, of course, also exist practical agreement that is merely verbal. In either case the disagreement is likely to surface in actual practice.

(vi) Complete practical agreement based on agreement about basic moral principles, all the relevant facts, the same understanding of rules of logic, correct reasoning, and a common understanding of the terminology used.

As we will see, in some situations considerations such as these can also help us to 'debunk' explanations of what at first seem to be strong moral intuitions.

2.2. Applied Ethics Turned Upside Down

All this is important as such, but there is an even more significant lesson to be learnt from applied ethics, of crucial importance in the present context. The answer to the practical question at hand depends on a correct understanding of the moral principles that are applied. However, it is not possible to know, without applying them to real and hypothetical cases, which moral principles are true and which are false. Applied ethics, however, *can* help us to justified beliefs about moral principles. But then we must move not top down but bottom up, from the conclusion to the premises. This will be the standard method used in this book.

If we hold a strong and considered (in a sense to be explained) moral intuition about how the practical question should be answered, then a principle that explains the content of this intuition gains some evidential support. And the principle that gives the *best* explanation of the content of our moral intuition gets inductive support by this content (we make an inference to the best explanation). We may also speak here of 'abduction'.

By an *intuition* I mean an immediate (not preceded by a conscious reasoning) reaction to a particular case; a reaction to the effect that *this is right, this is wrong*, and so forth. It is crucial that our intuitions have a propositional *content*, then. But I will also generalize the notion of an intuition to what has sometimes rather been called rational insights, i.e. immediate reactions to general propositions, varying in generality, and including claims such as the one that *it is always wrong to tell a lie*.

In having propositional content, intuitions are similar to perceptions (on many theories of perception, at any rate). They are also similar to perceptions in that they sometimes remain after we have lost our faith in them (like the observed stick in the water that looks bent even after we have learnt some optic theory). And, again, they are similar to perceptions in that they are often theory-laden. If we want to take the content of an intuition as evidence for a moral theory, the intuition must not be the result of a conscious inference from the theory put to test, however. I will return to this requirement at the end of this chapter.

Applied ethics, turned upside down, is the tool we need to resort to if we want to improve our general and principled moral understanding. This is what I will do in the present book, in a restricted manner: I will focus on three moral theories, conceived of here as bold conjectures, and they will be tested against the content of our considered moral intuitions about various different forms of killing.

I am interested to see if they yield the right or the wrong implications in each case, and I am interested in finding out, when there is overlapping consensus, which one among them gives the *best* explanation of our data (intuitions).

It should be kept in mind, though, that when I say that one theory in particular gives the best explanation of our data (the content of our considered moral intuitions), this judgement is restricted to the competition I have arranged. It explains our intuitions in this restricted field better than the rival theories also put to the same test.

When we make the move bottom up, from the conclusion to the premise, in an attempt to find the best explanation of our data, it is often helpful to turn not only to real cases but to crucial thought experiments as well. This will be done in many places in the book and is the main theme in Chapter 3, where I discuss the so-called trolley cases. My discussion there does not only shed light on the theories I want to put to test, but also provides me with critical resources I can use when I discuss our intuitions in relation to more mundane applications of the theories, to problems to do with suicide, abortion, capital punishment, and so forth. Here a warning to the reader is in order. These chapters, each devoted to a particular practical problem, such as the problem of whether or when suicide, abortion, capital punishment, and so forth is morally all right, may give the impression that I try to cover the entire discussion around each problem. This is not so. I use these problems exclusively to test the theories I am interested in. This means that I discuss important contributions to the debates when they are informed by these theories, but when they are not so informed I leave them to one side. Nor do I attempt to make difficult empirical assessments necessary for a definitive declaration of what is or what is not recommended by utilitarianism. The important question I do raise, however, is what kinds of empirical facts are *relevant* to an assessment of the question, according to each theory. This sheds important light on the theory itself.

2.3. Coherentism—Justified Belief

The use of the method of an inference to the best explanation, the resort to abduction, goes naturally together with a coherentist criterion of justification. On a standard notion of coherentism, if p is a member of a set of all the beliefs B, of a person S, at a time t, then the more p coheres with B, the more justified is S in his belief at t in p. Or, if there are some incoherent members of B that are in no way relevant to the truth of p, this should not mean that S is not justified in his belief in p. A way of handling this would be to require that p should cohere with a—conservatively—revised version of B.

Given this proviso, we may say that the more p coheres with B, the more justified is S in his belief in p. And coherence is not merely a matter of consistency, but a matter of how deeply p is imbedded among the rest of the beliefs as *evidence* for them, or as *explaining* them. The justification we find for our beliefs, when they form part of a coherent set, has to do with the simple fact that, the more coherent our web of beliefs is, the higher the intellectual *price* of giving up any single member of the web. I defend this view elsewhere.[1] It should be observed that even if a person is strongly justified, at a certain time, in a certain belief, this belief might well be false. *Justification* (for a person at a time, in a belief) is one thing; the (absolute) *truth* of the content of the belief in question is quite another thing.

What is the relation between the method here advocated, the abductive method of an inference to the best explanation, on the one hand, and John Rawls's idea of a reflective equilibrium, on the other hand?[2] Well, the coherentist notion of justified belief just *is* an idea of reflective equilibrium. This is simply another name for the same *criterion*. However, some philosophers (including Rawls himself) speak of a 'method' of reflective equilibrium. And some

1. Torbjörn Tännsjö, *From Reasons to Norms. On the Basic Question in Ethics*, Chapter 8.

2. John Rawls, *A Theory of Justice*.

claim that the 'aim' of our intellectual endeavour should be to arrive at a reflective equilibrium. All this is extremely misleading.

Our goal when we pursue normative ethics, is the truth about what we ought to do and why we ought to do it. We do not aim at any reflective equilibrium. We would not have succeeded in our endeavour if we ended up with all our ideas in reflective equilibrium, but, alas way off the mark. This is a possibility, since justification does not *guarantee* truth. To end up justified in false beliefs would indeed be a failure in one's intellectual enterprise.

Furthermore, when we make an inference to the best explanation of our data, namely the content of our considered moral intuitions, there is no way that we could just give up on the data, no way of 'negotiating' about them, no way of 'going back and forth' between theory and our more particular judgements in order to obtain a perfect 'fit' between them. The theory should fit the data, *as they appear to us*, otherwise we must consider the theory disconfirmed by them.

Of course, there may be something wrong about some of our intuitions, and we should consider that possibility seriously. I will say a lot about this in the present book. However, if there remains any singular recalcitrant intuition once we have exposed them all to what I will call cognitive psychotherapy, we must reject the hypothesis that could not account for it. Or, if we find ourselves holding a very strong belief in the theory, we may presume that our recalcitrant intuition *must* be mistaken; we must believe, then, that it can somehow be explained away (even if, for the time being, we do not know exactly *how* to provide the necessary explanation). This is the *only* permissible manner of setting it to one side.

The same goes for intuitions held by other people, who are equally competent as yourself, equally knowledgeable, and so forth, but who hold intuitions inconsistent with your own. You are not allowed to put them to one side unless you are prepared to judge that somehow these people *must* have made some kind of mistake.

3. CONSIDERED INTUITIONS

If I am right, we cannot gain justified moral belief, let alone moral knowledge, unless we resort to the method I have advocated, where we put moral principles to test, in both real cases and in thought experiments, and where we systematically try to arrange with crucial tests, where different moral principles, given the relevant non-moral facts, yield conflicting practical conclusions. Here the content of our considered intuitions should serve the role of observation in science. But are we allowed to rely at all on our immediate intuitive responses? Well, if not, there is no possibility that we should gain justified moral beliefs.[3]

It might be thought that it is an example of what the British philosopher Gilbert Ryle would have called a category mistake to believe that an intuition can be evidence for a moral theory. Intuitions are psychological events and a moral theory does not have any implications about how we actually feel, or think about moral matters. This objection is made rather frequently. Peter Singer writes, for example:

> A scientific theory seeks to explain the existence of data that are about a world 'out there' that we are trying to explain . . . A normative ethical theory, however, is not trying to explain our common moral intuitions. It might reject all of them, and still be superior to other normative theories that better matched our moral judgements. For a normative moral theory is not an attempt to answer the question 'Why do we think as we do about moral questions?' . . . A normative moral theory is an attempt to answer the question 'What ought we to do?'[4]

3. This is a bold claim, of course. For an argument against it, see Herman Cappelen's *Philosophy Without Intuitions*. For a good response to Cappelen, see Folke Tersman, 'Should We Worry About Opposing Intuitions?'.

4. Peter Singer, 'Ethics and Intuitions', pp. 245–246.

A similar argument has earlier been used by R. B. Brandt when, in a footnote to his *Ethical Theory*, he compares the role of intuition or feeling in morality to observation in science, making the following qualification:

> Physical theory, taken with a description of the experimental setup, may logically imply 'The ammeter will point to 30' and we can observe whether or not this is the case. Whereas, although in ethics we may reject 'There is no obligation to do X' by appeal to the fact that we feel a strong obligation to do X . . . we cannot say that ethical principles entail anything about how we shall feel—at least not in any direct way.[5]

The argument is popular, then, but mistaken. The simple answer to it is that it is the *content* of our moral intuitions that is taken as evidence. And the content of an intuition is a moral proposition to the effect that this is right or this is wrong, and such propositions *are* implied by moral theories. So the content of intuitions can be evidence for the truth of moral theories; there is no logical problem involved in this claim. And yet, for all that, the content of every intuition is not evidence. Only the content of a *considered* intuition is evidence. An intuition is considered, I will say, when it has passed scrutiny from the point of view of something I will speak of as cognitive psychotherapy. In this kind of therapy we get clearer about the origin of our reaction.

Here I take for granted that we are justified in our belief in the content of *some* of our moral intuitions. We have reason to accept their content; we are justified in taking them to track the truth. As noted above, this is not the place to defend this bold claim. Let me elaborate a little about what I consider to be the best defence for this position. We hold some very simple and firm moral beliefs, such as the one that it is wrong to torture a sentient creature for no reason

5. R. B. Brandt, *Ethical Theory: The Problems of Normative and Critical Ethics*, p. 249n.

whatever. We cannot give up on these beliefs. This is psychologically impossible. But since ought implies can, this means that we need not give up on them. We are permitted to hold them. This is not a positive reason to stick to them, however. But there exists also a positive reason to stick to them, to the extent that they are consistent with the rest of our beliefs. Our epistemic justification is practical. We are justified in relation to our epistemic goal in holding beliefs. Our epistemic goal is, roughly, to hold a realistic view of the world, to believe important true propositions, and to avoid believing false propositions. Now, if I believe that it *is* wrong to torture a sentient creature for no reason, moral nihilism comes with a price. It means that I must give up on this belief. But since I hold it, it would be *irrational* (in relation to my epistemic goal) to give it up. If I could give it up, and if I *would* give it up, I would stop believing what I consider an important truth.[6]

This is so only if I do not know of any knock-down argument in defence of moral nihilism, of course. I know of no such argument. Consequently, I stick to my belief that we, human beings, have a (fallible) ability for telling right from wrong. Regardless, this is not the place to go into this problem, which I have discussed at length elsewhere.[7] One could perhaps add that there appears to exist some empirical evidence to that effect in the study of infants, who seem to be capable of making moral distinctions very early in life. Just as we develop very already as small children a rudimentary capacity to count, we seem to develop a similar capacity to make a distinction between right and wrong action.[8]

Admittedly, we have better positive reasons to stick to some of our observational beliefs, because we know more about their causal history, than to our moral intuitive beliefs. And we have better

6. In Chapter 8 of my *From Reasons to Norms*, I elaborate on how we should best understand our epistemic goal, but I reach the conclusion that we cannot ever state it with full precision. It is likely that it varies to some extent from person to person and from situation to situation.

7. In my book *From Reasons to Norms*.

8. See Paul Bloom, *Just Babies*, about this.

positive reasons to stick to some of our linguistic intuitions than to our moral intuitions. It is less daring to say that we should allow our intuitions to decide what it means to have knowledge, say, than to allow them to be decisive when we want to know what to do. And yet, this does not mean that we have *no* reason to stick to some of our moral intuitive beliefs. Once again, there seems to exist no alternative to this kind of approach.

Even if we believe that our moral intuition is, by and large, reliable, we should not always trust its deliverances. Just as we have to be sceptical with regard to some of our observational beliefs, we need to be sceptical with regard to some of our moral intuitions as well. This means that we need to ponder the question of when to rely on them and when not to do so. In order to answer this question, it is important to know more about their *origin*. In this our moral beliefs are no different from our observational ones.

4. COGNITIVE PSYCHOTHERAPY

The proper way of approaching our intuitions, then, is to observe our reactions to the practical examples we confront, once we know about the origin of our intuitions. We should not rely on our intuitions before we know all that can be known about how they have come about. We should expose them to what I have liked to call a kind of cognitive psychotherapy.[9] Only if they survive this test should we count them as evidence. This is reminiscent of Henry Sidgwick, who once wrote:

> But though probably all moral agents have experience of ... particular intuitions, and though they constitute a great part

9. This is the term I use in my *Understanding Ethics*. My use of the term is inspired by Richard Brandt. I heard him presenting the idea in a talk in Stockholm in the early 1970s, and he writes about it in *A Theory of the Good and the Right*. Brandt wanted us to submit our preferences to cognitive psychotherapy. My intention is, rather, to submit our moral intuitions to it.

> of the moral phenomena of most minds, comparatively few are so thoroughly satisfied with them, as not to feel a need of some further moral knowledge even from a strictly practical point of view. For the particular intuitions do not, to reflective persons, present themselves as quite indubitable and irrefragable: nor do they always find when they have put an ethical question to themselves with all sincerity, that they are conscious of clear immediate insight in respect of it. Again, when a man compares the utterances of his conscience at different times, he often finds it difficult to make them altogether consistent: the same conduct will wear a different moral aspect at one time from that which it wore at another, although our knowledge of its circumstances and conditions is not materially changed. Further, we become aware that the moral perceptions of different minds, to all appearance equally competent to judge, frequently conflict: one condemns what another approves. In this way serious doubts are aroused as to the validity of each man's particular moral judgements.[10]

The remedy, according to Sidgwick, is that we should set these doubts to rest 'by appealing to general rules, more firmly established on a basis of common consent'.[11] He soon finds, however, that when we turn to general rules, what we will find is, once again, disagreement among competent judges. Does this mean that we should go for some very different method? In a way, this is what Sidgwick does, when he wants in a foundationalist manner to find a few 'axioms' upon which he can base a moral theory. Today, foundationalism must be considered a friendless non-starter, however. Instead, we should examine all our intuitions, and see if there is a subset of them, to wit, the set of our *considered* moral intuitions, the members of which we can treat as evidence; and we should investigate if

10. *Methods of Ethics*, p. 100.
11. Ibid.

the content of our *considered* intuitions can be best explained with reference to some general moral principle.

How can we find this trustworthy subset? We expose all our moral intuitions to cognitive psychotherapy.

The result of our session in psychotherapy may be just that we gain knowledge about the place of our intuitions in the culture in which we have been brought up. But it may also include knowledge gained from neuroimaging of our brains and studies in experimental psychology. No such information can *contradict* the content of any of our intuitions. Such information provides no *evidence* against them. But it can help us to undermine the *justification* for the content of some of the intuitions, in the same way that my knowledge that psychologists sometimes project holograms in front of me—in order to be able to mock me and my philosophy lectures where I claim to know that there is a table in front of me—would undermine my justification for my belief that there is a table in front of me.

There are in fact two ways our credence in an intuition may go away. We may simply lose the intuition, when we learn more about its origin in our thinking. Or, we may still retain it but stop treating it as evidence any more. This is what happens when we learn about optics, as I suggested above. We still see a stick in the water as bent, but we do not believe, for this reason, that it is bent any more. Something similar can happen to some of our moral intuitions. Examples of this will be given in the book.

Tradition can be one source of error. In particular, if we learn that people think differently about a phenomenon such as abortion, if they belong to different cultures, we should become suspicious about our own intuitions about abortion. We should try to transcend our narrow cultural horizon.

Partiality may be another source of error. When I am contemplating what I should do in a given situation, and choosing a particular option would result in a cost to me, we should not trust my answer if I claim that I need not make this option. This is so even when we want to tease out our intuitions in relation to theories to the effect that there exist agent-relative obligations. For instance, we should not ask whether *you* are obliged to sacrifice one of *your* limbs in order to save the life of a stranger. We should, rather, ask whether an agent *in the abstract* is obliged to do so. This allows you to imagine yourself *either* in the role of the agent or in the role of the individual whose life is at stake.

Hence, we should not ask questions such as whether people in the rich world ought to make heavy sacrifices in order to save lives in the poor world. Here we all know only too well to what camp we belong. In particular, it would be ridiculous to pose this question *merely* to people in the rich world.

There is at least one more possible source of error to keep in mind. When we confront competing moral purported principles in a crucial test (such as a thought experiment) to see if they fit the content of our considered intuitions (which have passed our test of cognitive psychotherapy), we must beware. In many situations it is highly likely that we have simply *deduced* the content of an intuition from one of the theories put to test. If this is the case, the content of this intuition lacks *independent* evidential force. The word 'intuition' is now a misnomer.

Finally, when our problem is that clever people seem to disagree with us, we should try to ascertain that we and they do not speak at cross-purposes. Subtle terminological differences, as well as the use of different types of deontic logic, may cause what seems to be genuine disagreement, but which can be shown, once we get clear about the matter, to be merely verbal.

But what if we find, after having gone through the process of cognitive psychotherapy, that we hold some intuitions that are inconsistent with the intuitions of other people who have gone through the same procedure? They are just as clever as we are. We do not speak at cross-purposes. Must we then give up our intuition?

I think not, but if we retain it, we must impute some error to the other party (even if we are not capable of identifying it). I commented on this in passing above. The same is true in the intrapersonal case, as I then claimed. If I hold one recalcitrant intuition at variance with a theory I think otherwise well-confirmed, I cannot reasonably accept the theory unless I impute some kind of mistake to myself (even if I cannot identify it). In the interpersonal case I must also be open to the following strange possibility.

If I am in disagreement with one person, then this is perhaps not enough to undermine my justification in my belief. After all, I hold it, and since I believe that I hold a true belief, it is irrational to give it up. I should do so if I possessed *evidence* to the effect that my belief was *false*. But the fact that one person disagrees is not as such evidence to the effect that the belief is false. I can hence impute an error to this person just because he disagrees with me. I can do so repeatedly with many people. However, if each of them seems to get things right more often than not, then this should give me pause. If it is just one clever person who dissents with me, I can think that I am a clever person too, so this fact is, as it were, cancelled out. However, if I am in disagreement with *several* clever people, I may come to think that, after all, they rather than I must be right, and provide, as an *argument* to this effect, the Condorcet Jury theorem. I must believe that I am the one who is wrong even though I have no clue as to what it is that has gone wrong with my thinking. According to the theorem, a majority among people who decide about an issue will be right more often than any of them in particular. This is true if they decide independently of one another and if everyone is better than chance at finding the right answer. As the number of individuals increases, we approach certainty in the majority verdict.[12]

Intuitions have a special favoured position in our moral thinking that is similar to the position held by observations in science. Even on a coherentist notion of justification, we grant them this favoured position, because of our belief that, *by and large*, they track the truth. Of course, the fact that an intuition has passed the test of cognitive psychotherapy does not *guarantee* that it tracks the truth. There are no such guarantees available to us. However, when it has

12. See, for example, Tom Christiano's entry 'Democracy' in the *Stanford Encyclopedia of Philosophy*, for a very quick introduction to the theorem and for references to further reading: http://plato.stanford.edu/entries/democracy/.

failed to pass the test, then, as a matter of fact, we give it up, or, if it stays with us, we simply stop treating it as evidence.

5. CONCLUSION

In this chapter I have used 'applied ethics' as a name for the kind of approach I defend. This may seem a bit rhetorical. However, if I am right, there is a rationale behind this piece of rhetoric. I have argued that applied ethics, as I conceive of it, is possible and useful. It is capable not only of leading us to answers for practical questions and explanations for why we ought to do this rather than that, but also of helping us to bring more consistency and clarity into existing public controversies about practical issues. Moreover, and most importantly, applied ethics, as here described, turned upside down, can help us to a deeper understanding of normative ethics. But then we need to have recourse to moral theories that yield definite implications, at least in abstract thought experiments.

This optimistic claim that applied ethics turned upside down can lead us to a deeper understanding of normative ethics has not been established, of course. It is predicated on the assumption that there exist true deterministic moral principles yielding definite implications in practical cases. In this chapter I have not attempted to show that this is the fact, let alone endeavouring to show *which* (deterministic) moral theory is the true one. For all we know, at this preliminary stage of my investigation, intuitionists of the Ross variety, claiming that there are moral principles but only of a prima facie kind, yielding no definite implications in particular cases where they conflict, or particularists, denying that any true moral principles at all exist, may be right.[13] If I am right, however, in my eventual claim that utilitarianism gives a plausible account of the ethics of killing, a first step towards showing them wrong has been taken.

13. I return to intuitionism and particularism in the concluding Chapter 12. I also discuss these views in depth in Torbjörn Tännsjö, 'Applied Ethics. A Defence'.

Chapter 2

Three Bold Conjectures

1. INTRODUCTION

If the best way of making progress in normative ethics is through the testing of bold conjectures, and given that this will be done in the present context in relation to a specific problem, the problem of killing, then which are the most promising candidates for the trial? Which are the *best* bold conjectures to confront with the problem of killing? Three candidates come to mind. I will speak of them as deontology, an ethics of rights, and utilitarianism, respectively—or, for short: theories about duties, rights, and utility. They can be seen more as research programs than as finalized theories, so I will try them out in different versions. The idea is to find the best versions of each one in relation to the problem discussed: when should we, or should we not, kill, and why?

Why these three theories or research programs? First of all, they are all intuitively plausible. In their explanations of why it is wrong to kill (when it is, according to each theory), they point at facts that seem morally relevant: the intention behind the act, the violation of rights, the consequences for the victim and the world at large. Secondly, they give, at least in principle, definite answers to all the problems I raise. In this they are different from views such as, for example, virtue ethics. Virtue ethics in the moral sciences shares a weakness with psychoanalysis in the social sciences: it doesn't lend itself to falsification. You cannot find clear refuting cases.[1] Thirdly,

1. This is not to say that the virtues lack moral importance; as we will see in the discussion about murder, virtues are of importance to all the three competing

they give promising explanations of various conflicting intuitions people claim to have in the area. They are clear, general, and fairly simple. And, finally, the problem I have chosen for confrontation with the theories, the ethics of killing, is such that it provides us with crucial tests of them. The three theories give, in many cases, interestingly *different* (inconsistent) answers to the questions posed.

Furthermore if we combine elements from these three theories, we can construct something that has been called *common sense* morality. I will try that tack as well.

It is worthy of note that, while the ethics of killing may seem to provide the best possible chances for a successful outcome of the test with regard to deontology and the moral rights theory, the ethics of killing seems to provide a correspondingly hard ground for utilitarianism. After all, if there are any actions that are absolutely prohibited, as deontology claims, some kinds of killing should be among them. And if there is *anything* we own and hence have a right to dispose as we see fit, it should be ourselves, as is taught by the moral rights theory; so the implications of the moral rights theory with regard at least to subjects such as murder, suicide, and assisted death should be regarded as initially *very* plausible. This can be contrasted with utilitarianism, with its implication that even murder is sometimes right, which may seem to fly in the face of common sense moral thinking. So if it can be shown, as I think it can (even though, as the reader will note, this turns out to be a real cliff-hanger), that utilitarianism in the final analysis does gain the upper hand in the competition I have arranged with, this should be a finding of no small consequence.

It may be objected to this project that these theories are all of them way off the mark. The true ethics of killing is provided by some other theory. I doubt that, but there is no possibility in the present context to provide any rationale behind this scepticism with regard to other theories. The reader will have to live with the

theories in this book. There is no reference to any virtues in the statement of their respective criteria of right and wrong action, though.

selection I have made, or simply stop reading here. However, in the final Chapter 12, I will consider the possibility of striking some kind of intellectual *compromise* between the theories. As was suggested above, with elements from each of them we can construct a kind of common sense morality. I will ponder if there exists any such alternative to each and every one of them, constructed out of elements from these three theories, which is superior to all of them. My own assessment of this possibility will be an outright rejection, however.

A final comment on my selection of theories for my test. My method in this book is similar to the one used by Henry Sidgwick. I have indicated both how my method of ethics is similar to, and differs, from his. A difference between my approach to normative ethics, and his, is, however, that while he seems to have thought that, in the final analysis, ethical egoism poses the strongest challenge to utilitarianism, I say nothing at all about ethical egoism in the book. The reason is that I do not find ethical egoism at all intuitively appealing. This is particularly clear in the area I here discuss. The idea that I ought to kill a fellow human being if, and only if, it serves my own best interests, does not strike me as very plausible. I think, furthermore, that those who are yet drawn to egoism tend to see it as a substitute to moral thinking rather than as a moral view in its own right. They are moral nihilists, they think that *all* putative moral theories are false—and they want to explore the possibilities for rational egoists and moral nihilists to agree about a way of living together, not too remote from ordinary moral thinking. This is a project developed by David Gauthier in his book *Morals by Agreement*. But my project is different. I want to know which moral theory is the true one. And ethical egoism doesn't seem to be of much interest in such a contest.

Those who happen to think otherwise should also consider the possibility that, for evolutionary reasons, we had better debunk whatever intuitions we happen to hold in favour of ethical egoism. This is only what should be expected from us, given the survival value of such a moral view. This is a theme in Katarzyna de

Lazari-Radek and Peter Singer's recent article, 'The Objectivity of Ethics and the Unity of Practical Reason'.

The theories with which I compare utilitarianism—deontology and the moral rights theory—cannot be set to one side by any similar simplistic move.

2. DEONTOLOGY

The simplest answer to the question of why it is wrong to kill—when it is wrong to kill—is that this action, the action of killing, represents a prohibited *kind* of action. There are certain actions that we, moral agents, are not permitted to perform (and there are actions we ought to perform), irrespective of the consequences of particular instances of them. And if there are any prohibitions of this kind at all, the most natural one must be the one given in the commandment that thou shalt not kill. If killing is not forbidden, then anything goes, one may think. Then the end must justify the means.

Of course, all sorts of counterexamples come to mind. What about capital punishment, what about killing in war, and so forth? In order to cater for these exceptions, if we want to stick to the idea that it is wrong, absolutely, to kill, we must work out a subtler version of the idea, which allows us to explain the exceptions we want to make in a manner that is not completely ad hoc. Perhaps it is possible to do so. This is a possibility I will try out in this book.

Now, the idea that it is wrong to kill (in certain ways), irrespective of the consequences of the individual act of killing under consideration, is an idea with strong support in the big monotheistic religions, and there are many philosophers who have tried to work out a defence of this idea. The most important thinker in this tradition is Immanuel Kant, both in his defence of the deontological approach in general, and in his defence of the prohibition against killing in particular. I will discuss his ideas repeatedly in this book. But there exists what one may call a Thomistic deontological tradition as well, often termed in the present discussion as the

Sanctity-of-Life Doctrine. I will examine this version of deontology as well.

It may seem that deontology, in both versions, is a very narrow theory, implying sometimes that an action is wrong, but, in many cases, yielding no normative implications whatever, since none among the alternatives contemplated means that any killing will take place. However, as we shall see, both Kantianism and the Sanctity-of-Life Doctrine come with additional ideas, allowing us to consider them as complete moral theories. More about this soon. First, however, a few words on Kant.

2.1. Kant's Deontology

I discuss Immanuel Kant's philosophy without pretending to be a Kantian scholar, and without any claims to the effect that in my interpretations of his philosophy I make best sense of his real intentions and ideas. I do claim, however, that the version of his theory I go for is the one that makes it as plausible as possible, in our search of an ethics of killing.

I will work out this idea about the absolute wrongness of killing in detail in chapters to come. Here I will just give a very rough sketch of the view I start with in my discussion. First, however, a brief comment on a point where I part company with many contemporary Kantian scholars. It has to do with how we should understand what is often considered as the heart of Kant's deontology, his so-called categorical imperative.

It is often thought that the categorical imperative, in its first Kantian formulation, is in itself supposed to provide an answer to the question of why actions are right and why actions are wrong. This is how Kant famously states the imperative:

> There is, therefore, only a single categorical imperative and it is this: *act only in accordance with that maxim through which you can at the same time will that it become a universal law.*[2]

2. Immanuel Kant, *Groundwork*, p. 31, emphasis in the original.

The idea, then, is that an action is right, if and only if, and because, it is such that the agent can will that the 'maxim' behind it becomes a universal law. This idea does not make good sense of Kant and I doubt that this is what he meant. It is more probable that he conceived of this version of the categorical imperative as a kind of heuristic device that helps us to find out what it is that makes actions right and wrong (the maxim behind the action). The problem with the idea that the first formulation of the categorical imperative should state a basic moral principle has to do with the role of such principles. Remember that we want them to *explain* the rightness or wrongness of particular actions. This means that they specify right- or wrong-*making* characteristics. Now, the fact that an act is an act of murder may well function as an explanation of why it is wrong. It is wrong, then, because it is an example of intentional killing of an innocent rational human being. This is not so with the fact that the agent could not will that the maxim behind it became a universal law, however.

I do not say that we have very strong intuitions about what the right- and wrong-making characteristics of our actions are. If we had such strong intuitions, the problems in normative ethics would have been solved long ago. However, we have at least a hint about what *kind* of characteristics could play this role. The fact that an action is an action of killing (or murder) is a plausible candidate to such an answer, as well as the other ideas to be examined in this book (it could be wrong because it violates a basic moral right, or because it makes the world, as such, a worse place). However, the fact that the agent could not will that the maxim behind it became a universal law is of a different order.

The problem with the idea that the wrong-making characteristic should be that the agent could not will that the maxim behind the act be universalized, is that what is here referred to is too detached from the patient, the agent, and what does actually happen in the situation. This invites the response: So what? What if the kind of action is not repeated? Then what was wrong with what I did?

Perhaps the imperative is supposed to help us to an understanding of a more general characteristic behind all wrong actions: they are 'irrational', in some sense. But, once again, it is hard to see that the *irrationality* of an act of murder could really explain its wrongness. And it would be strange if an act of murder and an act of lying would both be wrong for the very same reason (their irrationality). It would be less strange to say that an act of murder and an act of suicide are wrong for the same reason, for example that they mean the intentional killing of an innocent human being. So I will pay no respect to the categorical imperative in this formulation. I will, instead, focus on those substantial (categorical) views he actually defended.

2.2. The Second Formulation of the Categorical Imperative

There is another strand in Kantian thought, apart from his explicit claim that it is wrong to kill, which has bearing on the ethics of killing. It is expressed in his second formulation of the categorical imperative:

> So act that you use humanity, whether in your own person or in the person of any other, always at the same time as an end, never merely as a means.
>
> (*Groundwork*, p. 38)

This is an enigmatic view. On the face of it, it could very well function as the specification of a wrong-making characteristic. There is nothing strange in the idea that an action is wrong *because* it means that (the humanity in) a person is treated as a mere means. However, it is far from clear what this *signifies*. In contemporary discussions about Kant, in particular within the field of bioethics, we often find the idea that, in order to avoid treating (the humanity in) someone merely as a means, we should seek consent from her, before we use her for any purpose whatever, either for her own purposes, or for the purposes of others. However, this was certainly not Kant's own view. In fact, it sits very poorly with his idea about capital punishment, as I will explain in the chapter devoted to this subject. We do not seek consent (either actual or hypothetical) from the murderer before we execute him. We could of course say that when someone commits murder, she implicitly consents to being executed, if found out. This may resonate with Kant's idea that we 'legislate' for ourselves. However, this notion of consent stretches credulity, and we would certainly not want to rely on it in a more mundane discussion of typical problems in bioethics.

This understanding of the theory is also hard to reconcile, as we will see, with Kant's view of suicide. Certainly, he who kills himself deliberately consents to being killed. And yet, this is wrong, according to Kant, and it is wrong exactly because it means that the person who kills himself is using (the humanity in) himself as a mere means. In the chapter on suicide I will try to make sense of this.

2.3. Retributivism

There is a third strand in Kant's moral philosophy, which I will take as part of deontological thinking: his retributivism. This aspect of his theory will be explained when the time has come to apply it—when I discuss capital punishment and killing in war.

2.4. Perfect and Imperfect Duties

The hard core of Kantian deontological thought I will concentrate on is mostly the simple idea that it is just plain wrong to kill, regardless of the consequences, and I will try to find out the best elaboration of this idea. In doing so, I will not rely on Kant's own heuristic device, the first formulation of the categorical imperative. I have not found it helpful. I will also acknowledge, however, that Kant thinks that, apart from such *perfect* duties, as the one to the effect that one should not kill innocent human rational beings, or treat (the humanity in) them as mere means, he also thinks that there exists an *imperfect* duty of beneficence,[3] which can roughly be seen, I suppose, as a duty to maximize happiness among your fellow human creatures. It is not quite clear when this duty applies (there is room for vagueness), however, but it is clear that we are never allowed to fulfil it in a manner that means that we violate a perfect duty. Moreover, if, in a clear case, you violate an imperfect duty, then what you do is forbidden. And prohibitions do not come in degree. Hence, when you violate an imperfect duty, you act wrongly, period. When this weakly 'utilitarian' strand of thought is added to Kant's deontological prohibitions, we get a complete moral theory, allowing us to derive implications from it in all the cases to be considered in this book.

2.5. The Sanctity-of-Life Doctrine

I will also speak in many places in this book of the Sanctity-of-Life Doctrine. This is a term used by both those who defend and those who attack the kind of ideas I will discuss. Hence, I will not hesitate to use it. We may also speak of it as a 'Thomistic' version of deontology.[4] However, it should be noted that the religious associations the term gives rise to ought not to be seen as part of the meaning of the doctrine. Many people who believe in this doctrine also believe in various different religious principles, but the Sanctity-of-Life Doctrine, as here conceived of, is a moral (deontological) doctrine, and it can be defended regardless of any religious beliefs. It has no religious implications whatever. The idea is that some kind of life, to wit, *human* and *innocent* life, must not be taken.

Why should innocent human life not be taken? The explanation, according to a typical defence of the doctrine, is that it is 'sacred', or has a certain 'dignity', or 'value'. These are all expressions used to explain the wrongness of killing. However, as was just noted, the word 'sacred' is a bit misleading, because of its religious connotations. And the word 'value' is even more likely to mislead. It

3. *Groundwork of the Metaphysics of Morals*, p. 33.
4. See, for example, John Finnis, *Fundamentals of Ethics*, Chapter 5.

is tempting to think here of something's possessing value as something's to be pursued or even maximized. If those who defend the Sanctity-of-Life Doctrine think of the value of innocent human life in *those* terms, then they are open to the following kind of attack levelled at them by Jonathan Glover:

> I have no way of refuting someone who holds that being alive, even though unconscious, is intrinsically valuable. But it is a view that will seem unattractive to those of us who, in our own case, see a life of permanent coma as in no way preferable to death.[5]

Nevertheless, those who adhere to the doctrine can, and usually do, avoid this kind of objection by holding that the value of human life is different from what Glover here refers to as life's being 'intrinsically valuable'. They can stick to their view that even a life in permanent coma possesses the kind of value they speak about. Human value, or dignity, is not a value to be pursued. It is rather like a taboo; the appropriate attitude to something exhibiting it is to keep your hands off it. When you are in contact with something exhibiting this kind of value, you realize that you are not allowed to intrude on it; you are not allowed intentionally to kill an innocent human being for any reason whatever.

David Velleman has argued along these lines. On his version of the theory, it is the 'rationality' of a person that is destroyed in a suicide. Our rationality is the source of our dignity.[6]

One may of course wonder whether anything is gained by the claim that innocent human life (or our rationality, in the Kantian version of the theory)[7] is sacred (or has a certain dignity or value),

5. Jonathan Glover, *Causing Death and Saving Lives*, p. 45.

6. David J. Velleman, 'A Right to Self-Determination'.

7. At least this is the standard interpretation of Kant to which I will stick in this book. There have been attempts made to show that he really adhered to what has been called The Sanctity-of-Life Doctrine, however. See Patrick Kain, 'Kant's Defense of Human Moral Status', about this.

and, hence, must not be taken. The fact that a life is human and innocent gives it dignity, according to this line of reasoning, and the dignity possessed by this life in turn explains why it must not be taken. Why not instead say that the mere fact that a life is human and innocent renders it wrong to take it?

It seems as though, in many cases, nothing at all is gained by the introduction of the middle step in the argument, the idea of dignity, sanctity, or value. However, as we will see, the best way of making sense of Kant's objection to suicide relies on this middle term in the argument. We treat *ourselves* as mere means when we kill ourselves: when we do, we sacrifice our dignity only in order to gain a better quality in our lives. And this is wrong, according to Kant.

2.6. The Principle of Double Effect

The deontological theory I focus on, regardless of whether it can find a support in Kant's categorical imperative, in any of its versions, or in the Thomistic tradition, is the view that it is wrong intentionally to kill an innocent human (rational) being. But what does it mean to kill intentionally? This can be clarified with reference to the principle of double effect, which is usually taken to be a part of the Sanctity-of-Life Doctrine. This is also how I will understand the doctrine. To kill intentionally is wrong, but when the death of the person you kill is merely a foreseen, but not intended, side effect of a morally permissible kind of action, and when there is a reasonable proportion between the (badness of the) death you foresee and the good you intend, and provided you do not use the death you foresee as a means to the good thing you intend, then the merely foreseen killing may be all right. It should also be added that, if there had been a way of securing the intended effect, without killing, this way should have been chosen.[8]

8. An authoritative statement of the principle of double effect can be found in F. J. Conell, 'Double Effect, Principle of', in *The New Catholic Encyclopedia*, pp. 1020–1022. I will be true to the spirit of this entry.

How should we understand the requirement of proportionality—in actualist terms, or in probabilistic ones? Is it the actual casualties among innocent people that should stand in a reasonable proportion to the gain made in a just war, for example? Or, should we look at the expected intended gain and compare it to the actual merely foreseen losses? If we are interested in a criterion of right action we should understand it in actualist terms, I submit. However, if our interest is in methods of decision making, or in legal matters, and in particular in punishment, as when we are discussing laws of warfare, we had better understand the requirement in terms of prospects. Agents are bound to act on the evidence that is available to them, and we should not punish agents with bad luck. I will return to this in the chapter on killing in war.

There will be many occasions to return to the principle of double effect in the discussion of the Sanctity-of-Life Doctrine in this book. I will try to stay close to the characterization here given. Indeed I will defend this standard notion of the principle of double effect against critics claiming that it is *too* permissive with regard to killing as well as criticism to the effect that it lacks a *clear meaning*. It is meaningful, I will argue, and it makes the best of the Sanctity-of-Life Doctrine.

When I view the doctrine of double effect as part of the Sanctity-of-Life Doctrine, this means that I can see the doctrine as a complete moral theory. The addition of the principle of double effect means that the Sanctity-of-Life Doctrine yields implications with regard to all the problems to be discussed in this book. The principle of double effect forbids the agent to 'tolerate' merely foreseen harm of her actions, if the harm does not stand in any reasonable proportion to the good effects she intends and strives for. Just like Kant's inclusion of an imperfect duty to maximize the happiness among our fellow human beings makes his deontology depart less from utilitarianism than it would without it, the principle of double effect means that the Sanctity-of-Life Doctrine, too, is closer to utilitarianism than what first meets the eye.

It must be kept in mind that the Sanctity-of-Life Doctrine is not a view to the effect that it is 'worse' to kill intentionally than to kill with foresight. It is a normative view. The idea is that it is wrong, *simpliciter*, to kill intentionally. It can be wrong, *simpliciter*, to kill without intention as well. It is wrong when the requirement of proportionality is not met. What kind of killing is worst? The question makes poor sense. Prohibitions do not come in degree. We may ask, however, what kind of killing is most blameworthy. What kind of killing should be punished more severely? It may well be the case that the killing without intention, but way beyond proportion, is more blameworthy than a single act of intentional killing.

One may wonder *why* it is wrong to intend the death of an innocent human (rational) being. One may wonder, even if one grants that it is a sad fact that an innocent human (rational) being gets killed, about what is so special with acting from the wrong (evil) *intention*. I suppose Thomas Nagel has given the best statement of the rationale behind this aspect of deontology when he claims:

> to aim at evil, even as a means, is to have one's action guided by evil. One must be prepared to adjust it to insure [*sic*] the production of evil: a falling-off in the level of the desired evil becomes a reason for altering what one does so that the evil is restored and maintained. But the essence of evil is that it should *repel* . . . so when we aim at evil we are swimming head-on against the normative current.[9]

This completes my rough account of deontology. In the rest of the book I will belabour in detail the view here roughly put forward.

3. THE MORAL RIGHTS THEORY

Each individual subject (or person) 'owns', in a moral sense of the word, herself. Hence, she is at liberty to do as she sees fit with

9. Thomas Nagel, *The View from Nowhere*, pp. 181–182.

herself, so far as this does not mean that she violates any rights of anyone else. This is the hard core of the moral rights tradition elaborated upon by John Locke in his *Two Treatises on Government*, and most famously defended in our time by Robert Nozick in his *Anarchy, State, and Utopia*. There is a difference between the two, however, that is important in the present context. In Nozick's version of the theory, self-ownership is unrestricted. We are allowed to kill ourselves, if we like. In Locke's version it is restricted in the following manner:

> But though this be a State of Liberty, yet it is not a State of Licence, though Man in that State have an uncontrollable Liberty, to dispose of his Person ... yet he has not Liberty to destroy himself.[10]

In my discussion of the theory I will focus on Nozick's version of it. This version strikes me as the most plausible one. I suspect that Locke is here just yielding (perhaps not even sincerely so) to religious prejudice. If there is anything we *fully* own, it must be ourselves. But note that it is only the hard core of the theory, the idea of self-ownership, that I will discuss. Of course, unless the theory is somehow expanded, it cannot be seen as a complete moral theory. But there are many different ways of expanding it to include also a complete theory of justice.

One may wonder whether this is not just another version of deontology, in its Kantian version. And Nozick sometimes makes a reference to Kant in his defence of the theory. Does this mean that what we here meet with is Kantian deontology? It does not. Kant rejected in strong words the notion of self-ownership:

> Man cannot dispose over himself because he is not a thing; he is not his own property; to say that he is would be self-contradictory; for insofar as he is a person he is a Subject

10. John Locke, *The Second Treatise of Government*, Chapter 2:311.

> in whom the ownership of things can be vested, and if he were his own property, he would be a thing over which he could have ownership. But a person cannot be a property and so cannot be a thing which can be owned, for it is impossible to be a person and a thing, the proprietor and the property.[11]

The moral rights theory, then, is a moral theory in its own right. But how are we to understand self-ownership? Does this idea make any sense at all?

3.1. Self-Ownership

G. A. Cohen has presented a formidable attack on Nozick's libertarian theory of rights. However, in his attack on Nozick's theory of rights, he is careful not to base it on Kant's rejection of the notion of self-ownership. The notion of self-ownership is not inconsistent, Cohen claims. The argument I quoted above from Kant can be reconstructed, according to Cohen, in the following manner.[12]

(1) Man is a person.
(2) Nothing can be both a person and a thing.
(3) Hence, Man is not a thing.

But:

(4) Only things can be owned.
(5) Hence Man cannot be owned.
(6) Hence, Man cannot own himself.

This argument is question-begging, according to Cohen. Kant is using as a *premise*—(4)—the idea that only things can be owned. But this is what should be *shown*. I tend to agree. At least it is difficult

11. Immanuel Kant, *Lectures on Ethics*, p. 165.
12. *Self-Ownership, Freedom, and Equality*, p. 212.

to understand how one could have reasons to accept (4) unless one already has reasons to accept (6).[13] However, the idea that a person could own herself still strikes me as odd. Doesn't the relation of ownership require two distinct relata, the one who owns, and that which is owned?

A way of meeting this concern would be to claim that self-ownership means no more and no less than that everyone has a right to do with himself as he sees fit. But then the notion of self-ownership cannot be evoked as a rationale behind these rights.

Is there any other way of making sense of self-ownership? I think there is. Suppose I am an organism. This means that I have (possess) a body, a heart, a personality, and so forth. Now, even if I cannot own myself, strictly speaking, I can own what constitutes me, all my parts, as it were. This is in line with how Warren Quinn has accounted for the core of the theory:

> A person is constituted by his body and mind. They are parts of aspects of him. For that very reason, it is fitting that he have primary say over what may be done to them—not because such an arrangement best promotes overall human welfare, but because any arrangement that denied him a say would be a grave indignity.[14]

I will continue to speak of self-ownership in this book, but when I do so, *this* is how I understand the notion. It is not really an idea of my owning myself, but rather an idea of my owning the parts making up, or constituting, myself.

If the core of the moral rights theory is the notion of self-ownership, then we have no clear understanding of the theory if we do not know where to draw the line between the organism and the rest of the world. I own all the vital organs of the organism

13. I owe this modification to Jens Johansson.
14. Warren Quinn, *Morality and Action*, p. 170.

I am, of course. But do I also own my hair? What about the skin cells I leave behind all the time? I suppose that on a standard understanding of the moral rights theory, I own them. We may safely here assume, however, that implicitly I give others consent to use them, once I have left them behind. Actually, it might be difficult in many situations to avoid giving implicit consent, since we rely in many situations on conventions. I can forbid you to see my naked body, but if I appear naked in the street, I have implicitly consented to your watching it. You have no right to listen when I quarrel with my wife, but if I quarrel with her before an open window, I have consented to your listening to us. It is up to me to shut the window, if I want to protect my privacy.[15] The same goes for transgressions of my boundaries. When you breathe, you leave molecules (C_2O) that enter into my lungs. This is certainly a transgression of my boundaries. But if I want to avoid it, it is up to me to wear a gas mask (or stop breathing).

Where, exactly, this line between my body and the rest of the world should be drawn has been considered to be a problematic aspect of the moral rights theory.[16] However, the notion of implicit consent is helpful if you want to take up a very inclusive view on which body parts belong to yourself and a correspondingly very strict view on crossings of your boundaries. In the present context we need not bother with this problem any further. I will take it for granted that those who adhere to the theory can give a satisfactory answer to these questions. And since I will here focus on the right to the entire living organism and to the organs vital to the normal functioning of this organism, many of these subtle questions about nails, hair, and skin cells left behind lack relevance to my investigation.

15. On implicit consent to boundary-crossings, see Judith Jarvis Thomson, 'The Right to Privacy'.

16. See Kasper Lippert Rasmussen, 'Against Self-Ownership: There Are No Fact-Insensitive Ownership Rights over One's Body', for an excellent discussion on this point.

3.2. The Ownership of Things Other than Yourself

G. A. Cohen, who defended the claim that the notion of self-ownership is coherent, doesn't himself defend any moral rights theory based of self-ownership. He doesn't reject such a theory, either.[17] But more typical 'left' libertarians stick to self-ownership,[18] even if they quarrel with the idea that you can gain a right to the fruits of the labour of people other than yourself (such as your employees). *Some* such expansion of the theory is necessary if we want to conceive of it as a complete moral theory. The libertarian moral rights theory does not stop at self-ownership. According to the theory we can also acquire individual property rights to material things. The right way to acquire property is to be the first to get hold of it, or to receive or purchase it from someone who already owns it. There is also a right to restitution. If something that belongs to you has been taken away from you, your right to it has been violated, and you have a right to take it back. Furthermore, you have a right to defend what you own. And since you own yourself, this includes a right to self-defence. No one is allowed to kill you, at least not unless you have hired him to do so or have consented to it for one reason or the other. So you are allowed violently, if necessary, to resist any attempt at your life. In this the moral rights theory is different from both deontology and (as we will see) utilitarianism. There is room for self-defence in deontology and utilitarianism as well, but only as a means, when important values are at stake. In the moral rights theory self-defence is a moral category in its own right.

The right to self-defence is not predicated on any notion of guilt or culpability on the part of the one who attacks you. It is a mere matter of protecting your boundaries against invasion. You are also

17. G. A. Cohen, *Self-Ownership, Freedom and Equality*, pp. 230 and 240.

18. See, for example, Peter Vallentyne, Hillel Steiner, and Michael Otsuka, 'Why Left-Libertarianism Is Not Incoherent, Indeterminate, or Irrelevant: A Reply to Fried', pp. 201–222.

allowed to exercise pre-emptive force. However, you are only allowed to do so if, as a matter fact, the attacker would have attacked you had you not exercised this force.

You are free to protect your boundaries against natural events, attacks from animals, and even against an innocent person who has been violently thrown towards you. If necessary, you are allowed to pulverize such a person. I believe this is the most charitable interpretation of the moral rights theory. After all, this seems to follow if we want to be true to the rationale behind the moral rights theory: the idea of self-ownership.[19]

What if we consider the case from the point of view of the person who has been thrown towards you? She realizes that when your heads meet she will be killed. She cannot control the trajectory she follows but she, too, has a weapon that could pulverize—you. Is *she* allowed to use it? Yes, she is. She is allowed to protect *her* boundaries. So, if you both simultaneously fire your arms and pulverize one another, you both exercise—with lethal effect—your right to self-defence. However, since this is probably a controversial aspect of the theory, I will not take advantage of it in my argument against it. *I* will tiptoe around *this* aspect of it.[20]

However, even if, according to this (controversial) aspect of the theory, you have a right to destroy in self-defence an innocent person who has been thrown at you, you are not permitted, on the moral rights theory, to *redirect* a threat to your own safety onto a bystander. I will return to this in a discussion in the next chapter about Judith Jarvis Thomson and her recent stand towards a trolley case: the Switch (to be explained in the next chapter).

There are many problems with the extension of the theory beyond self-ownership. I will glance over these problems, however, since they are irrelevant to the question of killing. Here only the hard core of the theory matters: the idea of self-ownership. One

19. Robert Nozick does not take an explicit stand on this issue. See his *Anarchy, State, and Utopia*, pp. 34–45, where he 'tiptoes' around it.

20. See Suzanne Uniacke, *Permissible Killing* about this.

might think that, if there is any truth to the theory at all, this is the part that should be true. If there is anything we can 'own', in a moral sense of the word, it is ourselves. Even those who resent the theory because of its putative neo-liberal implications with regard to the ownership of material things (property) may want to ponder the question of whether persons do not at least own *themselves*. Moreover, only if the theory comes out successfully from the crucial test (in relation to the ethics of killing) I have here set up is there any point in elaborating on it further.

3.3. Moral Rights and the Risk of Boundary-Crossings

It is wrong to kill a moral subject who has not consented to it. Killing is an obvious example of a boundary-crossing. It should not take place without consent. Is it also wrong to expose a moral subject to the risk of being killed, if she has not consented to it? I think not. I here part company with Nozick himself and many adherers of the moral rights theory, who think that some kinds of risks are acceptable while others are forbidden. I think the theory is more plausible if understood, like I will do with utilitarianism and (implicitly) have done with deontology, as taking the *actual* (not the probable) consequences as decisive for the moral status of actions. In a complex society, we all the time expose one another to the risk of being killed; we do so when we drive our cars, in particular. This does not mean that it is wrong to drive your car, or at least it is not wrong because of the slight risk you expose others to, when, *cautiously* you drive your car. However, if the risk you expose others to would materialize, if you kill a bystander when you hit him with your car, however improbable it was that this should happen, then you have indeed violated his right to life. Actively you have killed him.

I opt for this understanding of the theory because it strikes me as not only much simpler than Nozick's own version (where it is far from clear which risks are acceptable and which risks are not) but also more intuitively plausible. However, in the examples I discuss risk will play no role, so I suppose this choice of interpretation is of little consequence in the present context. It will not affect my arguments in any important way.

3.4. Moral Rights and Compensation

There is another strand in Nozick's understanding of the theory that I find problematic for 'immanent' reasons. I see no point in accepting that a boundary-crossing that has been compensated for *is* a violation of rights. Suppose I need to trespass on your property, in order to save a life. Suppose I need to push you to the side when I come to someone's rescue. Suppose I even need to harm you slightly. Suppose there is no time to ask you for your permission. I harm you slightly and save a life. Does this mean that I violate your property rights, your self-ownership? Yes, it does, if you are not prepared to consent to what I have done. But suppose you give your consent *post factum*. If you do, I did not violate any of your rights.

Suppose instead that you demand and get fair compensation from what I did to you (perhaps from the person whose life I saved)—does this mean that your rights have still been violated? I think not. If you get fair compensation for crossing my boundaries, there is no violation of rights.

What, then, is 'fair' compensation? This is up to the person to decide, who is the victim of an act of trespassing. The basic notion, then, is, as it should be, consent.

Nozick does not accept this. His main reason for not accepting all boundary-crossing acts that are compensated for has to do with fear.[21] We may fear being used as a tool when a life is saved, even if we know that we will be fully compensated for the harm done to us. This may be so. But to produce fear in a person who does not give consent is in itself a violation of the right to self-ownership, one might argue. So even the fear should be compensated for. But then I see no problem anymore with such boundary-crossing acts.

21. Robert Nozick, *Anarchy, State, and Utopia*, p. 71.

If we are compensated for them, and even for the fear they cause in us, to be exposed to them is no different from going to the dentist in order to secure a healthy status of your teeth at the cost of some temporary fear.

Nozick also adds that if we allow boundary-crossings, given that they are compensated for, this 'embodies the use of persons as means'.[22] Again, I see no problem in this, if consent is indeed given (in the form of fair compensation). It is the use of one another as *mere* means that should be problematic, from the point of view of the moral rights theory, not the use, as such, of one another as means. It is morally repugnant, rather, to urge that if I can save a life by pushing a person, and then compensate him for the inconvenience, I should still not push him. If possible we should avoid this implication. And we do if we see trespassing that gets fairly compensated as morally all right.

If boundary-crossings that get compensated are no violations of right, we may also stick to the idea that 'all rights are equal'. It is wrong to violate rights, period. There is no such thing as some rights-violations being more wrong than others. For an action to be wrong means that it is morally prohibited, period. Prohibitions do not come in degrees. However, some boundary-crossings, such as pushing a person to the side when you save the life of another person, are all right, provided the person pushed is duly compensated. Even serious acts of boundary-crossings, such as the sacrifice of one person's limb for the sake of the life of another person, may be all right, provided compensation is paid. However, it is hard to see how the killing of one person, in order to save the life of another, could get compensated. The one who has been killed cannot afterwards give consent to the killing—hence an absolute prohibition against killing.

On this understanding of the moral rights theory we avoid a problem of 'asymmetry' discussed by Kasper Lippert-Rasmussen. Rasmussen is worried by the idea that while some rights-violations,

22. Robert Nozick, *Anarchy, State, and Utopia*, p. 71.

such as kicking a person unconscious for a while, can be outweighed with reference to the little harm they do to a person, killing is not treated in a similar vein, even though it may rob a person of exactly the same time of experienced life. However, if we grant that boundary-crossings that get compensated for are no violations of rights, then there is no asymmetry there to explain.[23] If the person knocked unconscious is given compensation, then her rights have not after all been violated. If she refuses any amount of compensation available, however, it is simply wrong to knock her unconscious, even if this would save a life.

3.5. A Problem with the Theory

The moral rights theory and deontology are similar in that they operate with side-constraints on our actions. According to both traditions, there are types of actions that we are not allowed to perform, irrespective of the consequences of the performance of particular instances of them. But while deontology has the agent, or even the act itself, at focus, the moral rights theory has what one could call a patient perspective. Our obligations are there because of the existence of basic rights, founded on self-ownership. The notion of rights is basic. This may be seen as both a strength and a weakness. It *is* a weakness in one respect, at any rate. Robert Nozick himself struggles with the objection that, if rights are so important, then why should there be side-constraints? This is how he articulates the problem:

> How can a concern for the nonviolation of C [a side-constraint] lead to the refusal to violate C even when this would prevent other more extensive violations of C?[24]

23. Kasper Lippert Rasmussen, 'Why Killing Some People Is More Seriously Wrong than Killing Others'.

24. Robert Nozick, *Anarchy, State and Utopia*, p. 30.

Why not indeed violate rights, if this means, on the whole, that fewer rights are violated? Many philosophers who defend theories of rights have bent over backwards in attempts to answer this question,[25] but, it seems to me, in vain. It has been claimed that, when we refuse to violate the rights of a person, even to stop other violations from taking place, we show the utmost respect for this person and his rights. And this is true, of course. But, as has often been pointed out, at the same time we show our complacency with regard to those individuals, who because of our resistance to violate the rights of this person get *their* rights violated. A deontological thinker like Kant need not bother with this problem. He is not interested in the patient. In his strict deontological philosophy, the obligations are there, and if we do not abide by them, we lose our moral standing. It is the agent who matters, not the patient.

Even if I see this theoretical problem with the moral rights theory as a thorn in its side, I will not discuss it any further. Again, I will look more directly at its moral implications and try to assess how plausible they are.

4. EXTREME CIRCUMSTANCES

Deontology (in both its Kantian version and its version as the Sanctity-of-Life Doctrine) and the moral rights theory share the feature that they operate with absolute constraints on our actions. There are things we must not do, regardless of the consequences. Some see this as a merit in the theories, and Kant, for example, is famous for the claim that justice should reign 'even if all the rogues in the world should perish'.[26] If our exclusive focus is on the act itself, and on the person who performs it, the agent, it makes sense

25. This includes Frances Kamm and Thomas Nagel. For references and an overview, and for a good criticism of their attempts, see Kasper Lippert Rasmussen, *Deontology, Responsibility, and Equality*, Chapter 2.

26. Immanuel Kant, *Perpetual Peace*, p. 133.

to adopt this absolute view of the constraints. By abiding by them I do what I ought to do, and that's what morality is all about. I keep my hands clean. But others see this aspect of the theories as deeply problematic. They want to hold on to one of the two types of theories, but only with the proviso that, if *terrible* consequences would ensue if one did not kill an innocent human being, or if one did not violate a right, it would be acceptable to do so. This proviso means that the rationale behind the theories gets somewhat compromised, of course. The proviso could be seen as too much of a concession to utilitarianism, the next theory to be discussed. It might be objected that the incorporation of an imperfect duty to maximize happiness, acknowledged by Kant, and the principle of double effect, wedded to the Sanctity-of-Life Doctrine, are enough. To make any further move in the direction of utilitarianism is to get too close for comfort.

Many people who adhere to deontology believe in God. They may comfort themselves with the thought that if they assume responsibility for their own actions, someone else, God, takes responsibility for the rest of the world. And yet, perhaps the best versions of the theories do indeed incorporate such a proviso. After all, even the *possibility* of such bad consequences of abiding by the theories may be seen as a problem for the theories. Robert Nozick, who had no religious backing of his moral rights theory, did indeed contemplate the possibility of such a proviso added to his theory:

> The question of whether these side constraints are absolute, or whether they may be violated in order to avoid catastrophic moral horror, and if the latter, what the resulting structure might look like, is one I hope largely to avoid.[27]

In my discussion of the theories I, too, will leave it open whether they do incorporate such a proviso or not. This means that I will not hold against any of the theories that it is absurd to say that we should observe the constraints even if this means that heavens will

27. Robert Nozick, *Anarchy, State and Utopia*, p. 30n.

fall. I will avoid such examples in my discussion, hence leaving room for interpretations of the theories with the proviso in place.

5. UTILITARIANISM

Utilitarianism is the theory that we ought to maximize the sum total of happiness in the universe. This is the classical version of the theory upon which I will focus in this book. This choice of focus has to do with the fact that the classical version of the theory strikes me as the most plausible one. However, in many ways, what I say about classical hedonistic utilitarianism is applicable also to versions of the theory, which operate with ideas that differ from the hedonistic idea that it is happiness, and happiness only, that we should maximize. Hedonistic utilitarianism competes with other versions of utilitarianism, according to which it is desire-satisfaction, or some items on an 'objective list' (such as knowledge, friendship, and achievements) that should be maximized.

5.1. The Simple Hedonistic Utilitarianism

The version of hedonistic utilitarianism I discuss takes as its point of departure the thought that there exists a single scale, our happiness scale, upon which sentient beings can all be plotted. At each moment, I am at a certain hedonic level. My total experience at this moment has a definite hedonic tone. If I am above the line where life begins to be worth experiencing, my happiness is positive. If I am below, it is given in negative terms. On this version of the theory, which I have defended in many places, we need not calculate how well a person fares at a moment by adding together various different pleasures and pains he had at the time; what *causes* your hedonic level at a time can be extremely varied, but it is the total *effect* on you that counts. It puts you in a certain mood. At each moment you are in a definite mood. You can go wrong in your description of it, but it feels the way it feels.

Given this very simple notion of happiness, we can speak of a sum total to be maximized (in a day of my life, in a life, or in the universe).

A problem with any idea about maximization is, of course, to do with measurement. Does it make sense to say at which hedonic level I am right now? Are intrapersonal and interpersonal comparisons of happiness possible? The classical utilitarian takes for granted, not that it is possible in practice to make such assessments, but that they make sense in theory. There is a true answer to the question of how happy I am right now. This is how they used to explain this.

The needed hedonic unit is typically (for example in Bentham and Edgeworth) conceived of as *the least noticeable difference with regard to happiness.*[28] It is taken for granted that a least noticeable difference has the same magnitude (1) irrespective of where it takes place along the scale from agony to bliss. In the present context I will take for granted that something of the kind works. It is also assumed that the unit is the same for all sentient beings. Hence, both intrapersonal and interpersonal comparisons of happiness make sense.

Of course, if we add to the picture of what it is that should get maximized—if it is not only happiness, but also, say, knowledge, friendship, and so forth—then the problem with a measurement and with interpersonal comparisons is magnified. I will not enter into this problem. I will take for granted that there are at least some versions of utilitarianism that make sense.

This is a general trait of this book. I will now and then touch upon difficult metaphysical and methodological problems associated with the three theories I examine, but I will labour under the assumption that these problems *can* be solved, one way or another. My exclusive interest here is in the *normative* plausibility of the theories. I want to assess their implications in particular cases.

28. I discuss and qualify this view in Chapter 5 of my *Hedonistic Utilitarianism*. See also my entry 'hedonism' in *The Encyclopedia of Utilitarianism* for further discussion (and complication).

This does not mean that these methodological problems are not important. If I had had space enough, and my readers had had patience enough, I would have gone deeper into them. If several moral hypotheses (theories) turn out all of them to be intuitively adequate, we would have to resort to methodological considerations in our adoption of one of them in particular, as the one that *best* explains our considered intuitions. Only utilitarianism will turn out to be intuitively adequate in the field I here examine—the ethics of killing—so the main remaining task is to try to sort out methodological worries in relation to *it*. That must be a task for another time, however.

5.2. Criteria of Right Action and Methods of Decision Making

According to the utilitarian criterion of right action, what we do is right if and only if it maximizes the sum total of happiness in the universe. The fact that it maximizes the sum total of happiness in the universe is what *makes* it right, furthermore. Obviously, it is not easy to tell in a particular case whether an action satisfies this criterion or not. So utilitarianism implies practical scepticism. However, utilitarians tend to argue that there is a way of handling the problem that practical scepticism poses. We construct a method of decision making such that, when consistently abided by, we believe, it is likely to lead to better outcomes than any competing method would have led to. In many situations the recommendation is to try to maximize, not happiness, but expected happiness, where we take into account our subjective beliefs about the consequences of the alternative actions we are facing.[29] However, the method is bound

29. A clear account of this idea, which has been implicit in all classical statements of utilitarianism, was first given in R. Eugene Bales's 'Act-Utilitarianism; Account of Right-Making Characteristics or Decision-Making Procedure?'. It is debatable, but beyond the scope of this chapter, to discuss whether this move really meets the argument that utilitarianism cannot guide our choices. For a critique, see Fred Feldman, 'Actual Utility, the Objection from Impracticality, and the Move from Expected Utility'.

to be complicated. In some situations it has bad consequences if you calculate the expected outcome of your actions (such as in your dealings with your spouse, your children, or your friends). Then you allow yourself to be spontaneous, at least to some degree. Moreover, in many situations it probably has better consequences if you abide by some rule or habit than if you calculate. Thus, this is what you will do if you abide by the favoured method of decision making.

I will accept that this idea makes sense, even though there are both metaphysical and methodological problems with it.[30] Once again, I will simply assume that such problems, facing each one of the three approaches under scrutiny in this book, can be solved. I want to assess them from a *moral* point of view.

It should also be kept in mind that, even if utilitarianism cannot be 'applied' to real cases, it does yield definite implications when confronted with thought experiments; and this is the kind of confrontation of theory with 'practice' that we will mainly meet with in this book. Here utilitarianism does no worse than deontology or moral rights. I see this as a merit in all the three theories discussed in this book; when we want to make an inference to the best explanation of our data (the content of our considered intuitions), it is important that a theory has this kind of intuitive content. Theories that do not satisfy a 'practicality' requirement are wanting, for this very reason.

Even if many versions of utilitarianism are covered by implication in this book, there is one version of it that is not covered at all, to wit, rule-utilitarianism. I will say a few words about it here but then take no further notice of it. The reason is that it is highly implausible.

5.3. Why Not Rule-Utilitarianism

Rule-utilitarianism is the view that a particular action is wrong if, and only if, it is forbidden by the set of rules the general obedience

30. I discuss them in my *From Reasons to Norms*, Chapter 6.

or acceptance of which would maximize the sum total of happiness. This can't be right.

Suppose it has the best consequences if everyone takes to the street in an attempt to topple a tyrant—or the acceptance value of this rule is optimal. Then I should take to the streets. But, if, as a matter of fact, no one else does, then this may have very bad consequences indeed. This provides, as such, a strong objection to rule-utilitarianism.

Moreover, just as we noted in relation to Kant's first formulation of his categorical imperative, rule-utilitarianism cannot state any plausible answer to the question of what it is that *makes* an action wrong. To say that the action was wrong because it was at variance with a rule such that, had everyone obeyed or accepted it, the consequences would have been the very best, is not a plausible way of answering the question of what *made* the action wrong. Again, we have distanced ourselves too much from the patient, the agent, and what really took place in the situation.

It might seem that there exist cases where rule-utilitarianism has more plausible implications than act-utilitarianism. I think of a situation where we have coordination problems. Suppose two persons can together achieve something valuable. If both cooperate, the desired outcome will materialize. However, if only one does his share, and the other one defects, we end up in a very bad situation. Not only have we not achieved the desired end, one person has wasted his resources as well. If both defect, the result is bad, but less bad than if one does his share and the other one defects.

In the situation, if each person cannot affect what the other does, and both, as a matter of fact, defect, each one has done his act-utilitarian duty. But this means that the result of each one doing his act-utilitarian duty can be suboptimal. Had they instead done their rule-utilitarian duty, the result would have been optimal. Does this speak in favour of rule-utilitarianism?

It does not. First of all, rule-utilitarianism has a similar problem. Even if all do their rule-utilitarian duty, the result may be suboptimal. Suppose *all* take to the streets, where it had been enough if, say,

75 percent had done so. In that case, the remaining 25 percent could have done something better than wasting their resources. The outcome is suboptimal.

Furthermore, there is a way of seeing to it that act-utilitarianism, if generally practiced, does indeed lead to optimal outcomes. We should count, not only what each individual agent does, in the situation, but also what people do together. It is true that, in the envisaged situation, each person does the right thing if he defects. However, *together* the two persons act wrongly. They should have cooperated. So if everyone does what he should, individuals and collectivities alike, then act-utilitarianism does guarantee optimal outcomes.

Can collectivities act? Yes, they can. I have argued this point elsewhere, and will not belabour it in the present context. Collectivities can act, they can act wrongly, and there is even a point in having sanctions that set collectivities right.[31]

5.4. Contractualism and Rule-Utilitarianism

In the preceding section I have dealt with rule-utilitarianism as a view motivated by consequentialist concerns. So understood, it fails. However, in the present discussion we often meet with attempts to defend rule-utilitarianism in a different manner. It is taken to be the natural outcome if we adopt a contractualist stance to morality. If we think that a correct moral theory is a set of rules we would accept under certain circumstances, or a set of rules such that no one can reasonably reject them, if they sincerely attempt to regulate life together with other human agents, then it is perhaps possible to claim that what we would opt for is rule-utilitarianism.[32] It may also be claimed that this view, rule-utilitarianism, is not only a version

31. See my 'The Myth of Innocence. On Collective Responsibility and Collective Punishment'. See also Björn Petersson's discussion about this proposal and defence of a somewhat less radical but similar claim in 'Collective Responsibility and Omissions'.

32. For a vigorous defence of rule-utilitarianism along such lines, see Brad Hooker, *Ideal Code, Real World: A Rule-Consequentialist Theory of Morality*.

of utilitarianism, but also a version of Kantianism (of Kant's categorical imperative, in its first formulation). This is the theme of Derek Parfit's highly influential book *On What Matters*.

I am very sceptical about this approach. It is not clear to me what conclusions we should draw from the fact that a set of rules would be generally accepted under some more-or-less ideal circumstances. Some contractualist philosophers are moral nihilists. This seems to be true of David Gauthier, who offers the set of rules we can agree about as a substitute for morality.[33] He furthermore claims that this substitute is more like common sense morality than we would have expected. As I noted in the previous chapter, this kind of contractualism is of no interest in the present context. Here an attempt is being made to find the truth in morality.

In other versions of contractualism, it is less clear how the result of the hypothetical contract is thought to function. Is the idea perhaps that what we would contract on must be a true morality? Suppose a set of rules (for example, rule-utilitarianism) is such that it could not 'reasonably be rejected' by people in the search of a set of rules intended to regulate their lives together (to use Thomas Scanlon's way of putting it).[34] It strikes me as just plain wrong to conclude that the kind of morality that would be accepted under such ideal circumstances must be *true*. Moreover, if the result turned out to be rule-utilitarianism of some kind, we would have to conclude that the version of rule-utilitarianism agreed upon, could still not help us to explain *why* some actions are right and some actions wrong. It is not a right-making characteristic of an action, even on this view, either that the action conforms to an ideal set of rules, or that it conforms to rules that people would opt for, under ideal circumstances. What makes, say, an act of murder wrong, if it is wrong, is not that it is a variance with an ideal rule, but that it is an act of murder (provided there is a rule against murder). In this I suppose even a contractualist rule-utilitarian must concur.

33. See his *Morals by Agreement*.
34. *What We Owe to Each Other*, p. 4.

But if this is so, contractualism, even if it would favour rule-utilitarianism, doesn't really provide us with an alternative to the moral principles discussed in this book. Rule-utilitarianism cannot, as such, be put to the kind of test I here arrange. What should be put to test are really the attempted moral explanations of the rightness and wrongness of particular actions that adherents of this view are prepared to give with reference to each one among the rules contained in the optimal set of rules we have contracted for (or could contract for). What should be put to test are those individual rules, such as the rule that one should not steal or murder, and so forth. Do they best explain the content of our considered intuitions? If they do, we get evidence, not for rule-utilitarianism, but for these rules themselves.

5.5. Utilitarianism and Killing

According to utilitarianism, killing is all right if it maximizes the sum total of happiness. So if an act of killing is wrong, it must be wrong because, in the circumstances, it robs the universe of happiness. This is often the case. And when it is the case, it often has to do with the fact that, when a person is killed, she is deprived of all the happiness her future life would have contained. This is true of all victims of murder who would have led lives, had they not been killed, that were, on balance, worth living (they would have contained a positive sum of happiness). Here we deduct negative happiness (misery, the state where life is not worth experiencing) from positive happiness (states worth experiencing).

On the version of utilitarianism here discussed, the loss suffered by one individual may be morally outweighed, however, by the larger gain by someone else, or by a sum of small gains pertaining to many people. On this total view merely hypothetical individuals count in the moral calculus. According to this view, loss in quality of life may be morally compensated for by gain in the number of lives lived. All this is of little significance in many discussions about the moral status of killing, but it becomes relevant in discussions to be undertaken in this book about abortion, where I will discuss it at length.

According to utilitarianism many acts of killing are in fact wrong, either because they deprive the victim of future possible happiness, without any compensating gain for others, or because of the bad side effects on those other than the victim. In particular, when someone is murdered, this often means suffering for those who are near and dear to the victim. This counts from the point of view of utilitarianism, and it is an important part of the utilitarian account of the ethics of murder.

Furthermore, when it comes to legislation, the effects of the laws are of importance from the point of view of utilitarianism. We ought to make the laws that help us maximize the sum total of happiness. This means, as we will see, that utilitarians take up a strong *legal* stance against murder—even against individual acts of murder that are *morally* permitted. Utilitarianism is different from both deontology and the moral rights theory in that it condones such a system of double standards. It recommends the criminalization of some actions that are, according to the utilitarian criterion of right action itself, morally all right.

6. THE CRUCIAL TESTS

We now have the three bold conjectures in rough outline, and it is time to put them to test. The idea is to confront them with various different kinds of killing, to see what implications they yield, and to assess whether they can explain our considered moral intuitions about the cases at hand.

The task is to discuss the implications of the theories and, at the same time, to try to put our own moral intuitions under scrutiny—to submit them to cognitive psychotherapy. It is, furthermore, helpful to know what other people think about the cases. Here my empirical surveys will provide important input if we want to try to transcend our own narrow cultural horizon.

It is also interesting to know whether there are any systematic cognitive mistakes, which underlie our intuitive reactions to the cases. Are some of our reactions mere expressions of disgust, like our fear of snakes? Or, do they have their origin in a lack of moral imagination in relation to large numbers? In such cases, even if we cannot avoid them, we should perhaps not trust them in our pursuit of moral truth.

Let us now put the theories to test. And let us start with the most abstract cases, the so-called trolley cases.

Chapter 3

The Trolley Cases

1. INTRODUCTION

How do we test moral theories? We conceive of them as bold conjectures and we put them to crucial tests and investigate whether the implications they yield stand up to a confrontation with the content of our considered moral intuitions, I have claimed. We treat the content of our intuitions as evidence. Before we do so, however, before we put any trust in our intuitions, I have also insisted, we need to submit them to cognitive psychotherapy. After all, they may merely be the result of tradition. We may have been inculcated in them in a manner that means we would hold them regardless of whether they are correct or not.

When it comes to intuitions about such things as abortion, capital punishment, and killing in war, it is obvious that we have a hard time distancing ourselves from the views that have been instilled in us. We will see this in this book. When you survey the views of people from different cultures on such matters, you get what you expect: systematic differences that seem to reflect varying cultural backgrounds. Such differences should raise our suspicion. If we are lucky, and duly suspicious, then we might succeed in actually transcending our own narrow cultural background. We might arrive, in a cool hour, at intuitions with a content that we feel we can trust. But it would also be nice if we could arrange crucial experiments in an area where cultural biases are more or less absent. It has been suggested that this may be the case with certain abstract thought experiments, in relation to which cultural variations are indeed not that important. I think of examples such that we can describe them without using expressions that trigger any idiosyncratic cultural cues. In fact, it has been suggested that the so-called trolley problems are of this kind. In relation to them, a consistent pattern of responses emerges, irrespective of cultural background.[1] Then, at least, what lead us to our responses are not cultural *idiosyncrasies*. I make this claim about the trolley examples with a caveat to be explained below. Perhaps our reaction to the trolley cases is, after all, more dependent on cultural background than has been supposed. In particular, it seems as though a Chinese tradition has reinforced the kind of deontological responses we find in relation to some of the trolley cases. Or, perhaps the other way round? The Western tradition has reinforced a more 'utilitarian' response?[2]

Setting the uncertainties about the Chinese to one side, it might be a good idea to test our moral hypotheses in relation to such thought examples and hence hope to avoid some cultural bias. That is what I will do in the present chapter. However, as I have noted, there are biases other than the cultural ones to correct for. There also exist some kind of cognitive mistakes we make when we react to cases such as these. In this chapter they will be our focus. The reason for this is that, as a matter of fact, we know a lot about how people tend to arrive at their judgements about these examples. What we know about our reactions to these examples should help us to the *right* debunking strategy. It should lead us to an idea about which intuitions to trust, and which not to trust, and why.

1. For references to this research, see, for example, Greg Miller, 'The Roots of Morality'; the main source is Marc Hauser, Fiery Cushman et al., 'A Dissociation Between Moral Judgments and Justifications'.

2. See Henrik Ahlenius and Torbjörn Tännsjö, 'Chinese and Westerners Respond Differently to the Trolley Dilemmas', presenting empirical findings about reactions to the trolley cases gathered from average Chinese, Russian, and US citizens. The Chinese have been found in general to be more 'deontological' than the Russians and Americans.

2. A CRUCIAL TEST

Here are the three standard trolley examples I want to use as a crucial test: The Switch, The Footbridge, and the Loop. They are extensively discussed in a debate inaugurated by two important moral philosophers, Philippa Foot and Judith Jarvis Thomson.[3] I describe them in the form I here use them, in the opening paragraphs of sections 4, 5, and 6, respectively. These are also the versions I used in my survey of opinions among the Chinese, the Russians, and the Americans.[4]

Suppose for a moment that the way people react to these examples does not reflect their different cultures or genders. This does not mean that all agree about them, however. The point is that the same pattern of answers surfaces, irrespective of what kind of people we ask about them. A vast majority believe that we should flip the switch in the Switch and that we should not push the big man in the Footbridge, and a majority (but not a vast one) believe that we should flip the switch in the Loop.

We may now try to construct a crucial experiment where we confront various different bold moral conjectures with the trolley examples. I will focus here, as elsewhere, on deontology, the moral rights theory, and utilitarianism.

I confront these three families of moral theories with the answers to the trolley cases. How does each of them fare in relation to the ordinary reactions to the examples?

On the face of it, it seems as though all three approaches have problems with the majority view. The utilitarian answer does not square well with our reactions to the Footbridge case, deontological thinking—at least (as we will see) in some version of it—sits ill with the majority reactions to the Loop, and the moral rights theory

3. For the first contributions to this discussion, see Philippa Foot, 'The Problem of Abortion and the Doctrine of the Double Effect' and Judith Jarvis Thomson, 'Killing, Letting Die, and the Trolley Problem'.

4. Ahlenius and Tännsjö, ibid.

has problems already with the Switch (I will soon explain why). But can we rely on these reactions? Why trust the majority? In order to know whether the majority has got it right, we need to know which ones among the intuitions we encounter are reliable. Again, we need some cognitive psychotherapy.

3. OUR REACTIONS TO THE TROLLEY CASES EXAMINED

Joshua D. Greene at Harvard University and his collaborators have studied extensively how we reach our verdicts in the trolley cases. Here are, in a very simplified form, some of their results about what happens when people react to the cases.[5] It seems as though a dual model makes best sense here. On the one hand, controlled cognitive processes drive our utilitarian judgements, while non-utilitarian judgements (don't push the man in the Footbridge Case) are driven by automatic, intuitive emotional responses. This is shown also in other (personal) cases, where we are reluctant to kill upfront, in a physical manner, requiring the exercise of physical personal force, even for a seemingly good reason. Different parts of our brains are responsible for these different responses, as can be seen from neuroimaging of our brains. 'Utilitarian' responses are associated with increased activity in the dorsolateral prefrontal cortex, a brain region linked to cognitive control.[6] By cheering people up, before we confront them with the cases, or by making them angry, it is possible to move them closer to the utilitarian camp. By keeping people busy with intellectual tasks while they are giving their verdicts on the trolley cases, it is possible to move them closer to the non-utilitarian camp. Moreover, those who reach the utilitarian

5. For an overview of his results, and for his own interpretation of them, see his impressive book *Moral Tribes: Emotion, Reason, and the Gap Between Us and Them*.

6. Greene, J. et al., 'The neural bases of cognitive conflict and control in moral judgment'.

verdict have to overcome their own initial emotional resistance to the conclusion. And people suffering from focal bilateral damage to the ventromedial prefrontal cortex (VMPC), a brain region necessary for the normal generation of social emotions, easily reach the utilitarian solution when asked about the cases.[7]

When we know more about the origin of our moral intuitions, can this help us to select the right moral hypothesis, utilitarianism, the Sanctity-of-Life Doctrine, Kantianism, or a libertarian moral rights theory? It can.

The results from neuroimaging of our brains and experimental psychological studies do not contradict the content of any of our intuitions. They provide no evidence against them. But they can help us to undermine the *justification* for the content of some of the intuitions.

Let us try this approach in order to find out which ones among the common intuitions to the trolley cases have their justification undermined by the scientific results showing us how they have come about?

The proper way of approaching our intuitions is to see what our reactions to the cases are, once we know about the origin of various kinds of intuitions. We should not rely on our intuitions before we know all that can be known about their origin. Consequently, we should expose them to a kind of cognitive psychotherapy.

Here is a brief sketch of how one could proceed with the psychotherapy.

4. THE SWITCH

The Switch. A trolley is running down a track. In its path are five people who have been tied to the track. It is possible for you to flip a switch that will lead the trolley down a different track. There is a single person tied to

7. Koenig et al., 'Damage to the prefrontal cortex increases utilitarian moral judgements'.

that track. Should you flip the switch and have one person killed in order to save the five?

	China	*Russia*	*United States*
Yes	52%	63%	81%
No	36%	20%	13%
Don't know	12%	17%	6%

There seems to be no reason to discard our reaction to this case. Like most people, my intuition is that one ought to flip the switch. This is an immediate reaction on my part. It is theory laden, of course, but not consciously deduced from any moral theory. It depends on my sympathy with the victims and with the simple mathematical and moral thought that it is worse when five are killed than it is when one is killed, all other things being equal. Even among the Chinese, a majority concurred in this judgment.

The content of this intuition is explained by utilitarianism. It is also explained by the deontological Sanctity-of-Life Doctrine, according to which you are not allowed intentionally to kill even to save lives (since the killing of the person on the side-track, if you flip the switch, is merely a foreseen and not intended side effect of your action). However, the deontological theory only explains why one *ought* to flip the switch since it has a utilitarian component built into it in addition to the idea of deontological constraints. In the Sanctity-of-Life version of deontology it is the principle of double effect, with its insistence on proportionality, that does the trick. If you do not flip the switch, you may claim that you merely foresee the death of the innocent five on the track. However, given that you could have saved them, at the cost of one life, the requirement of proportionality is arguably not satisfied if you choose this option. In standard Kantian thinking the utilitarian addition comes in the form of an 'imperfect' duty of beneficence. This in itself is a complicated notion. A judgement in the individual case is also required in order to sort out the implications of it. But even Kant should say that we ought to flip the switch, it seems to me, since in so doing we promote happiness in the world and we do so without violating any constraint. In particular, when we redirect the trolley, we do not use that single person on the track as a *means* to the rescue of the five.

What about the moral rights theory? It has often been taken for granted that, on that theory, you are at least allowed to flip the switch. However, according to this theory, you *need* not do it. This is at variance with how people ordinarily see the case. As a matter of fact, according to this theory, in its strict Nozickian version, you need not flip the switch even if there is *no one* on the track onto whom, in order to save the five, you redirect the trolley. This strikes most people as absurd. Of course, the libertarian may search for some compromise with utilitarian thinking and argue that you ought to save lives, if the costs to you are not very high. However, such a compromise is likely to seem ad hoc. If you feel that you need to resort to it, then it is better to opt for utilitarianism in the first place.

But is it true that, according to a moral rights theory, you are allowed to flip the switch in the Switch? Judith Jarvis Thomson has questioned this recently, and very plausibly.[8] She invites us to think of a situation where it is possible for a person either to redirect the trolley to a track where he is himself situated, or to a track where a stranger is situated. He is allowed, on the moral rights theory, to redirect it into the track where he is situated, of course, but in the circumstances, where he is also present on a side-track, he is not allowed to redirect it into the track where the stranger is situated, not even to save the five, Thomson claims. However, the presence of the extra track, which the person is on, cannot make any moral difference, she also claims, so we are not allowed in the standard case to flip the Switch.

8. Judith Jarvis Thomson, 'Turning the trolley'.

This understanding of the moral rights theory is a congenial one, it seems to me, since the moral rights theory relies on a distinction between doing and allowing harm, and even in the Switch, if we flip the Switch, we do harm to an innocent person. Or, if we want to be strict, we should put the point, not in terms of harm, but in terms of boundary-crossings not consented to. This is so since the notion of harm plays no essential role in the moral rights theory. We are sometimes allowed actively to cause harm—if it happens without any transgression of any personal boundaries. And we are sometimes allowed to transgress personal boundaries and do harm—if it takes place with consent. However, in this case, it is clear that there is both transgression of boundaries and that it takes place without consent.

What if we were one among the five threatened by the trolley? Would we then be allowed to redirect the trolley? We would not. We may avert the threat to our life by destroying the trolley, if we can, even if there is a driver on board, since the trolley (with its driver) is about to invade our personal territory. Or at least this seems to me to be a way of making best sense of the theory.

It might be objected that if there is a driver on board, who, too, is an innocent victim of the accident, which he did in no way cause, then we are not allowed to kill him. But this is not so according to the moral rights theory. The moral rights theory doesn't deal in the notion of innocence. If the trolley with its driver poses a threat to me, if it is about to cross my boundaries, without my consent, then I may stop it. This is like getting rid of a foetus who has invaded my body (if it is where it is, say, because of rape). However, my right to destroy the trolley with the driver on board does not give me a right to redirect the trolley onto some person *who doesn't threaten me*.

Now, if this understanding of the moral rights theory is correct, and it seems to be correct, then the theory is in deep trouble. It is in trouble, I submit, since we *ought* to flip the switch in the Switch.

What am I to say of my difference here with Thomson? How did she reach her judgement? Well, even if it is *her* considered intuition that we are not allowed to flip the switch, I can't give up *my* intuitive response on this ground alone. And even if I have not asked her, I strongly suspect that her immediate reaction to the case is still that one ought to flip the switch. However, she does not take this reaction as evidence. She must think that she has found a way of debunking this reaction of hers and others. I suppose the thought experiment with the extra track on which the person supposed to flip the switch himself is situated, is meant to do the trick. But is it successful? I think not. Most people seem to be unperturbed by it. Perhaps the idea that it is wrong to flip the switch is not something she or anyone else intuits, then, but rather something she has *deduced* through an intricate argument from her favoured theory!

A reason to believe that this has actually happened is the following. First of all, we should adopt a detached view of the case.[9] We should cast it in the third person. This is what Thomson does when she states the case. However, when she starts to argue, she leaves the third person perspective and casts the reasoning in the first person. She attributes and repudiates the following argument to the person capable of either sacrificing his own life or the life of the stranger on the other side-track:

> Hmm. I want to save those five workmen. I can do that by . . . throwing the switch to the left, saving the five but killing myself. I'd prefer not dying today, however, even for the sake of saving five. So I'll choose . . . saving the five but killing the one on the right-hand track instead.[10]

We should not speculate, as Thomson does, about what we would do in the circumstances (where *we* could either save *our own* neck or save the lives of *others*). We should, instead, focus in a detached manner on the person who can flip the switch in order either to kill himself or

9. This is rarely done. My own questionnaire violates what one may call the requirement of impartiality. Sometimes this is of no consequence, but in Thomson's example it seems to be of the very last consequence. We tend to think: 'Would *I* sacrifice *my* life for the five? No, but then. . .' But this line of argument is misleading.

10. Ibid., p. 364.

the stranger—or allow the five to die. Most people would agree with Thomson that this person is allowed to sacrifice his own life in order to save the five. But does he have an *obligation* to do so? The utilitarian answer, of course, is that he can do as he pleases. He can either sacrifice his own life or the life of the stranger on the side-track. But he *is* under an obligation to save the five, one way or the other. Many people believe that utilitarianism makes too heavy a demand on us. They would say that the agent is under no obligation to sacrifice his own life. This is also Thomson's view. Yet he who says so must also face the question of whether he should sacrifice the stranger on the side-track or allow that the five on the main track die, once he himself has decided to stay alive. In order to reach the conclusion that he should allow the five to die, we seem to need the assumption that it is wrong to kill one individual actively, even in order to save (several) lives. But this is what the moral rights theory tells us. The moral rights theory, and the moral rights theory only, provides us with this assumption.

If this is so, however, then Thomson's judgement about the Switch has no epistemic value, which is *independent* of her moral rights theory. It is not really an intuition at all.

There may be another aspect to Thomson's discussion. She makes this further claim about the agent who contemplates saving his own neck while sacrificing the person on the other side-track, in order to save the five:

> Since he wouldn't himself pay the cost of his good deed if he could pay it, there is no way in which he can decently regard himself as entitled to make someone else pay it.[11]

This comment seems to me irrelevant to the normative question of whether the agent should flip the switch or not. It has all the more to do with what kind of people we want and ought to be. It has to do with character traits. It may very well be that a person who is not prepared to sacrifice his own life in order to save the five should feel

11. Ibid., p. 366.

ashamed when he sacrifices the stranger. He should feel ashamed not of what he does but because of the character traits he realizes that he has. However, flipping the switch, when there is no other way to save the five, may still very well be what he ought to *do*. Unless we resort to the idea that it is wrong actively to kill even in order to save lives (the moral rights theory), it is difficult to avoid this conclusion. To flip the switch is what he ought to do.

THE SWITCH

Majority view: You ought (it is wrong not) to flip the switch.

My immediate reaction: You ought (it is wrong not) to flip the switch.

My (our?) considered intuition (to be explained): You ought (it is wrong not) to flip the switch.

5. THE FOOTBRIDGE

The Footbridge. You are on a bridge under which the trolley will pass. There is a big man next to you and your only way to stop the trolley is to push him onto the track, killing him to save five. Should you push him?

	China	*Russia*	*United States*
Yes	22%	36%	39%
No	68%	45%	56%
Don't know	10%	19%	5%

If we trust the content of the majority reaction to this case, this means that we have evidence against utilitarianism (which is inconsistent with it) and in defence of deontology as well as in defence of the moral rights theory (which both explain it). Or, is this perhaps a superficial understanding of the deontological theory? Part of deontology, at least in the form of the Sanctity-of-Life Doctrine, is the principle of double effect. Doesn't the principle of double effect leave room for this kind of killing?

The crucial thing in the Sanctity-of-Life Doctrine is that we do not kill intentionally. It seems to be part of the received wisdom that this is what we do if we push the big man in the Footbridge. But is that correct?

In order to find out whether we kill intentionally in the Footbridge, we should consider the standard counterfactual test. If we could have pushed him and used his body in a manner that would not have meant that he would have been killed, would we then have opted for this method? I think even those who claim that they ought to push him meet this requirement. If, before they push him, they could have dressed him up in some kind of armour that would have saved his life when he was hit by the trolley, they would have done so. But then his *death*, when neither time nor armour is available, is not intended. It is merely a foreseen additional effect of their using him as a tool to stop the trolley. Note that this is different from murder, suicide, euthanasia, and abortion, where death is—as we will see—indeed intended. So, as a matter of fact, the Sanctity-of-Life Doctrine cannot explain why it is wrong to push him. According to this theory, it is not wrong, and, given that we also want to save lives when we can do so without intentionally killing people, we ought, according to the Sanctity-of-Life Doctrine, to push the big man in the Footbridge.

I rely here on a standard interpretation of the theory, where it can be clarified with an example taken from medicine: It is always wrong intentionally to kill a patient, but it may be right to provide aggressive palliative care with the intention of relieving pain, even if it can be foreseen that the patient will die from the care in question. This may be right provided that, in the circumstances, it is a good thing to have the patient free of pain, and provided that there is some reasonable proportion between the (first) good effect (the patient's being free of pain) and the (second) bad effect (death being somewhat hastened), and provided the death of the patient is not sought as a means of achieving the good effect.[12]

It has sometimes been objected that this version is unreasonably permissive. Jonathan Bennett has pointed out this liberal aspect of the theory.[13] This has invited criticism, like the following one from Jonathan Glover:

> When we are on a desert journey and I knowingly use all the drinking water for washing my shirts, my act may be described as one of 'washing shirts', or 'keeping up standards even in the desert', and our being out of water may be thought of as a [merely] foreseen [but not directly intended] consequence.
>
> But it is at least equally acceptable to include the consequence in the description of the act, which may then be described as one of 'using up the last of the water' or of 'putting our lives at risk'.[14]

Those who adhere to the principle of double effect would undoubtedly say that, irrespective of whether we describe the action as 'using up the last of the water', or as 'putting our lives at risk', crucial to its normative status is whether the intention *is* to kill the members of the expedition or not. If it is not, then the intention is not forbidden, *as such*. We are not confronted with an example of *intentional* killing. It is the *actual* intention of the agent that is decisive.

Thus, even if the principle of double effect, on the standard understanding of it, is more liberal than what many thinkers have supposed, the rationale behind does not get compromised. While acting on it we are capable of being *repelled* by what is evil—the killing of innocent human beings. We do not *intend* the death of anyone, if we are true to the requirements made by the principle, even when it is given a liberal interpretation.

12. Once again I rely here on the authoritative statement of the principle of double effect in *New Catholic Encyclopedia*.

13. Jonathan Bennett, *Morality and Consequences*, pp. 110–111.

14. Jonathan Glover: *Causing Death and Saving Lives*, p. 90.

However, even if the actual intention is to keep up standards, and the death of the people in the desert is not intended, this does not mean that the action is right. We must also assess the importance of the intended first effect (keeping up standards), and compare it to the merely foreseen bad effect of the action (the death of the members of the expedition). Unless there is a reasonable proportion between these two effects, the action is not permissible. Consequently, it must be hard to make a case for the claim that the requirement of proportionality is fulfilled in the given example. I think, therefore, that we should stick to the standard version of the doctrine. It is a way of making best sense of it.

It should be noted that when we apply the counterfactual test we keep the actual basic motivational structure of the agent fixed. We can then ask whether the agent would have dressed the big man in armour before pushing him, in order to tease out the content of the given motivation. We are not allowed to introduce counterfactuals that presuppose that the motivational structure would be different, however. Here is a good example.[15] I want to torture a person. If I cannot torture him I want to kill him. I cannot torture him so I kill him. Was my killing intentional? It may seem that it was not. After all, if I could have tortured him, I would not have killed him. This counterfactual is not admissible, however. This counterfactual means that we speculate about what the agent would have done, given a different (in the situation) basic motivational structure. I do not claim that it is crystal clear how the test should be used in all circumstances but, as in other places of this book, I do not take upon myself to solve all the metaphysical problems engendered by the normative theories I discuss. My interest is in their moral implications and I assume that the metaphysical problems can be solved, in one way or the other. So let us now move on to Kantianism.

In a Kantian version of deontology, we do find support for the majority opinion. For certainly, if we push the man in order to stop the trolley, we use him as a mere means. We use him as a mere means

15. I owe it to Daniel Ramöller.

to a noble end, but that does not mean that, according to Kant, we are doing the right thing. We are not allowed to use people as mere means, not even in order to save lives.

It should be noted that the Kantian view I here *distinguish* from the principle of double effect has been seen also as a possible *interpretation* of the principle.[16] I think we had better keep them apart, however. After all, they present us with two *different* moral perspectives.

According to the moral rights theory, we are not allowed to push the big man. That would be a violation of his right to life. If Thomson is correct in her understanding of the moral rights theory when she applies it to the Switch and claims that we are not allowed actively to kill a person even in order to save five lives, it is even more obvious that we are not allowed to push the big man onto the tracks. This, too, is active killing of a moral subject, against his will, or at least without his permission, in order to save lives.

But is the majority intuition in the Footbridge case reliable? It is not. It is of the kind that we can and should debunk.

What is problematic with our reaction to the Footbridge has to do with the fact that our reluctance to push the big man seems to stem from a primordial emotion we all exhibit. We do not want to kill in this nasty and immediate manner, not even to save lives. In particular, it seems that our reluctance is triggered by the fact that we need to exercise physical force against the big man in order to get him to the track.[17] But this means that things we should all realize are morally irrelevant are taken by us to be relevant, such as physical force exercised in our contact with the victim. As we will see, there is no moral difference between the Footbridge and the Loop on *any* of the moral theories discussed here, in *any* of their versions,

16. Warren S. Quinn, 'Actions, Intentions, and Consequences: The Doctrine of Double Effect'.

17. See Joshua D. Greene, Fiery A. Cushman, Lisa E. Stewart, Kelly Lowenberg, Leight E. Nystrom, and Jonathan D. Cohen, 'Pushing moral buttons: The interaction between personal force and intention in moral judgement' about this.

which indicates that there is none. And yet we intuit one. We must be wrong.

Our emotive reluctance to push people onto the tracks is of a kind that is therefore suspect from an epistemic point of view. It is rather like an instinctive fear of snakes than like an observational response. Our reluctance is not triggered by any feature in the situation that is of direct moral relevance. Rather, it is triggered by a trait that, in many ordinary cases, happens to correlate with what is of moral relevance. It may be rational, therefore, to have this reluctance, and it may lead us to the right verdict in many cases, but it is not rational to rely on it in our search of the moral truth, like the present one.

However, in my discussion about the Switch I admitted that our intuition to the effect that we should flip the switch also relies on emotions (our sympathy for others), together with some simple math. What is the difference between this intuition, to the effect that I ought to flip the switch, and my unwillingness to push people onto the track? The content of the intuition that I should flip the switch is not directly handed over to us by evolution, in the way our reluctance to push has been handed over to us. However, it is received wisdom that both my capacity for sympathy and my capacity to count are indeed given to me by an evolutionary process. But is the fact that both my capacity for sympathy and my capacity to count are the results of evolution something that should make me suspicious of them? It is not. They are capacities that help me to understand the world around me and to react appropriately to it. In particular, evolution has helped us in the ability to count. This does not mean that we do not believe that 3+5 *really* equals 8.

A crucial premise in my argument is that our reluctance to push is different. It is an immediate emotive[18] response with a particular

18. The fact that it is emotive, if it is, is not really important to the argument. It is the fact that it is a heuristic device, tracking something that is of no *direct* moral relevance (although of *indirect* relevance of a sort to be explained below) that is of importance. For a criticism of the idea that it need be emotive, see Guy Kahane, 'On the Wrong Track: Process and Content in Moral Psychology'.

function. We may speak of it as a heuristic device. Even if it does not track anything of direct moral relevance in the situation, it helps us to what is more often than not the right reaction, without any need for theoretical thought.

Selim Berker has repudiated this premise. He is reluctant to attribute this premise to anyone in the discussion about the trolley cases, partly for reasons to do with charity (he thinks it is mistaken), partly for lack of clear textual support. Regardless of this, I can say for sure that *I* rely on it. I find it very plausible. There is also more to say about it, when the empirical evidence is in. This is how Greene et al. comment on the mechanism, when they conclude their study on the importance of the exercise of physical force (in combination with intentions) to our moral intuitions:

> Why is it that the combined presence of personal force and intention pushes our moral buttons? The co-dependence of these factors suggests a system of moral judgment that operates over an integrated representation of goals and personal force—representations such as 'goal-within-the-reach-of-muscle-force.' . . . A putative sub-system of moral judgment . . . might operate by rejecting any plan that entails harm as a goal-state . . . to be achieved through the direct application of personal force.[19]

Here a caveat is in place. I have argued that in the Footbridge, there need not be any intention to kill the big man. But if this is true there need not be any intention to harm him, either. But Greene et al. stress that it is the combination of the intention to harm and the exercise of personal force that triggers our reluctance to push. My conjecture is that even an intention to use a person as a mere means, in a manner that indicates that the person is killed, and hence certainly harmed as well, in combination with the exercise of personal

19. 'Pushing moral buttons: The interaction between personal fore and intention in moral judgement'.

force, triggers the reaction just as well. I suppose I must leave this issue for further research, however.

Setting these subtleties to one side, why is Berker, who accepts most of the empirical findings reported by Greene et al., still reluctant to admit that the emotional response functions in this way—like a heuristic device, given to us by evolution? This is what he has to say about it:

> [I]t is question begging to assume that just because emotional processes in other domains consist in heuristics, therefore emotional processes in the moral domain consist in heuristics. How can we proclaim these emotional processes to be quick but sloppy shortcuts for getting at the moral truth unless we already have a handle on what the moral truth is?[20]

I discern two distinct objections here, one to do with emotions in general, and the other with a putative circularity. I discuss them in order.

First of all, regarding emotions, we should beware of hasty generalizations. The claim is not that all emotional processes consist in heuristics; the claim is just that this is true of the mechanism triggering our judgement that it is wrong to push the man in the Footbridge. This claim seems very plausible. The empirical evidence from Greene at al. substantiates it.

Now to the concern that the argument is circular. It is true that my argument is based on two moral assumptions. Both seem to be innocuous, however.

First of all, I claim that the mechanism delivers the right answer in most (mundane) cases. How can I make this claim, unless I already have recourse to the moral theory of which I am on the search? But the claim that, *usually*, it is wrong to kill physically and deliberately and upfront (and unprovoked) *is* very reasonable. Even if we cannot tell why this is so, we have no reason to distrust our

20. 'The Normative Insignificance of Neuroscience', p. 317.

judgement about the particular cases: the consequences are devastating, we see no reason why this kind of behaviour should be warranted, and so forth.

Second, I claim that the judgement that it is wrong to push the man in the Footbridge is triggered by facts that are of no *direct* moral relevance (the exercise of physical force). How can I be so sure that this fact is of no direct moral relevance?

It seems clear that we can identify some aspects of the situation as of *no* direct moral relevance (the exercise of physical force), even before we have worked out a complete and intuitively adequate moral theory. The exercise of physical force should make no moral difference, we intuit. It is clear that we have some such pre-theoretical sense about what traits cannot reasonably be taken to be right- or wrong-*making*. I commented at length about that in the previous chapter. The exercise of physical force is indeed such a trait of no *direct* moral relevance.

Note also that I do not claim that the heuristic device delivers the *wrong* answer in the Footbridge. My claim is more modest. I argue that we should not *trust* its deliverances in abstract thought experiments like these, for which it has not evolved. We should be sceptical about its *reliability*. It is obvious that there is something wrong with it. There are no moral differences between the Footbridge and the Loop (we shall see). Yet it only kicks in in the Footbridge. So there is bound to be *something* wrong with it, from the point of view of reliability. And yet, in ordinary life, it is helpful for us to possess this device.

Here another observation may be in place. It may seem as though I here take for granted that, from an evolutionary point of view, an inhibition to kill upfront and intentionally with the use of physical force has survival value. Is that so? It is tempting to argue that, in order to promote your own interests, you should be prepared to kill, at least when you can get away with it. And this may be so. But often you don't get away with it. The person you attack is stronger than you, and he kills you rather than the other way around. So, unless you are under attack yourself, it is unwise to attack a stranger physically and upfront.[21] Or, even if you succeed, your action might come to be looked upon with anger by other people. You are found out and punished. And more importantly, if you develop the kind of character where you are prepared to kill intentionally and violently, even in cases where you are not yourself under attack, you may be found out, not for killing, but for having this kind of character. You will then be exposed to ostracism. We are at least semi-transparent.[22]

Heuristic devices of the kind here identified are rational in the sense that when we react on them, by and large, we escape from certain dangers. We may be afraid of all snakes, irrespective of whether they are dangerous or not, and hence avoid being killed by those who are dangerous. In a similar vein, it may have survival value not to push fellow human beings onto tracks, even if now and then one would save some lives by doing so. But, in a pursuit of the truth, such as the one in normative ethics (in the seminar room, so to speak), when time allows a careful contemplation of the facts, it is wise to rely on our theoretical reflection, which has helped us to a realistic view of the world in other (natural and mathematical and logical) respects.

A problem with the deontological and moral rights theorists' attempt to offer moral explanations of the content of this intuition is also, of course, as just stressed, that people tend to accept that we flip the switch in the Loop. I will return to this. But this fact means that, even if a deontological theory in its Kantian version, or a moral rights theory, can explain our reaction to the Footbridge, this is not a *good* moral explanation. These theories have problems in *other* cases. The moral rights theory has problems already in the Switch, as we have seen.

Our reluctance to push the big man is no evidence in support of either deontology or the moral rights theory, then. What are we to say of the opposite reaction, exhibited by a minority, who claim that the big man should be pushed?

21. This is an explanation stressed by Paul Green in *Just Babies*, p. 184.
22. This is a major theme of David Gauthier's book *Moral by Agreement*.

I am myself a utilitarian (as will be seen in the final chapter). I think the big man should be pushed onto the tracks. I don't think I should count the content of this judgement of mine as evidence in favour of utilitarianism, however. The intuition that I should not push the big man remains, in a way, even when I have decided to consider it not reliable. It doesn't go away. It is like the stick that looks bent in water. Even if I know that it is straight, it still *looks* bent to me. And more importantly, I suppose that my judgement that the big man should be pushed is not really the content of any intuition at all. The problem with it is that, most likely, it has been produced by my belief in the theory I want to test: utilitarianism. This is why it takes time and effort to arrive at it. And this is why, in a sense, the gut feeling that I ought not to push the big man still stands in the way of it.

But if it is derived in this manner from utilitarianism, it lacks independent evidential value. It is not only theory laden, but has stemmed from the very theory I have tried to put to the test.

What are we to say about the fact that people suffering from brain damage that has caused their antisocial personality easily reach the verdict that it is all right to push the big man? I suppose we should say that, in this very special situation, they have an epistemic advantage over the rest of us. They lack the heuristic device that makes it difficult for us to react in a rational manner to a case such as this one.

This does not mean that we should take their answers as evidence for the theories that urge us to push the big man, however. The fact that they have difficulties identifying with other people, the fact that they lack empathy, should give us pause. It is likely that they see the trolley problems not as posing difficult moral puzzles, but as a simple exercise in math.

What are we to say of the putative fact[23] that people who reach the utilitarian verdict in the Footbridge case seem to be *less* prone to help

23. Kahane, G., Everett, J. A. C., Earp, B., Farias, M., and Savulescu, J., '"Utilitarian" Judgments in Sacrificial Moral Dilemmas Do Not Reflect Impartial Concern for the Greater Good'.

others than people at large in many other contexts? They give less to charity than people at large, they are less prone to make sacrifices for the environment, and so forth. Doesn't this show that they have not deduced their verdict from utilitarianism? If they are not utilitarians, how could they have used utilitarianism as a premise in their argument?

I owe this objection to Guy Kahane. I am not convinced by it, however. Regardless of how they live their lives, they may have used utilitarianism as a premise in an argument in this particular situation. When confronted with the Footbridge case, they do apply a simple kind of utilitarian thinking (that they would not allow to mould the way they live their lives in other situations).

What if it could be shown that they have not applied utilitarianism in these cases? What if they have weighed reasons for and against the conclusion that they should push the big man in the manner a deontologist of Ross's variety (to be explained in the last concluding chapter) would do, and ended up in the verdict that they ought to push? This conjecture is also due to Guy Kahane.[24] And if this is so, could we not take the content of their intuitions as evidence?

A problem with this idea is, however, that Ross's kind of intuitionism, as we will see, doesn't allow us to say anything about mere thought experiments, where we have abstracted from all the concrete details that, according to Ross, when taken into account, will lead us to the right judgement. If we would have asked him about the trolley cases, I suppose he would have been silent. Thus, those who believe that we should push the big man could not have argued in the manner described by Ross. It is more plausible to think that they have deliberated along roughly the following lines. 'If I push him, I kill him actively and in a way that would feel very nasty. Moreover, I use him as a mere means. But, what the heck, when it comes to the saving of lives, the end justifies the means. One should save as many as possible. But then I ought to push him.' This is too close to utilitarianism to allow us to say that the conclusion is not derived from it.

24. See again Guy Kahane, 'On the Wrong Track: Process and Content in Moral Psychology'.

Anyway, since *I* believe that *I* have deduced the conclusion that I should push the big man from utilitarianism, *I* hesitate to take the content of this intuition as evidence in defence of utilitarianism. Justification starts and ends at home.

Thus, the upshot is that there is no evidence either for or against utilitarianism (or any moral theory) to be gained from the Footbridge case. When I make my final verdict about the Footbridge, I am in the same camp as I suggested that Judith Jarvis Thomson is in when she states her final verdict about the Switch. We have only derived our different (conflicting) conclusions from different theories.

THE FOOTBRIDGE

The majority view: It is wrong to push the man onto the tracks.

My immediate reaction: It is wrong to push the man onto the tracks.

My (our) considered intuition (to be explained): none.

6. THE LOOP

The Loop. *As in the first case, you can divert the trolley onto a separate track. On this track is a single big man. However, beyond the big man, this track loops back onto the main line towards the five, and if it weren't for the presence of the big man, flipping the switch would not save the five. Should you flip the switch and have the big man killed in order to save the five?*

	China	*Russia*	*United States*
Yes	34%	54%	60%
No	52%	23%	32%
Don't know	14%	23%	8%

Here *my* intuition is that we should flip the switch and most people—setting the Chinese to one side—agree. Again I see no reason to discard this intuition. It has been arrived at in much the same way that the intuition to the simple Switch case was arrived at. We use our ordinary capacity for sympathy and simple math. Again, the content of this intuition is explained by utilitarianism. It is inconsistent with the moral rights theory. If we redirect the trolley towards the big man, we kill him actively, in order to save lives. That is not permissible, according to this theory. But this is not a plausible conclusion. This is good news for utilitarianism, then, and it spells problems for the moral rights theory.

What are we to say of the loop from a deontological point of view? Well, if I am right in my claim that we are allowed to push the big man, even according to the Sanctity-of-Life Doctrine, the loop should not be a problem.

On a more strict Kantian theory, pushing is wrong in the Footbridge case, and also, it may seem, in the Loop. In that case, deontology is in deep trouble here.

Is it true that, according to (Kantian) deontology, we should not flip the switch in the Loop? Frances Kamm has argued[25] that there is a crucial difference between the Footbridge and the Loop. According to her doctrine of a 'triple' effect, we ought not to push the big man in the Footbridge, but we are allowed to flip the Switch in the Loop. How is this possible?

The main thrust of Kamm's argument seems to be that, in the Footbridge, we intend the death of the big man in that we act *in order* to have him killed, while in the Loop, we don't. Here we only act *because* he is there and will be killed when we flip the switch. If I am right in my claim that we do not intend the death of the big man in the Footbridge, then the claim that we do not intend his death in the Loop is completely trivial. Yet on the Kantian version of deontology, Kamm's argument seems to fail. For, certainly, both in the Footbridge and in the Loop, one person is used merely as a means to the saving of lives. This

25. *Intricate Ethics: Rights, Responsibilities, and Permissible Harm*, p. 102.

is not permissible on this theory. Matthew Liao clearly makes a similar point in his 'The Loop Case and Kamm's Doctrine of Triple Effect':

> Even if one grants that in Loop, we are redirecting the trolley because the one will be hit, but not in order to hit the one, it seems that we are nevertheless taking advantage of the one's being on the track. This seems especially the case, when, as in Loop, it is not even in part *their* good we seek to achieve.[26]

Finally, it seems that utilitarianism, which gives an explanation of the content of the majority intuition in the Switch and the Loop, where we can rely on our intuitions even after they have been submitted to cognitive therapy, explains, not only our data, but also the *relative* success of deontological (Kantian) thinking. Utilitarianism explains the relative success of deontological (Kantian) thinking since it can make *moral* sense of our reluctance to push the big man in the Footbridge. It does so with its claim that, even though it is right to push the big man, it is indeed right to try to become a person who will not do the right thing in these very special circumstances. This means a genuine advance in our thinking, of the kind taken as a desideratum by Karl Popper, when we test bold conjectures.[27]

To avoid misunderstanding I should perhaps add that I have not here showed that those who hold the minority view—the view that it is wrong to flip the switch in the Loop—have made any cognitive mistake. They may be justified in their belief that it is wrong to flip the switch in the Loop. It is only that this is not my intuition, nor the intuition held by the majority. When I stick to my intuition, I need also believe that they *must* have made *some* mistake. What kind of mistake? My conjecture is that they have conflated the problem of what it is right to do in the circumstances with the

26. 'The Loop Case and Kamm's Doctrine of Triple Effect'. The paper contains a careful examination of Kamm's position, beyond the scope of this chapter.
27. *Objective Knowledge*, p. 16.

problem of what sort of character one should develop. It may well be that we had better not be people who are prepared to flip the Switch in the Loop (more about this kind of intellectual mistake in the next chapter). And yet, for all that, it seems to me, this is what we ought to do.

THE LOOP

Majority view (with a Chinese caveat): You ought (it is wrong not) to flip the switch.

My immediate reaction: You ought (it is wrong not) to flip the switch.

My (our) considered intuition (to be explained): You ought (it is wrong not) to flip the switch.

7. CONCLUSION

It seems that the moral rights theory, as well as Kant's idea that it is always wrong to treat a human being as a mere means, is at variance with our considered intuitions about the trolley cases. Utilitarianism and the Sanctity-of-Life Doctrine have both proved to be consistent with our considered intuitions about the trolley cases. We see this (I hope) once we go through the kind of cognitive psychotherapy I have advocated and ponder carefully the origin of our intuitions.

A problem with the crucial test provided by the trolley examples, which consists, really, of three independent thought experiments, is, however, that one of these thought experiments has proved to be useless (the Footbridge). Here a sound debunking strategy has robbed us of all possible available evidence.

Chapter 4

Murder

Suppose a woman is stalked by her ex-husband. He does not threaten to kill her, but he never leaves her alone and she thinks that this makes life meaningless for her. She asks the police for help but receives none. She then kills her ex. She comes forward, assumes responsibility for her action, but claims that she had no choice. Is it possible that she did the right thing?

	China	*Russia*	*United States*
Yes	10%	27%	44%
No	86%	68%	51%
Don't know	4%	5%	4%

Should she be punished?

	China	*Russia*	*United States*
Yes	86%	78%	67%
No	9%	16%	28%
Don't know	5%	6%	5%

In my survey I asked a rather abstract question, so what my respondents reacted to was a mere thought experiment. Alas, the case is not very exceptional or far from realities, however. Here is a real-life case, which comes close to my imagined one:

Nurse practitioner convicted in ex-husband's shooting death

It took jurors less than an hour Thursday to find Tracy Devon Brown, 35, guilty of killing her ex-husband by firing a shotgun through the plate-glass window of his front door.

Brown, a nurse practitioner with two master's degrees, now faces up to life in prison for the March 8, 2009, killing of Victor Brown at his northeast Bexar County home.

Jurors are expected to begin deliberating her sentence Friday.

Although Brown declined to testify, her attorney described her throughout the trial and in closing arguments Thursday as a battered wife who was at wits' end when the abuse continued after her divorce and multiple police calls.

The violence eventually spurred mental illness, which contributed to the shooting, defense attorney Stephanie Boyd said. She asked for a not guilty verdict on behalf of Brown and for all people who are abused.

'Where were (authorities) when all of this was going on?' Boyd asked jurors. 'Where was Bexar County, Texas? Somebody continued to let it pass over and over and over.

"Tracy Brown had done all she could to protect her children. She went through all the right channels.'

Boyd also referred to testimony from Brown's 14-year-old daughter, who told jurors Wednesday there was constant violence in the home. One time, the teen said, she fractured her hand when she fell off the bed as Victor Brown was beating her with a belt.

'My mom, she seemed really scared,' the teen said, adding that her own fear of her stepfather led her to sometimes sleep in her mother's room or with a knife under her pillow. 'I always thought that he would try to come to the house.'

But prosecutors Jan Ischy and Marilisa Janssen countered that there was never any proof that Victor Brown was abusive. Regardless, they pointed out, he wasn't the one on trial.

(*My SA News*, accessible on the Internet at: http://www.mysanantonio.com/news/local_news/nurse_guilty_of_shotgun_killing_101609478.html; accessed on 3 September 2010)

This is the kind of action I will discuss in this chapter. I want to examine the implications of the three theories for this kind of action, and initiate a discussion about how we should assess our intuitions in relation to them (to be continued in the final chapter). This kind of action is an act of murder, or so I will argue, but that does not settle its moral status. Is it possible that Tracy Brown did the right thing? Should acts such as the one she performed be illegal? And, even if illegal, should they be punished? What do our theories under examination say about this? Before we can answer that question, we have to be clearer about what is meant, in the present context, by the word 'murder'. It is of note that here something is introduced that was lacking in the previous chapter: the intention to kill (an innocent human being/person). If my argument in the previous chapter was correct, we there met with the (lethal) use of an innocent person as a mere means, objected to by a strand of Kantianism. We also met with active killing, objected to by the moral rights theory. But we did not meet with any *intentional* killing (of an innocent human being/person), typically objected to by all strands of deontological theory. Such killing will be at the heart of the present chapter.

1. WHAT DO WE MEAN BY THE WORD 'MURDER'?

Here is one possible definition of 'murder':

> **murder**, v.t. Kill human being unlawfully with malice aforethought; kill wickedly or inhumanly. (*Concise Oxford Dictionary*)

Perhaps this describes the ordinary use of the term, but I doubt it. Anyway, for my purposes, this definition is not suitable. The definition is in some regards too narrow, in other regards too inclusive.

First of all, the idea that murders must be committed with "malice aforethought"—a difficult expression for a person who does not have English as his native tongue—is too restrictive. Think of the woman who kills her ex. Think of Tracy Brown. She need not act out of any malice aforethought. She may well feel pity for her ex. It's just that she must get rid of him, for her own sake and for the sake of her children.

Secondly, the idea that the killing in question is wicked or inhumane is also too restrictive. The killing may be swift and not even, from the point of view of the victim, noticeable, and it is yet murder.

Thirdly, and I now turn to ways in which the definition is too inclusive. In order to qualify as murder, the killing must be intentional—the intention behind the action must be that the victim is robbed of his life. It is not sufficient, in order to perform an act of murder, to strike a person with malice aforethought and in a way that leads to the death of the victim; if death is not *intended*, it is not murder. The intention must be to *kill*.

Fourthly, the killing in question must be *active*. If I strangle a child I find on my doorstep, this is murder. If I fail to provide aid to poor children in foreign countries, who then die from infectious diseases, I do not commit murder. This is so even if I refuse to send aid only because I *like* the thought of these children dying (the thought of their death perversely enhances the quality of my life). My act may then very well be immoral, but it is not an act of murder. The distinction between acts and omissions is not as straightforward as it may seem, and in a later chapter on assisted death I will return to it. In the present chapter—as I did in the previous chapter—I take it at face value.

Fifthly, the victim must be a born human being. The killing of a foetus (in abortion) or the destruction of an embryo (outside the womb of a woman) is not classified, in the present context, as murder. I discuss abortion in its own chapter.

Sixthly, the victim must be distinct from the perpetrator. You cannot murder yourself. I discuss suicide in its own chapter. I do not include suicides in the class of murders.

Seventhly, the killing of the victim should not be performed at request of the person who is killed. If the victim asks to be killed, as in assisted death, it is not murder. I discuss assisted death in its own chapter.

Eighthly, the killing must not have a legal sanction. If it has, and even if the sanction *should* not be there, the killing is not an act of murder. In the circumstances, the killing is punishment, not murder. I discuss capital punishment in its own chapter.

Note that all this means that a very similar action may be murder in one culture but not murder in another. Think, for example, of the case when a father or a brother kills a young woman (daughter or sister) because her sexual behaviour is considered to be a threat to the honour of the family. In some countries such killing is authorized, and hence not murder, while, in others, it is unauthorized, and hence murder.

Ninthly, the killing should not happen in self-defence (in defence of your own life or the life of someone close to you). If it does, it is not murder. Killing in self-defence is a kind of killing I discuss in the chapter on killing in war.

Finally, the perpetrator must not, when she performs her killing, act under the influence of any severe mental disorder; in particular, it should be true of her that she could have avoided the action. Unless this requirement is fulfilled, her action lacks normative status. Or, one may say, it is *trivially* all right, since there was no alternative open to the agent.

This may seem to take us into deep metaphysical waters. Are we ever free to act differently from how we do? If we cannot ever act differently from how we actually do, then all our actions would be morally all right, since wrongdoing presupposes that I should have acted differently from how I did. I will not go into such problems in the present context, however. It must suffice to note that the entire discussion in this book proceeds under the assumption that there is a sense of 'could have acted differently', which is such that there are examples of wrongdoing, according to all the views I discuss.

My definition of murder, then, looks like this.

Murder is the active, intentional, and, not requested for, killing, performed not in self-defence, of another human being without legal sanction, not performed under the influence of any serious mental disorder rendering the act unavoidable to the agent.

I do not want to say that murder must, by definition, be illegal, then, since I want to discuss whether, according to the theories I examine, such actions should be legal or illegal. I suppose that, as a matter of fact, the actions I discuss *are* illegal in all well-ordered societies. But this is an empirical fact and not something rendered true by my definition.

Note that an act must fulfil *all* these requirements in order to count as murder. Even the active killing of an individual, against his wish, is not murder, if it is not *intentional* killing. An instructive example of this is life-saving killing, discussed especially by Kasper Lippert-Rasmussen.[1] A doctor who saves the life of a patient in a critical situation by giving him a blood transfusion with HIV-infected blood (the only blood available) actively kills the patient (twenty years hence, we may assume). Yet, she doesn't commit murder. The death of the patient from AIDS is not intended; it is a merely foreseen side effect, which the doctor would have avoided had it been possible (had a safe supply of blood been available).

What are we to say about the three trolley cases in relation to my definition of 'murder'? If my characterization of them, in the previous chapter, to the effect that not even in the Footbridge case does the killer intend the death of his victim is correct, then we must conclude that they do not constitute cases of murder. So the crucial element added to the discussion in this chapter is indeed to do with the *intention* to kill.

I asked a Swedish professor of criminal law how the killings in the trolley cases would be assessed from a *legal* point of view. He was inclined to think that they would all qualify as cases of murder, even if he thought that probably no charges would be pressed either in the Switch or in the Loop.

We now have a rough idea about what it means to commit an act of murder. I therefore turn to the question of whether, according to the theories under examination, it is always morally wrong to commit such an act and to the question of whether, according to

1. *Deontology, Responsibility and Equality*, see especially Chapter 4.

the theories, murder should be illegal and, in that case, why. I discuss what the three main moral approaches—deontology, the moral rights theory, and utilitarianism—have to say about this matter.

2. DEONTOLOGY AND MURDER

It might seem that in a discussion about murder, as the notion has been defined in the present context, deontology should appear extremely plausible. If there is any (conventional) action type that is wrong in all its instances, period—irrespective of the consequences in the individual case—it should be murder. This is what deontology claims. And not only does deontology claim that murder is wrong, it also explains the wrongness of murder. Murder is wrong since all acts of murder are examples of intentional killing of innocent human beings, or, on the Kantian version of deontology, of innocent rational beings.

Or, is that really true? As I have defined murder there is a possibility that the person who gets killed is not innocent, after all. The person who gets killed may deserve to die, because she is herself a murderer. And the killing of her may still constitute murder, if it takes place without legal sanction. We may think of a society where there is a ban on capital punishment, and where, say, a relative of a victim of murder kills the murderer. Is such killing right or wrong, according to deontology?

This depends on how we interpret the doctrine. It depends on the stance it takes up to capital punishment, in the first place, but also to individual attempts (without any legal sanction) to see to it that justice is done. I return to these questions in the next chapter. Here I assume, for the rest of the discussion, that the victim of the act of murder really is innocent (does not *deserve* to be killed). If this is the case, deontology does not only imply that the action is wrong, it also explains why it is wrong. The victim is an innocent human (rational, in Kant's version of the theory) being. This is what *makes* the action wrong.

There are many problems with deontology that will be discussed in chapters to come. They have to do with how we distinguish intentional from not intentional killing, human beings from non-human beings, rational beings from non-rational beings, and so forth, but in the present chapter we can glance over them. I take it that it is clear that any act, here classified as murder, is an act of intentional killing, and, since I discuss only the killing of individuals who have been born, we need not here enter into discussions about when human life starts, whether they are rational creatures, and so forth. We are not in a position where we can evaluate the deontology in its two main forms, Kantianism and the Sanctity-of-Life Doctrine, until we have dealt with these problems, of course, but we can assess whether its implications with regard to *murder* are plausible or implausible. And we can compare them with the implications from the competing theories, the ethics of rights, and utilitarianism.

2.1. Implications of Deontology for Murder

Are the implications from deontology with regard to murder intuitively plausible or not? Remember that the implication is that *all* acts of murder are wrong (with the possible exception for the murder of people who deserve capital punishment but who cannot otherwise receive it).

If we should question this implication, we should look at instances of murder where, intuitively speaking, it seems as though they are right. Are there any such examples?

Well, think of Tracy Devon Brown, mentioned at the opening of this chapter. Think of the abstract thought experiment I presented to the Chinese, the Russians, and the Americans. Is it possible that a woman who murders her ex in order to get a better life for herself and her children is doing the right thing?

Here the cultural variations are substantial. Only 10 percent among the Chinese find this plausible, and only 27 percent among the Russians do, while as many as 44 percent among the Americans find it possible that some murders are morally right. This means that, before we form any definite opinion, we ought to try to transcend our own narrow cultural horizon, and view the matter with fresh eyes.

If we then end up with the verdict, that I personally do, that it *is* plausible to assume that some murders are morally right, we should be able to explain, of course, why many people have reached the opposite verdict. I think there exists a good explanation for this, and I will return to it when I sum up the chapter. For the moment it must suffice to say that, when *I* ponder the question, I find it plausible that there exist examples of murder where this action is right.

Most people would probably think otherwise. Typically they would claim, I believe, that there must have existed other options. They will say that not only in relation to my abstract thought experiment presented to the Chinese, the Russians, and the Americans, but also and even more obviously so in relation to the real-life case of Tracy Devon Brown. However, if we have problems avoiding the thought that there must have existed other options, we can simply *stipulate* that there are no such options. Moreover, if we have difficulties avoiding the impression that there must exist other options in all the cases I have presented so far, we may instead think of a (real-life) case where the conflict is *obvious*.

Think of a mother living with two small children in abject poverty in a country where starvation is endemic. There is no way that she can feed them both. She can decide to feed herself and one of her children and allow that the other child starves to death. Or she can painlessly kill one of her children. In either case it is possible for her and her only surviving child to go on with their lives. Suppose she kills one of the children, drawn at random. That amounts to murder. Suppose instead that she allows the same child to starve to death. That is not murder. The latter option is not only more painful for the child, we may assume, but it is also more costly to the woman and the surviving child. It means that the mother has to spend time with the dying child. This means that she will have additional problems of feeding herself and the child that will survive. Would it not be better if she killed it?

If this is emotionally possible for her, a big IF indeed, *my* intuition is that she should kill one of her children in order to save the life of herself and the other child, rather than allowing one of the children to starve to death, which means a cost not only to this child itself, but to herself and the other surviving child as well. I return at the end of the chapter for my attempt to debunk the intuition (held by many?) that her action would be wrong.

2.2. Deontology and the Legal Issue

I did not simply ask the Chinese, the Russians, and the Americans about their opinion on the normative status of an act of murder (the killing of the ex by the stalked woman), but also about whether the actions should be punished. The moral doctrines I discuss have answers to these questions as well. On deontology it is clear that murder should be illegal. The reason that it should be illegal is that it is always wrong to perform an act of murder. And it is then also natural to assume that, whenever someone performs an act of murder, she should be punished. Severe wrongdoing should never go unpunished. There is also a retributive aspect to the doctrine, in particular in its Kantian version, to be discussed in more detail in the next chapter on capital punishment.

Are *these* implications plausible? It is plausible, I would say, to assume that murder should be illegal (in any conceivable well-ordered society). As a matter of fact, murder is illegal in all well-ordered societies. That's why it is tempting to *define* murder as a kind of illegal killing, a temptation I have resisted. And it is also natural to assume that people who have been convicted of murder should be punished (even if the circumstances may render a lenient punishment appropriate). I have no quarrel with these claims. Nor had the Chinese, the Russians, and the Americans.

Note that even among the Americans, where almost half the population thought that the envisaged act of murder could be morally right, 67 percent felt that the woman should be punished. I share their intuition. But if deontology goes wrong when it claims that all acts of murder are wrong, it must also be wrong in its explanation as to why murder should be kept illegal. If some murders are right, the explanation as to why murder should be kept illegal cannot be that all acts of murder are wrong.

3. MORAL RIGHTS AND MURDER

The moral rights theory is in many respects similar to deontology in its implications for murder. According to the moral rights theory, all acts of murder are wrong. The explanation of why they are wrong is different, however. The explanation is that when a person is murdered, she gets her rights violated. The victim owned herself, and the active and involuntary (not requested for) killing of her meant an intrusion on her most private territory.

The moral rights theory is different from deontology in that it accepts that one person kills another person, actively and intentionally, if this takes place with the consent of the person who gets killed. The other person is allowed to invite us to his property (which includes his self, his body), as he sees fit. And this right to invite us includes a right to hire us to kill him. However, as I have defined murder, it is clear that only killing that takes place without a request from the person killed constitutes murder. So we may safely conclude that all murders are wrong, according to the moral rights theory.

3.1. Problematic Implications of the Moral Rights Theory

If I am right in *my* insistence that there are acts of murder that are morally right, then the moral rights theory has got it wrong. The acts of murder it has a problem with in general are, of course, acts of murder that have, on the whole, good consequences and, in particular, acts of murder that mean that we avoid further (future) murders (i.e., violations of rights).

Are there any acts of murder that obviate future murders? Could one not argue that, when a person is killed in order to prevent further murders, he must be killed in self-defence, or, at least, in defence of some rights? According to the moral rights theory, we are allowed to kill in order to protect rights. We are allowed, not only to kill in self-defence, but also in defence of someone else who is under attack. The latter option is allowed, but not required, by the moral rights theory.

This line of argument is insufficient to meet the objection, however. I have a right to kill a person who tries to kill me, in order to save my life, according to the moral rights theory, and I have a similar right to kill a person who attempts to kill a third person, if I am in a position to do so. However, we here speak of rather *immediate* threats. It is conceivable, however, that by killing a person who is no immediate threat to me or anyone else, I prevent future killings performed by *another* person. Consider the following example taken from my book *Understanding Ethics*.

> *Anna has devoted her life to Amnesty International. She is divorced. She has four children who have lived most of the time with their father. It has not been possible for her to take them with her on her missions to a South America ruled by dictators. She is now travelling in Argentina with her four children, however, only a few months after the establishment of a democratic regime. She is terminally ill and realises that she has only a short time left to live. She wants to show her children something of the kind of life she has had. Her lecture tour has come to an end. She spends the last night in Buenos Aires. Amnesty has provided her and her children with accommodation. They are staying with one of the local members of the organisation. After her children have gone to bed she takes a nightcap with her host, Pedro. Pedro now takes her by surprise. He has conned the local Amnesty group, he confesses. He is a former torturer and he has invited Anna to stay with him for a very special reason. He has had more than enough of her human rights talk, he says. He has gathered some of his former friends*

> *and he is now going to teach Anna a lesson: the end justifies the means. His friends enter the room, carrying automatic weapons in their hands. He offers a syringe to Anna. It contains a deadly dose of potassium chloride, he tells her. He now wants her to kill her eldest son Peter, who is asleep in the next room, suffering from a slight temperature. Pedro threatens that unless Anna kills her son, he will make sure that all her children are killed instantly. Anna realises that the threat is genuine. To her own surprise, she finds herself grabbing the syringe and walking into the nearby room. Her son wakes up, complains that he feels dizzy, and asks what is going on. Anna tells him that she is going to give him an injection. Then his fever will go away, she says. She injects the poison and her son dies. Pedro is satisfied. The next day Anna tells her three remaining children that their brother is dead. His fever turned out to be more serious than anyone had expected, she says. There is no time for ceremonies. The local Amnesty group will organise the funeral. Now they have to hurry. They immediately embark on the ferry to Montevideo. Anna returns the children to their father, who is waiting for them, and tells him that the fever killed their eldest son. He accepts her explanation. She then goes to a hospice where she is to spend her last few months. Several years have passed since this happened. Anna is dead. The three brothers and sisters lead good and protected lives together with their father. They rarely speak of their deceased brother, but they sometimes think of him. The thought causes some pain, but they all know perfectly well how to get on with their own lives. And they remember their mother with pride. She worked for a noble cause, they say. They know nothing of Anna's action. What are we to say of it? My considered intuition is that she did the right thing.*[2]

It is tempting to argue that a good mother should not kill one of her children, even to save the rest. Perhaps a good mother should not even be *capable* of doing this. This may well be so. I discuss this

2. Anna is not her real name.

at length elsewhere.[3] In that case we must conclude that, luckily enough, Anna was not a good mother. That fact helped her, in the situation, to save three of her four children. This was the *right* decision, or so it seems to me, at any rate. And how sad, if she could have saved three of her children, but had not done so! According to the moral rights theory, which sides here with deontology, however, she did the *wrong* thing. This implication of the theories strikes me as very problematic.

What are we then to say of the intuition many claim to have that it was wrong to kill him? Here it is tempting to 'explain away' the intuition that what she did was wrong, to the extent that we have it, with the conjecture that we have conflated the question of the normative status of her particular action with an assessment of her traits of character. If anything was wrong here, it was her general traits of character, not what she did in the situation.

These days we often hear that we need to turn to virtue ethics if we want to account for traits of character such as these (being a good parent). I do not think virtue ethics is a plausible theory in its own right. It gives no superior account of right-making characteristics of actions, if we compare it to utilitarianism, deontology, or the moral rights theory. In particular, the fact that a virtuous agent would not perform an act does not make it wrong, nor does the fact that a vicious agent actually performs it make it wrong.[4] The virtues that virtue ethics operates with are of general interest, though. All the theories here under examination—utilitarianism, deontology, and the moral rights theory—operate with their own ideas about what sort of people we should try to become. They come with their own lists of desirable character traits, giving their own rationale for the adoption of each respective list. The utilitarian one is straightforward. You should try to become a person who, on balance, does as little harm, and as much good, as possible—even if this means that, for sure, when your actions are true to your character,

3. In 'Sophie's Choice'.
4. I explain this claim in my *Understanding Ethics*.

you will now and then come to act wrongly. I return to this important point at the end of the chapter.

3.2. The Moral Rights Theory and the Legal Issue

The fact that, according to the moral rights theory, all murders are wrong, explains why they *may* all be prohibited. According to the moral rights theory, an action should *not* be made illegal unless it is a rights violation. The claim that no morally permitted act should be criminalized is essential to the moral rights theory. But since all acts of murder are wrong, it is morally all right, according to the theory, to have them criminalized.

When we render murder illegal, this is something that is permitted by the moral rights theory, then. However, moral rights theorists could have abstained from legislating in the first place, and, as it were, deliberately decided to remain in a state of nature with regard to murder. To do so would have been inexpedient, but it would have meant no violation of any rights. The moral rights theory is *consistent* with a system where murder is rendered criminal, then, but it cannot explain why (it does not imply that) we *ought* to render murder a criminal act. This strikes me as a bit odd.

4. UTILITARIANISM AND MURDER

It is reasonable to assume that, if utilitarianism is true, then many (most) acts of murder are wrong. After all, when a murder takes place, the person killed is robbed of future life, there are bad side effects for those who are close to the victim, and the murderer himself, if he gets caught, is often victimized. And if he is caught, he is sentenced to a long time in prison, or executed, which means a loss of his own life. However, it is also reasonable to assume that, if utilitarianism is right, there are some murders that are right. I think of examples such as the one presented to the Chinese, the Russians, and the Americans in my survey. And even more plausibly, the killing by Anna of one of her children was morally right. Moreover, it is also reasonable to assume that, if utilitarianism is right, there exist many situations where a murder should have taken place but did not.

Are these implications of utilitarianism problematic, or are they very reasonable implications? As I have insisted, I find them quite plausible. This is so if one remembers that utilitarianism also implies that murder should be illegal, and that a murderer, when exposed, should be punished. The rationale behind this claim is not that all acts of murder are wrong, then, but that such a legal prohibition maximizes happiness; it is needed in order for us all to feel safe. All this is in line with *my* considered intuitions.

4.1. Bernard Williams's Critique of Utilitarianism

It is notable that even a critic of utilitarianism, such as Bernard Williams, would have agreed that it is quite possible that Anna did the right thing in my example. This seems to follow from his concession about a similar example he has famously constructed with a person, Jim, who can save a group of people from being innocent victims of an assassination—by killing one innocent person. Williams notes that according to utilitarianism this is what Jim ought to do (there are no bad side effects, he has assumed). This is not the problem with utilitarianism, according to Williams. The problem is the way a utilitarian reaches this conclusion, which is too simplistic as far as Williams is concerned. When he makes this claim, he adopts the perspective of the agent himself (Jim). But here something seems to go wrong in his discussion.

Williams seems to believe that, according to utilitarianism, we ought always to ponder the question, how should I go about in order to maximize the sum total of happiness in the universe? And when the answer to this question is obvious, then it is clear what to do, irrespective of how outrageous the action seems to us, irrespective of whether we can think of ourselves as people ever doing this kind of thing. This means that utilitarianism 'alienates' us from ourselves and our life projects[5]—at least to the extent that we are ordinary human beings with an ordinary view of ourselves and with projects other than *just* making the world a better place.

Here the important point is that Williams seems to share the intuition that Jim and Anna are doing the right thing. This leaves us with the alienation complaint. The alienation complaint is catered for by utilitarianism, however, once it is observed that it is one thing what we ought to do and quite another thing how we ought to be (or, rather, what sort of people we should strive to become). As I have noted, it is quite reasonable to assume that a good mother should not be capable of doing what Anna did. She seems to have alienated herself from one of her life projects, the project of being a good mother, in a manner that may be morally problematic. The problematic thing, then, was that she had not developed such traits of character that her children could reasonably expect from her. This may have led to many moral mistakes in her life. Even so, this sad fact helped her to do the right thing in these *extraordinary* circumstances.

All this does not mean that there are no problems with the utilitarian view of murder, however. For I have now focused on cases where many people (at least Americans) are prepared to grant that murder could very well be morally defensible. However, there are also other cases of murder, condoned by utilitarianism, which I believe most people would find abhorrent. Think of the following example.

4.2. A Problematic Case

Assume that a physician discusses a situation with one of her patients, a man with a very bad prognosis. He will suffer terribly from his terminal disease and there is no way effectively to alleviate

5. *Utilitarianism: For and Against*, p. 116.

his refractory symptoms. The physician asks him to consider euthanasia as a way out of the situation. The patient rejects the offer, however. He says he realizes that the rest of his life will be an ordeal, and it would be better for him not to live through it, but it goes against both his moral conviction and his religious belief to accept euthanasia. He is prepared to go through the rest of his life, to the bitter end, even if it means torture. *He* is not a hedonistic utilitarian, he insists.

Suppose there is a possibility for the physician to kill this patient, against his wish, in a manner that is painless, not even noticeable for the patient, and assume furthermore that the physician knows for certain that she can get away with this instance of mercy killing (murder), which is of course illegal. According to utilitarianism she ought to do so. I suppose *most* people find this implication unacceptable. I confess that I share this intuition. Had the patient not been aware of his bleak future prospects, and had he not for that reason been adamant in his wish to stay alive, it might have been a rather straightforward decision to kill him, in his own best interest. Equally so if he had been indoctrinated into some ridiculous religious belief that forced him to his decision. But this is not the case in the example before us, we may assume. The patient realizes what his future will be like. And he is as clever and knowledgeable as I. We may think of him as one of my colleagues. We have often met in our seminar room. I have tried to convince him of hedonistic utilitarianism. As a matter of fact, he has read the manuscript of this book. He still wants to go on with his life. He sticks to his perfectionist view of a good life, he tells the doctor.

My intuition is that, in the circumstances, it is wrong to kill this patient against his wishes. He should be allowed to suffer the consequences of his (unwise) decision, it seems to me.

A utilitarian objection to the example immediately comes to mind. It is a mere thought experiment. In real life there is always a risk that the physician will be exposed, that the effects then are likely to be very bad indeed. Perhaps the very system of euthanasia will be put into jeopardy once the public knows her decision. But this is not a good objection. For what we are pondering here is indeed a mere thought experiment. Thus, we are allowed to postulate that the physician will get away with her murder. Consequently, the correct utilitarian verdict *is* that she did the right thing. And even such an implication, in such a merely hypothetical case, may strike many as intuitively wrong. I confess, as I just noted, that *I* do find it intuitively wrong.

4.3. Preference Utilitarianism—An Aside

In most places in this book I discuss utilitarianism in its classical, total, hedonistic form. I do so since I do not believe it makes much difference if, instead, I discuss it in some other version, such as one cast in terms of desire satisfaction (preferentialism) rather than happiness. It might be thought, however, that in the present context it makes a difference whether we consider the case with the doctor from the point of view of hedonism or preferentialism.

On a preferentialist version of utilitarianism, one may think that, since we human beings have an interest in going on with our lives, it is morally more problematic to kill human beings than to kill non-human sentient but not self-conscious beings, lacking any notion of their own future lives. It counts heavily against the killing of a person, on this view, if the person wants to go on with his life. Would this line of argument save us from the conclusion that we should kill the patient, who wants to go on with his life? I think not. And the reasons are as follows.

The most plausible version of preferentialism is the idea that what makes a life go well is the satisfaction of *intrinsic* desires. It is doubtful if any person has an intrinsic desire for continued life. It is more plausible to assume that people have intrinsic desires for such things as happiness, knowledge, friendship, and so forth. And, in the envisaged example, there will be no satisfaction of any such desires on the part of the dying patient.

Moreover, even if we assume that this patient does have an intrinsic desire for continued life—perhaps a very strong desire—this is just one desire among many others. This means that we may construe our example in a manner that allows us to say that, overall, there will be *more* satisfaction of intrinsic desires in the life of the patient if he is killed against his wish to go on with his life. We may construe the example such that the rest of the life of this dying patient will not contain any further satisfaction of the desires for knowledge, friendship, happiness, and so forth. On the contrary, on these counts, we may see to it when we construe the example, his life will be worth *not* living. The *only* preference that is satisfied if the physician does not kill her patient will be the patient's desire to go on with his life. Hence, even on preferentialism, the physician ought to kill him. I can't help feeling that this is wrong.

5. CONCLUSION

We have seen that all three approaches under scrutiny seem to have counterintuitive implications with regard to the moral status of acts of murder. However, I feel that deontology and the moral rights theory are in worse shape here than utilitarianism. The insistence that we are never allowed to commit acts of murder is *highly* improbable. We realize this once we think of murders making the world a better place (for a stalked woman and her children, say, or, even more plausibly, for Anna's children whose lives are saved). And the moral rights theory, given its patient-centred perspective, has a *special* problem with the idea that we are not even allowed to murder in order to obviate future acts of murder. Deontology has the same implication, but since it is agent-centred rather than patient-centred, this is not in the same manner a problem for it.

If I am correct in my insistence that there exist morally permissible acts of murder, then, in our attempt to find a rationale behind the idea that murder should be illegal (and be punished when the perpetrator is exposed), we must rely on something other than the idea that all acts of murder are wrong. Here I think the utilitarian solution to the problem is extremely plausible. The reason that murder should be criminal is that we would not feel safe in a society where people could contemplate to kill us, just to make the world a better place—and get away with it. Such a society would be terrible for *all* and this means that the utilitarian rationale for making (keeping) murder illegal, even if indirect, is an extremely *strong* one.

Now, if I am right when I insist that murder is sometimes morally permissible, how do I then explain that most people seem to think otherwise? Only 10 percent among the Chinese and 27 percent among the Russians were willing to admit that the stalked woman who killed her ex may have done the right thing. It is also tempting to 'explain away' some of the US acceptance of murder with the hypothesis that some of the respondents believed that the ex was not innocent after all when he was killed, and thus only got what he deserved.

I conjecture that the reason that people at large say that it is always wrong to commit an act of murder is to do with four things. First of all, we must take into account here a cultural factor. Some of them live in cultures where this belief has been inculcated in them. They live in what we could call strong deontological cultures. This is true in particular of the Chinese, as we saw in the previous chapter and as we will see from their answers also to other questions in my survey, in chapters to come.

Secondly, while many people support active killing in order to save lives (remember the Switch from the previous chapter), they hesitate to accept intentional killing. This has to do with a problem of distinguishing between two questions. On the one hand: Is it in general a good idea to act on the intention to kill people? On the other hand: could an individual action performed with a deadly intention be right? They find the distinction between good intentions and right actions problematic.

Is this distinction indeed problematic? The late American logician and philosopher W. V. Quine has insistently reminded us that it is difficult to compare particular sentences from different theories (in science). Even when the theories operate with the same terms, these terms may play different roles in the theories; it is then impossible to isolate their respective meanings; we have to understand

and assess the theories globally. The same could be true of some moral theories. There is no simple way to compare parts of them, such as their views on rightness and wrongness.

Whatever we may think about this view in general, in the present context it seems irrelevant. All three theories here under examination *do* operate with a focus on the rightness and wrongness of individual actions and, more importantly, the notion seems to play *the same role* in all three theories. They propose different and conflicting criteria of right action. It is true that, according to deontology, one way an action may be wrong is by having been performed with the wrong motive. However, other actions, performed with an acceptable motive, may be wrong as well. For example, merely foreseen killing is not wrong *as such*, but it is wrong *in fact*, if the bad effects you foresee are out of proportion in comparison to the good effects you intended (the principle of double effect). According to the moral rights theory an action is wrong if and only if it violates the rights of a moral subject. The distinction between right (permitted) and wrong (forbidden) actions plays the same role in all three theories.

This does not exclude the possibility that some theorists, and some people at large, use 'wrong' in a different sense. They may *mean* when they say that an action is 'wrong' that the action is performed from the wrong motive or by an agent exhibiting vicious character traits. If this is indeed so, then they cannot (morally) *explain* why an action is wrong with reference to the motive or the character of the agent. And, more importantly, this means that when we (I and the adherents of the theories here under examination) claim that a certain action is right, and these people using 'wrong' in the way just described claim that it is wrong, we speak at cross-purposes.

The distinction between what kind of motives you should have, on the one hand, and the rightness or wrongness of a particular act, on the other hand, is clear and straightforward, then, and it is put to use in each of the three theories here compared; once we ponder it, I think we should come to realize that even if intentional killing in most cases is wrong, some acts of murder may yet, for all that, be morally permissible. Our original intuition to the opposite effect should go away. Even if most actions performed from a bad motive are wrong, this is not *why* they are wrong. Note also that, if my argument in the previous chapter is correct, then those who object to the pushing of the big man in the Footbridge cannot evoke the idea that it is wrong to kill intentionally, if they want to provide a rationale behind their objection. So the intention does not, perhaps, play the role we often and incorrectly attribute to it.

Thirdly, there is another distinction that is important, but such that even many philosophers have had a problem keeping it in sight. I think of the distinction between the normative status of our actions, on the one hand, and what kind of persons we should attempt to become, on the other. Once we make the distinction between the normative status of Anna's killing of her child, on the one hand, and the value of her character (was she a good mother?) on the other hand, it should not be hard to see that while she may have been a bad mother, her action was right. I have made a similar comment on those who are prepared to, and capable of, pushing the big man in the Footbridge. Even if they do the right thing in this exceptional case, we may not want to socialize with them.

Finally, many people have difficulties with the distinction between the following two questions: 'Can an individual act of murder be morally permissible?' and 'Should murder ever be legal?' They—and their culture—may even find the distinction problematic. But the *distinction* is real, and it is real on all three theories. It is real also on the moral rights theory, even if, according to the moral rights theory, an action should be criminalized only if it violates a moral right.

One may feel that it is a strange instance of double standards when an action is considered, according to utilitarianism, morally acceptable but yet such that it should be illegal. From a logical point of view, there is no problem with this stance, however. This kind of double standard is typical of utilitarianism, and it does not seem to be quite alien to everyone. In particular, many Americans seem to accept it. Remember that as many as 44 percent of the Americans believed that the stalked woman who murdered her ex may have done the right thing. And yet, for all that, most of them think that she should be punished.

On the utilitarian view, even though some acts of murder are right, all acts of murder should be illegal. Moreover, on utilitarianism, it is wise to teach your children, not only that murder is illegal, but also that it is something you should not even contemplate. It is reasonable, if utilitarianism is true, to instil in your children a strong inhibition against murder. You should do what you can to make them persons who do not kill any of their children—not even to save the lives of the rest. Or, perhaps, you need not here be very active in your education of your children; it is probably rather a matter of not questioning a tendency already instilled in them (us)—by evolution.

It may seem, then, that utilitarianism gives us the best account of the ethics of murder. However, as I have insisted, we cannot accept that a theory has gained intuitive support unless it can explain *all* our considered intuitions. Recalcitrant evidence should never be 'negotiated away'. And in this chapter I have indeed concluded that there is *one* implication of utilitarianism with regard to murder that I find intuitively wrong—the implication that the physician, in my thought experiment, should kill her patient, against his wish.

Chapter 5

Capital Punishment

If it could be shown beyond reasonable doubt that the death penalty reduces the number of murders, would that mean that capital punishment would be morally acceptable?

	China	*Russia*	*United States*
Yes	71%	58%	64%
No	25%	35%	33%
Don't know	4%	6%	4%

1. INTRODUCTION

In this chapter I will discuss the following question. Think of a state, like the Scandinavian countries, with relatively low incidence of murder. Would it be a good idea to introduce in such a state a system of capital punishment, where murderers are sentenced to death and executed, once their guilt has been established beyond reasonable doubt? I assess the matter from the point of view of deontology, the moral rights theory, and utilitarianism in order to find out about their respective implications. To the extent that the conclusion depends on difficult empirical matters I will note which facts are relevant, according to each theory, but I will make no attempt to settle the empirical matters as such—which means that it is not quite clear what the implications of the theories are. Still, the discussion sheds light on the theories as such.

The reason to focus on a society with a low incidence of murder is that this helps us to steer clear of a lot of distracting facts. If we find good arguments for the death penalty in such circumstances, we need not bother with the question of whether other kinds of preventive measures, such as the introduction of a welfare state, should be resorted to instead of having recourse to the death penalty. It also avoids a discussion about death penalty in war or in relation to crimes against humanity. This is once again to avoid problems that can detract our attention from the more basic aspects of the question. Furthermore, I will not discuss whether the death penalty should be resorted to when it comes to crimes other than homicide. This, however, is more a matter of space than of principle.

It will become clear that, according to the most plausible version of deontological thinking, in what I will call its retributivist form, there are indeed good reasons to adopt a system of death penalty for homicide. From the point of view of the moral rights theory, we must conclude that there exists no principled defence of the death penalty. Finally, when attempting to assess the matter from the point of view of utilitarianism, which is a theory extremely demanding of empirical information, it seems as though no categorical answer to the question can, as yet, be arrived at. However, it is interesting to speculate about what a utilitarian would say about the death penalty, if it could be established that, by executing a few murderers each year, one could avoid a significant number of homicides. Such speculation will be undertaken and I will argue that a utilitarian should side with the majority opinion in my survey, and accept capital punishment, if it turns out to have a superior deterrent effect.

2. RETRIBUTIVISM

According to the retributive and deontological idea I will first focus on, there are certain kinds of actions such that instances of them are proscribed or prescribed, *simpliciter.* Any rational individual should be able to grasp why this is so, it is claimed. A way of finding out what is proscribed and what is prescribed is to consult one's rational capacities. Immanuel Kant is, of course, the main proponent of such a view. And the categorical imperative in its first version gives us guidance, he claims, when we ponder what we ought, and what we ought not to do.[1] As I remarked in Chapter 2, I find the categorical imperative less helpful than Kant himself did. So here I will focus on the *conclusions* Kant is drawing from it rather than on the categorical imperative as such (the premise of his argument). There is one prohibition and one prescription he finds obvious. The prohibition is against killing: no one is allowed to kill an innocent rational being, not even himself, not even to save lives, and not even at request. We have met this idea in our discussion of murder and we will return to it in chapters to come. Here the question is: what does this doctrine have to say about killing of people who are guilty of murder? On a retributivist reading of the doctrine, when a person is guilty of murder, he should be executed.

Perhaps Kant is too strict in his prohibition on killing. Perhaps Kant is mistaken when he claims that it is wrong to commit suicide, or when he claims that it is wrong to kill when an individual asks you to do so (as in euthanasia). I will discuss that in chapters to follow. Still, I will take for granted in this section that, according to deontological thinking, at least what we usually classify as 'murder' is wrong. And I will ponder if it is a congenial part of such a theory to accept that those who have committed murder should be executed.

2.1. Kant on Capital Punishment

Let me first focus on Immanuel Kant. Kant's defence of capital punishment is part of his general idea of crime and punishment. This is how he writes about this in his *Rechtslehre* (1797):

> Judicial punishment can never be used merely as a means to promote some other good for the criminal himself or for civil

1. Immanuel Kant, *Groundwork of the Metaphysics of Morals*, p. 31.

> society, but instead it must in all cases be imposed on him only on the ground that he has committed a crime.
>
> (*Metaphysical Elements of Justice*, p. 138)

This is, literally speaking, compatible with a view suggested by John Rawls to the effect that, while the punitive institutions should be designed to have the best overall effects, the individual sentence should never be decided on consequentialist grounds.[2] The criminal should only receive a sentence because of what he has done. However, I do not think such a reading of the passage is true to the spirit of *Kant's* thinking. His deontological point is that we ought to punish the criminal for the criminal's own sake, in order to see to it that justice is done. We treat him merely as a means, not as an end in himself, if our system of punishment is designed to obtain good consequences either for him or for society. We are not doing him (retributive) *justice*, unless we punish him for what he has done. One can make a parallel with *distributive* justice here, to see the point more clearly. Just as we are not doing justice to women if we pay them lower wages than we pay men for the same job, we are not doing justice to the criminal if we do not punish him.

Could one not argue, with reference to the version of the categorical imperative—where it is urged that you should use humanity, whether in your own person or in the person of any other, always at the same time as an end, never merely as a means—that if the culprit himself accepts a more lenient punishment than he deserves, we can give it to the culprit without treating him as a mere means? This is so at least if he himself assents to this aberration from justice?

No, this won't do. Consent is neither a necessary nor a sufficient condition for our not treating someone as a mere means to our purposes. There are concessions a person is not allowed to make. And if he still makes them, they are, from a moral point of view, null and void. And, of course, we need not seek consent from the culprit before we punish him.

2. 'Two Concepts of Rules'.

This is, I think, how Kant himself would answer the objection. We are not morally permitted to accept less punishment than we deserve (in the same manner that we are not allowed to have our physician kill us in euthanasia). If yet we do, our acceptance should not be taken for an answer. And irrespective of how Kant is best understood, this is the idea *I* want to discuss here. Given that idea, what are we to say about capital punishment? This is Kant's own answer to this question:

> Even if a civil society were to dissolve itself by common agreement of all its members (for example, if the people inhabiting an island decided to separate and disperse themselves around the world), the last murderer remaining in prison must first be executed, so that everyone will duly receive what his actions are worth and so that the bloodguilt thereof will not be fixed on the people because they failed to insist on carrying out the punishment; for if they fail to do so, they may be regarded as accomplices in this public violation of legal justice.
>
> (Ibid., p. 140)

Is Kant right about this? Is this the conclusion a retributivist should draw about the death penalty? Should she, as a matter of principle, defend the death penalty?

Even if some people who adhere, nowadays, to deontology, in particular if they opt for the Sanctity-of-Life Doctrine, are against the death penalty—such as are the most recent popes—I can't help finding this as a way of compromising the very doctrine they defend. There is indeed a strong presumption in favour of Kant's answer. It is congenial with the retributive idea that the criminal should get what he deserves. This is an idea of proportionality in punishing. And it is not just any theory about proportionality, but a very special one.

Many thinkers have argued that there should be some proportionality between crime and punishment. Philosophers of a utilitarian bent, such as Beccaria and Bentham, have held this view.[3] But at least one of them, Beccaria, was an abolitionist with regard to the death penalty. How is this possible?

The explanation is that utilitarians typically adhere only to a weak idea of proportionality. They claim that ordinal rankings of both crimes (with regard to how serious they are) and punishments (with regard to severity) can be made, at least roughly. And they then go on to argue that a system where a more serious crime receives a less severe sanction than a less serious one, would be counterproductive from the point of view they are interested in, to wit, the point of view of deterrence. As Bentham puts it:

> Where two offences come in competition, the punishment for the greater offence must be sufficient to induce a man to prefer the less.[4]

Both Bentham and Beccaria see punishment as a necessary evil. If we can fulfil the purpose of punishment without having recourse to the most serious kinds of punishment, we should avoid them. They disagree on an empirical matter, not a basic moral one. Beccaria was an abolitionist with respect to the death penalty. Bentham was sceptical too, but conceded that we might need to resort to it, though only in 'very extraordinary cases'.[5] J. S. Mill, on the other hand, is famous for his utilitarian argument in defence of the death penalty.[6] He thought that a lifelong prison sentence was a more severe punishment than death. These utilitarian thinkers all rely on a weak notion of proportionality. However, this weak notion of proportionality sits ill with the kind of retributive thinking Kant advocates.

3. Bentham's view on punishment is developed in many places, but it exists already in its basic form in *An Introduction to the Principles of Morals and Legislation*; for Beccaria, see Cesare Beccaria Bonesana, *An Essay on Crimes and Punishments*.

4. *An Introduction to the Principles of Morals and Legislation*, p. 168.

5. Ibid., p. 182.

6. In his famous speech before the British Parliament on April 21, 1868, in opposition to a bill banning capital punishment.

The retributivist must have a stronger notion of proportionality in mind, where comparisons are made also between the seriousness of a crime and the severity of the punishment. Here there should be a rough balance.

Of course, such a proportionate system of crime and punishment is difficult to work out in all details,[7] but when it comes to premeditated murder it should not be too difficult to see what, according to this theory, the relevant kind of punishment ought to look like. Here something like the *lex talionis* (i.e., eye for an eye) is at work. The murderer has intentionally killed his victim. He has acted upon a maxim, according to which it is in order to kill. But then, out of respect for him as an autonomous individual, he should himself be killed.

In the contemporary discussion about crime and punishment, there are many less straightforwardly retributive theories, where the punishment is seen as an expression of a message to the criminal or the general public,[8] and so forth, and where this conclusion may not follow as easily as it does from the standard theory. However, here the interest is precisely in the hardcore standard retributive theory. As a matter of fact, I think this theory is superior to more watered-down modern versions, but this is not the place to try to show this. Here it should suffice that the standard version of the theory is the one discussed.

Now, is this a plausible theory? It has some intuitive support, I concede. However, there is also a problem with the theory. The problem is that it is not sensitive to certain facts. Even if it should turn out that the death penalty has less of a deterring effect than some less drastic kind of punishment for murder, we would have to stick to it, according to this theory. But this strikes me as wrong. We cannot make the world a better place by inflicting unnecessary pain and death. I suppose Kant would just retort, however, that we are

7. See Jesper Ryberg, *The Ethics of Proportionate Punishment: A Critical Investigation*.

8. See, for example, Jean Hampton, 'An Expressive Theory of Retribution'.

not here speaking of unnecessary pain and death, but *morally* necessary pain and death.

2.2. Some Objections

One standard objection, with roots in retributive thinking, has been that, even if, in a just world, murder should be punished with death, in the real world, there is no way of constructing a system of capital punishment that is not biased with regard to certain discriminated-against groups in society. Thus, even if death penalty is the ideal, in a non-ideal world we have to stick to long time in prison as a reaction to murder. The focus on the bias against perpetrators from the minority group (and in favour of perpetrators from the majority group) is typical of retributivist thinking. Utilitarians have been more concerned with the fact that crimes against the members of the minority group are punished less severely than crimes against the members of the majority group. Here I focus on the former line of argument.[9]

This argument is not convincing. First of all, the most obvious reaction to this argument is to call for social reform. The discrimination should be abolished, not the capital punishment. And, while we wait for this to happen, we should try to see to it that at least legal practices are not discriminatory in this way. The main objective, then, is not to stop sentencing people from the discriminated-against group to death, but to do so as well with murderers from the privileged group. Strictly speaking, moreover, when people in the privileged group escape execution, this means that, according to retributive thinking, *they* are not given their due. They are not treated in the way they deserve to be treated. Thus, they are the ones the system discriminates *against*![10]

9. For an early distinction between these two lines of argument, and a discussion of each of them, see Randall L. Kennedy, 'McCleskey v. Kemp, Race, Capital Punishment, and the Supreme Court'.

10. I owe this observation to Jens Johansson.

A final worry may be that, even if all precautions are taken, it could sometimes happen that innocent people will be executed. Does this possibility mean that a retributivist must reject a system of capital punishment? I think not.

On one line of argument, the killing of an innocent is right, provided it is done in good faith. If this were so, the problem of innocent victims would be no problem at all. But this is not a plausible view. It is more plausible to say that, even if the execution of an innocent happens in good faith, it is still wrong. However, the retributivist can nevertheless claim that the establishment of a system of capital punishment is still right, even if it means that now and then a wrong action will take place. If the only option is never to give the murderer what he deserves, it seems to be sound retributive policy to have a system of capital punishment in place. Even if we can foresee that some innocent people will be executed, this is not an intended effect of the system. If, when we constructed the system, we had done what we could to strike a reasonable balance between the number of false positives (innocent people who are executed) and false negatives (murderers who escape the death penalty), then we would have done the right thing. In order reach this conclusion, the deontologist of a Kantian bent needs to borrow (the principle of double effect) from the Sanctity-of-Life Doctrine.

And yet, for all that, even if it is morally permissible, according to deontology, to establish an institution where murderers get executed, in spite of the fact that this means that, now and then an innocent person gets killed, what are we to say of the killing of this individual innocent person? It seems clear to me that, according to deontology, it is wrong. The person who is killed does not deserve to die. If we grant that it is wrong, does this also mean that those who are responsible for it deserve punishment themselves? Should *they* be executed?

No, this does not follow. You do act wrongly when you kill an innocent person, whom you wrongly believe to be guilty. But this is not a kind of wrongdoing for which you deserve capital punishment. This is not acting from any wrong (evil) motive. This is not murder.

As we remember, according to deontology, some actions are wrong because they are performed with an evil intention. However, there are other kinds of wrongdoing as well, such as killing as a merely foreseen side effect, but out of proportion. Perhaps the intentional killing of a person you wrongly believe to be guilty is even a case of *blameless* wrongdoing? This notion has a secure place in utilitarianism. It seems to have a place also in deontological retributivist thought.

3. THE MORAL RIGHTS THEORY

Each individual subject or person has a right to, or owns, herself. This is the hard core, we have seen, of the moral rights theory. According to the theory, you have a right to defend what you own. And since you own yourself, this includes a right to self-defence. No one is allowed to kill you, at least not unless you have hired him to do so or have consented to it for one reason or the other. So you are allowed violently, if necessary, to resist any attempt at your life.

According to the moral rights theory, what punishment would be appropriate for a murderer? What kind of theory of punishment in general is dictated by the moral rights theory? The answers to these questions do not seem to depend on what exact version of the theory we opt for. Irrespective of this, we can raise and answer these questions. And here are the answers to them.

While the deontological (retributivist) theory, as here conceived of, focuses exclusively on the criminal in order to give him the punishment he deserves, the moral rights theory here described focuses exclusively on the victim. This aspect of the theory of moral rights is rarely discussed, and many of its adherents, such as both Locke and Nozick, tend to combine it with a deontological theory of retributive justice. However, the theory of moral rights should also be taken seriously as such as a theory about crime and punishment. If taken seriously, and if rid of all retributive ideas, it would say something like the following.

3.1. Moral Rights and Capital Punishment

The victim has a right to what she has been deprived of, or else is due fair compensation. And the compensation should include not only the value of what has been removed, but also the costs of regaining it. If compensation is paid, the apparent rights violation is annulled, as it were. I discuss this aspect of the moral rights theory in Chapter 2. This move is a deviation from Nozick's own understanding of the theory, but it makes the best of it, I there argued.

The notion of compensation is easy to understand when applied to crimes such as theft, but what are the adherents of the moral rights theory to say of murder? Is it possible for murderers to compensate their victims?

This is in one obvious way impossible. And this means that if we want to abide by a strict version of the moral rights theory, then we must accept that there is no room for the punishment of murder. It is certainly true that when we want to guard ourselves against murder we may resort to all kinds of means, according to the theory. In order to protect my life, I may kill the person who attacks me. However, if I fail, and he kills me, then there is no further room for any just action against the murderer. As a matter of fact, this is true of the thief as well. Suppose he cannot compensate his victim. This does not mean that we have a right to put him in prison. Strictly speaking, there is no room for *punishment* in the moral rights theory. If he can pay me, on the other hand, he has to do so. And if he tries to hide away what he has stolen from me, we may keep him in prison until he surrenders and gives it back to me.

Could we not say that our murderer should pay compensation to our relatives? No, this argument sits ill with the moral rights theory. Our relatives do not possess us. The murderer has not deprived them of any property of theirs.

Could we say that the murderer, by committing his crime, has alienated or 'forfeited' his own right to life?[11] That may be a way of finding a version of the theory compatible with capital punishment. It does not strike me as plausible, however. Perhaps it makes sense in some legal setting but not when the stress is on *moral* rights. The notion that we can forfeit our moral rights sits ill with the rationale behind the moral rights theory, the idea of self-ownership. I can lose my right to something by losing my personality (as in progressive forms of dementia). And I can waiver (give up) my right to something I own by giving it away. I cannot lose my rights, however, if I do not voluntarily give them up, as long as I remain a moral agent. I have them *in virtue* of being a moral agent.

It should be noted that, when the moral rights theory accepts that we kill in self-defence, this right to kill has nothing to do with the merits of the person who threatens our life. It could be a murderer who attacks us, but it could also be, as we will see in the chapter on abortion, an innocent foetus, which just happens to be in the wrong place (her mother's womb) at the wrong time. There is no room for the notion of desert in the moral rights theory, as here (most plausibly) understood.

We noted that deontological retributivism is not interested in crime prevention. The punishment is there for the sake of the perpetrator, not for the sake of society. If the punishment has a preventive effect, then this is a second, and not sought for, effect. This explains why, sometimes, retributivists want *less* harsh punishments than do utilitarians. In a similar vein, the theory of moral rights, if taken seriously, is not interested primarily in crime prevention through punishment. According to the moral rights theory, the state ought not to use the criminal as a means to deterrence from future crime. In this it is similar to deontological ethics. Yet in another respect it is very different from the deontological theory.

11. For a recent defence of the forfeiture theory of punishment, and for further references, see Wellman, Christofer Heath, 'The Rights Forfeiture Theory of Punishment'. William Bülow drew my attention to this paper.

While the theory of moral rights makes plenty of room for the police, for locks and security vaults, for violent resistance whenever someone tries to thwart the rights of someone else, and if necessary for restitution, it makes no room whatever for what we can genuinely call 'punishment'.

3.2. Contractual Versions of the Moral Rights Theory

If this analysis is correct, then the theory of moral rights must reject, for principled reasons, capital punishment. For even if we want very much to do so, there is no way for us to compensate a victim of murder. If the murderer poses an immediate threat to others, we may detain him in self-defence, or in defence of the others, but there is no room for punishment, according to this theory. There is no way we can argue that he should be executed because he *deserves* to die. Still, there is a way for the adherent of the theory who wants to defend a system of capital punishment to do so. This can be defended if it is voluntary! We can imagine a society in which each member has become a member through a free and voluntary decision. Such a society can have any legal and other practices it sees fit. It can execute murderers, harvest organs for transplant purposes via a lottery where those who draw the 'winning' ticket must give up their vital organs to those who need them, and so forth. On the theory, each one owns himself. However, just like it is possible to give up your self-ownership and become a slave of some other individual, it is possible to give up your self-ownership and become the property of a collectivity, such as a state.

Would it be a good idea for freely consenting libertarians to establish a community where murder is punished with death?

Paradoxically enough, this question leads us to the next section. For it seems as though it would be a good idea to do so if, and only if, capital punishment has a superior deterrent effect. And this question is at the heart of the utilitarian query about the death penalty.

4. UTILITARIANISM

Utilitarianism is the theory that we ought to maximize the sum total of happiness in the universe. What are the implications of utilitarianism for the death penalty?

According to utilitarianism there are no conventional types of action such as breaking promises, or stealing or lying, that are wrong as such. This is true also of murder, as we have seen. An act of murder is right, if and only if it maximizes the sum total of happiness in the universe. This is probably true of some murders. Think of the killing of a murderer who is at large, who lives a poor life himself, and who is about to commit further violent crimes, when he gets killed. Moreover, as was pointed out in the previous chapter, it is probably true of each and any one of us that we *should* sometimes have committed a murder we did in fact not commit. I think in particular of situations where it was possible for us to kill a very nasty person and get away with it! This does not mean that we should *all* kill, but, given that most people don't, *each* of us faces this kind of heavy utilitarian obligation.

Does all this mean that utilitarianism is complacent with regard to murder? No, it does not. Even if some murders are morally right actions, *all* acts of murder should be criminalized, according to utilitarianism. And the reason is, as we saw in the previous chapter, that only if murder is made illegal will it be possible for us to be and feel secure in society. We do not want to trust the legal system to try to find out whether a particular act of murder produced good or bad consequences. We want a more general and reliable solution to the problem. If a murder is committed, and this is found out, there should exist a strict *legal* rule to the effect that the murderer ought to be punished, irrespective of whether his action was, *morally* speaking, right or wrong. Contrary to what is sometimes said, this is a *strong* defence of making murder illegal. It is strong since security, and the sense of it, is a public good. We all stand to gain from such a legal system. It is also a subtle theory, as compared to retributivism, in that it allows for the intuition that some murders are indeed morally right.

Since the utilitarian is interested in security, and our sense of it, it is clear that, to a utilitarian, it is of crucial importance to know whether capital punishment has a deterrent effect on murder. If it has, it may mean not only that some wrong actions (murders) are avoided, but also that we can all feel more secure in society. There will be less need to fear that we ourselves, or people for whom we care, such as our children, shall become victims of murder—or murderers.

Does the extensive use of capital punishment for murder mean fewer homicides and violent crime in general? Many thinkers have found this self-evident. First of all, they have thought, capital punishment is superior to long terms in prison with regard to its deterrent effect. This is partly due to irrationality among us human beings. We fear death more than anything else. James Fitzjames Stephen has made the point about deterrence in the following words:

> No other punishment deters men so effectually from committing crimes as the punishment of death. This is one of those propositions which it is difficult to prove simply because they are in themselves more obvious than any proof can make them . . . Was there ever yet a criminal who, when sentenced to death and brought out to die, would refuse the offer of a commutation of his sentence for the severest secondary punishment? Surely not.[12]

Furthermore, when a murderer is executed, he is definitely incapacitated. Finally, the execution of a murderer sends a clear message to society. Murder is not tolerated. How could any other sanction compete successfully with this?

And if it is true that the use of capital punishment means fewer homicides, there exists a strong utilitarian presumption in its

12. I have the quotation from Jonathan Glover's *Causing Death and Saving Lives*. Glover gives as the source of the quotation Fraser's Magazine, 1864.

favour. How could a utilitarian, convinced of the deterrent effect of capital punishment, argue against such a system?

4.1. Are There Special Problems with the Death Penalty?

One idea would be to argue that capital punishment is cruel and unusual. It inflicts more harm than it avoids. The idea must be, then, that the murderer suffers (much) more than his victims, when he is killed. This seems to be a non-starter, however. The execution of the murderer can be painless and similar to euthanasia. It then means that the murderer gets a better death than most of us. Is the very fact that you will be killed by others, at a certain moment, terrible as such? No, it seems to me. Death may be unwelcome in itself, but the fact that it takes place at a certain time, which you know of before it happens, and painlessly, should rather be a source of comfort than despair. It makes room for preparation, a review of your life, and a closing of relationships. Some people get the message from their *doctor* that they will soon die. It means that they have the same possibility to finalize their lives. This is usually seen as something positive. Some people think, when the doctor tells them that their illness is fatal and that an untimely death is what awaits them: 'Why did this happen to me?' The murderer has an advantage over them. He knows the answer to this question.

Jonathan Glover thinks differently about this. He assumes that most of us would 'rather die suddenly than linger for weeks or months knowing we were fatally ill' and Woody Allen has claimed something similar: 'It's not that I'm afraid to die, I just don't want to be there when it happens'.[13] This may be true of many people. However, it strikes me as an egoistic view. Even if, for your own sake, you want to leave without saying goodbye, this is not nice to those who are close to you.

13. Woody Allen, *Without Feathers*, p. 99.

But, the fact that your death is known beforehand to you is not the only thing that is bad with an execution, according to Glover:

> He has the additional horror ... *of knowing that his death will be in a ritualized killing by other people, symbolizing his ultimate rejection by the members of his community. The whole of his life may seem to have a different and horrible meaning when he sees it leading up to this end.*[14]

What about the claim that the execution is 'symbolizing his ultimate rejection by the members of his community'? Well, if he believes in a retributivist theory of crime and punishment, as many people seem to do, there is no ground for this claim. As a matter of fact, his execution can on that theory, as we have seen, be understood as an act of respect. He is given what he deserves. What if he believes in the theory of rights? Well, then he himself has agreed to what is about to happen to him. This is so in a real sense in the United States, where he could have chosen to murder in a state not practicing the death penalty. Finally, if he is a utilitarian, he can comfort himself with the thought that he doesn't die in vain. His death is lifesaving. It will deter several murders.

There is still a difference between ordinary death and execution. In the execution we know that death is not necessary. It would not happen if the authorities changed their mind. Does this render death from execution worse than 'ordinary' death? Perhaps it does, or perhaps it does only for some people. And yet, in this execution is similar, not different from, death caused by a murderer when he murders. He, too, could change his mind.

Could one, then, instead argue in the following manner? To the extent that the person who is executed really is guilty, then it is no problem that she is executed. But no matter how cautious we are, if we practice a system of capital punishment, it is highly likely that, at some time, an innocent person will be killed. And, given that the

14. Jonathan Glover, *Causing Death and Saving Lives*, p. 232, italics mine.

death penalty is irreversible, this is not morally acceptable. This is one of the reasons that Bentham was, if not an abolitionist, at least sceptical of capital punishment. It is a desideratum that a punishment should be 'remissible'.[15]

The observation that some innocent people will be executed if capital punishment is practiced is, of course, correct. But note that if we do not practice a system with capital punishment, we will instead send the putative murderer to a long term in prison. In case she is innocent, it may well happen that this will never be found out. This means that, in this case, even the prison sentence was irreversible. We can safely conclude that it was, once the person sentenced to life in prison has died.

Note, furthermore, that if we practice capital punishment, this may well lead to more severe requirements on the evidence for the guilt of the person sentenced for murder and hence to a system with fewer 'false positives'. If we abolish capital punishment, or do not adopt it, we are likely to tolerate more false positives. We may even be forced to do so, if we want to retain enough deterrent effects of the practice. Thus, perhaps we are allowed to conclude that capital punishment has the property of leading more seldom to the situations where innocent people are convicted of murder, while it still is superior with regard to deterrence of future violent crimes. If this is so, capital punishment seems again to have gained the upper hand in the utilitarian discussion.

It may be objected, of course, that, if you are innocent of the crime for which you have been convicted, it is still worse for you to be executed than kept for life in prison. Here we should bear in mind, however, an observation, to which I have already made a reference, made by J. S. Mill to the effect that this might be a misperception.[16] Not only may the time you spend in prison be filled with nasty experiences, the very fact that you know that you are innocent will add insult to injury. When the innocent person is executed,

15. *An Introduction to the Principles of Morals and Legislation*, p. 184.
16. Ibid.

he is spared both further nasty experiences and resentment. So the utilitarian balance may well tip in the direction of capital punishment, even when it comes to the punishment of innocents.

4.2. Entertainment Value

Perhaps this argument is too myopic. Utilitarians count what we could call the entertainment value of practices. For example, according to hedonistic utilitarianism, it can be right to arrange public killings of people in order to entertain an audience (as happened with the Roman gladiator games). If only the audience is large enough, and pleased enough, the sacrifice of the victims on the arena may be worth its hedonic price. This has sometimes been taken as a *reductio* of hedonistic utilitarianism, but some of its adherents, the present writer included, are prepared to bite this bullet (I would not like to be the victim, of course, but I think it would lack a sound rationale if I were to complain). Could this kind of argument be turned upside down when applied to capital punishment? Could we argue that, in a civilized society, the knowledge that some people get executed is so painful to the public at large that, in order to spare them their pain, we should allow a certain number of murders, that could have been avoided, to take place?

Since I am prepared to bite the bullet in the first case, I see this as a promising utilitarian argument against the death penalty, even if the death penalty deters from murder. However, in both cases, I have my doubts about the calculus. What happens to the victims (on the arena, or to those innocent people who get murdered when we abstain from capital punishment) is indeed terrible, and the joy or agony respectively among the audience is ephemeral. I doubt that the argument has the bite it is supposed to have.

Moreover, those who are not prepared to rely on it in the first instance (the gladiator games) should not rely on it in the second case (capital punishment). If they object to hedonism and claim that entertainment value should be discounted, they should discount it consistently.

Or, they may argue, perhaps, that there is an important difference. While sadistic pleasure is bad, sympathetic suffering is a good thing. This would certainly tip the balance in the gladiator case. But then the sympathetic suffering, when a murderer is executed, would count *in favour* of the system of capital punishment! What happened to the person executed would be bad for him, no doubt, but there is compensation for this in the fact that fewer people are killed. And it is a *comforting* fact that people suffer with him when he dies.

If all this is correct, it seems as though a utilitarian who is convinced that the use of the death penalty deters from murder must be in favour of the death penalty.

4.3. Is There a Superior Deterrent Effect?

This is not the place to settle this issue of whether the death penalty has a superior deterrent effect, of course. But we should not accept views such as the one put forward by James Fitzjames Stephen at face value. It is not *self-evident* that the death penalty is superior to long terms in prison if we want to obviate homicides. It has sometimes been claimed that the use of the death penalty has a brutalising effect on criminals. In order to avoid the death penalty, a murderer is prepared to resort to further murder. However, even long terms in prison may have a brutalising effect on murderers. After all, once you have received a sentence for life in prison, you are invulnerable. You may kill as you see fit, and there is no way of sentencing you to any stricter punishment, if the death penalty is not available.

It has been claimed that at least murderers who are irrational when they commit their crimes, murderers who kill in the heat of some emotion, will not be deterred by the threat of capital punishment. But this claim has been questioned.[17] Furthermore, even if a criminal is rational, it is not only the severity of the punishment

17. See Cass R. Sunstein and Adrian Vermeule, 'Is Capital Punishment Morally Required? Acts, Omissions, and Life-Life Tradeoffs', p. 712 for references.

he has to take into account when contemplating whether to kill or not, but also how likely it is that he will be caught, found guilty, and executed. If the death penalty is practiced, it is likely that fewer false positives are accepted, and hence he may be tempted to take the chance and kill. On the other hand, it has also been pointed out that, if the criminal's rationality is 'bounded', he may well misinterpret some very salient executions as a sign of the risk of getting executed being very high.

This is not the place to try to settle these empirical questions. In the final analysis, they should be solved through empirical studies, and not through speculation. There are indeed some recent US statistics indicating that the death penalty may be effective. A review of these findings by Cass R. Sunstein and Adrian Vermeule points to results such that one execution deters from something between five and eighteen murders.[18] These findings are questioned, of course. Not all arguments brought forward against them are convincing, however, as is clearly shown by Sunstein and Vermeule. It has sometimes been claimed that the statistical material does not show a deterrent effect in *all* cases. As a matter of fact, the deterrent effect is visible only in a few (six) states. This is not a good argument against the reliability of these studies, however. For, as it has often been pointed out, and as the authors note, the correct interpretation of this finding may be that only if there are enough executions will the system work. In those states where the deterrent effect has been said to surface, there are indeed enough executions (at least nine each year). So what we may have to reckon with here may be a kind of threshold effect. Interestingly enough, it seems, according to the authors, as though capital punishment, when it does deter, deters less rational people—killing in the heat of some emotion—as well as more rational ones.

Since I have no expertise in this area, it is impossible for me to assess these recent and highly controversial studies, hence I will abstain from any attempt to do so. It should be noted, however,

18. Cass R. Sunstein and Adrian Vermeule, ibid., pp. 703–750.

that even if they would turn out to be reliable when it comes to the situation in those states where the system seems to work, the *reason* that it works need not be *only* that here the number of executions is above a certain threshold. It may *also* be a result of the high incidence of murder in these states. So even if the death penalty has a deterrent effect when murder is a usual way of solving personal conflicts, it need not work in a state where murder seldom happens. If this is so, the utilitarian lesson to be drawn from the US experience is to introduce a welfare state, if that is a way of lowering the incidence of murder, rather than to resort to capital punishment.

From this it does not follow that capital punishment would not have any deterrent effect in a state with low incidence of murder, of course. We know next to nothing about this.

5. A TENTATIVE CONCLUSION

My gut feeling tells me that there is something inherently wrong with the death penalty. It is difficult to find a sound rationale behind this gut feeling, however. I have to conclude that it has probably been inculcated in me in the tradition to which I belong. I need to try to transcend my narrow cultural horizon and think about the matter from scratch. Consequently, this is how I want to sum up the argument in the chapter.

From a utilitarian point of view, it is hard to find any good reasons to object to the death penalty, if it could be shown to have a deterrent effect that is superior to the deterring effect of all conceivable alternative and less drastic forms of punishment. A group of moral rights theorists would be well advised, under such circumstances, to adopt the institution of capital punishment as a part of their social contract. Finally, there seem to be strong deontological reasons, to do with the retributivist rationale behind at least Kant's version of the theory, to adopt the death penalty regardless of its deterrent effect.

How should we assess these implications from respective theory? As I stated above, when I first started to think about capital punishment, my unreflective intuition was that capital punishment is never right. The content of this intuition is captured by one version of the Sanctity-of-Life Doctrine, in its present form. How did *I* think? I did indeed think that capital punishment must be wrong even if capital punishment turned out, with regard to its deterrent effect, to be more efficient than long turns in prison. I must have thought that there was something inherently terrible in the way people are killed when they are executed. I suppose I was here very much under the influence of Jonathan Glover's treatment of the subject in *Causing Death and Saving Lives*. It has transpired in the discussion about this matter, however, that there seems to be nothing especially nasty about being executed, in comparison with ordinary death, let alone in comparison with being murdered. So I have come to be inclined to believe that the correct verdict here is that capital punishment should be resorted to, if, and only if, it proved to have a superior deterrent effect. This is, of course, an implication from utilitarianism, which can, hence, explain the content of my considered intuition. The content of this intuition is at variance with deontology, however, in both its versions. The idea that we should *never* resort to capital punishment, regardless of its deterrent effect, now strikes me as squeamish. The idea that we *should* resort to capital punishment, again regardless of its deterrent effect (even if it does not have a superior deterrent effect), strikes me instead as much too bloodthirsty.

It is of note, however, that the content of my considered intuition can also be explained by the moral rights theory, allowing people to contract either for or against capital punishment, in view of its deterrent effect.

I return in the final chapter to a discussion about how we should assess these implications.

Chapter 6

Suicide

Are there situations where it is morally permissible to commit suicide?

	China	*Russia*	*United States*
Yes	51%	28%	38%
No	43%	66%	59%
Don't know	6%	5%	3%

1. INTRODUCTION

Suicide is a sensitive topic. When you take up a public liberal stance to suicide, people who are suicidal approach you and seek your advice. This in particular explains the initial difficulties, described in the preface to the book, of wanting to have questions put to the public at large about the ethics of killing. I am pleased that I could order the survey and have it done, however. The results are interesting, with the cultural differences in regard to suicide rather striking. While a majority among the Chinese believe that suicide is sometimes morally permitted, a majority among the Russians and Americans believe that there are no such situations. One is tempted to think here that there is something in the Christian moral culture that is operative in Russia and in the United States, but not, of course, in China. My hope, and belief, actually, is that neither my survey nor what I write in this chapter has or will provoke any irrational suicides. Judging from my own experience, there is some ground for such hope. People who are suicidal may gain from discussions about their situation. The worst thing is to be left alone with your thoughts. I truly believe I have actually stopped some people from committing irrational suicides. Or, did I stop them from committing *rational* suicides? I hope this chapter can shed some light on that question.

While there are clearly startling cultural differences on the view of suicide, interpreting them is far from easy. In particular, there is a problem with the findings from Russia and the United States. As we will see in a coming chapter on assisted death, a majority among all the investigated peoples—not only the Chinese but the Russians and the Americans as well—believe that assisted death should be a legal possibility. How is this possible, if they believe that suicide is always wrong? My guess is as follows. It is not that the Russians and the Americans are inconsistent. It is, rather, that they conceive of suicide in a manner that doesn't connect it to end-of-life decisions. When they claim that suicide is always wrong, they think of people who kill themselves, even though it would have been possible for them to go on with their lives. They do not think of terminally ill people at all when they think of suicide. Provided that I have interpreted this correctly, I will follow suit in this chapter. I will discuss suicide in situations where it had been possible for the person who took her own life to go on with it for an indefinite period of time. I will think of *healthy* people killing themselves. I think of people, then, who are healthy in the sense that they are not terminally ill, but who are also, for reasons to be given below, free of serious *mental* illness. My query, as usual, is what the implications are from deontology, the moral rights theory, and utilitarianism regarding the issue at hand. I will also initiate a discussion about which ones among our intuitions on the subject we should trust and which ones we should debunk.

Are there actual examples of suicide, if we confine our interest to people who are healthy? We sometimes learn from suicide research that everyone who commits suicide is *mentally* ill—and hence not responsible for her action. The action lacks moral status. Or, as I would prefer to say, in absence of any alternative, it is (trivially) all right. However, many, especially among the old people who commit suicide—are (also) physically ill. Perhaps some of these self-killings are avoidable? Well, it is hard to tell, but even if it is clear that those who kill themselves are often showing symptoms of depression, in some circumstances the explanation behind these symptoms need not be mental illness, one may conjecture, but rather the impression that life is indeed meaningless. Furthermore, as we will see, sometimes people kill themselves for what one may call other-regarding reasons. It is reasonable to assume that such actions have moral status; they are either right or wrong and hence they provide us with real examples of suicide.

Now, be this as it may, irrespective of whether there are suicides or not in real life, it is still possible to query about the normative status of this kind of action. Even if there are no suicides in real life, it is possible that there *should* be such cases. Until we have gone deeply into the question, we cannot preclude that, at least on one of the theories under scrutiny (utilitarianism), many, perhaps all of us, *ought* to kill ourselves.

In order to go systematically into the question, we need to be more precise about what it means to commit suicide, however.

2. SUICIDE—A DEFINITION

According to the *Concise Oxford Dictionary*, to commit suicide means 'intentionally [to] kill oneself'. This is close to the mark. However, several clarifications need to be made.

As I noted above, many, perhaps all, people who are said to commit suicide (a million each year, according to some statistics)[1] suffer from a mental illness that renders them incapable; they kill themselves intentionally, but they cannot help doing so.[2] If they would

1. WHO *World report on violence and health*, World Health Organization, Geneva (2002).

2. Keith Hawton and Kees van Heeringen, 'Suicide'.

decide not to kill themselves (as a matter of fact, many do) their decision would not be efficacious. They cannot avoid doing what they do. But then we should not speak of suicide, I suggest. So let me therefore stipulate that to commit suicide means to kill oneself intentionally, when one could have abstained from doing so.

What are we to say of people who commit suicide under some kind of pressure? The extreme case is Socrates, who would have been killed had he not killed himself. Did he commit suicide when he drank the cup of poison hemlock? He did, on my account. It is reasonable to assume that his intention was to die and it is reasonable to assume that his killing of himself did result—if *any* self-killing has ever done so—from an autonomous decision. After all, he could have refused, and suffered the consequences of his refusal.

We often hear reports in today's media about 'suicide bombers'. Here is a typical report, of the blast in Moscow's busiest airport on 24 January 2011:

> The prosecutor's office said the bomb had been classified as a terrorist attack—the largest since twin suicide bombings on the Moscow metro rocked the Russian heartland in March.
>
> 'The blast was most likely carried out by a suicide bomber.' State television said the blast was the work of a 'smertnik,' or suicide bomber. State-run RIA, quoting Markin, said the bomber most likely had a belt laden with explosives.
>
> (Reuters, Alexei Anishchuk)

Do terrorists commit suicide when they blow their deadly bombs, killing themselves as well as targeted victims (often civilians) belonging to the 'enemy' population? Or, are the words 'suicide-bombers' and 'smertnik' misnomers? According to the definition I will operate with here, they are misnomers. These terrorists do not commit suicide. And neither did Samson, as it is reported in The Tanakh (the Jewish Bible), commit suicide when he pushed the pillars over so that the building fell down on himself and the Philistines and killed them all. In all these instances, it is reasonable to assume that his own death is merely foreseen by the person who kills himself, in an attempt to kill the enemies. His own death is not intended. If it had been possible to kill the enemy while avoiding death, we must believe that the 'suicide' bombers, from Samson and onward, would have done so. Death must indeed be intended, and not merely foreseen, in order for an act of killing oneself to be counted as an instance of suicide.

This stipulation means also that what is sometimes called 'supererogatory' action, such as when you throw yourself on a hand grenade about to explode in order to save the lives of your fellow soldiers, does not count as suicide. Clearly, if you could save their lives in some other way, you would have preferred to do so, and stayed alive yourself. In such situations your own death is not intended; it is merely foreseen.

This does not mean that death you produce must be sought as an end in itself in order to count as suicide, however. It is hard to see that death could *ever* be seen as an end in itself. Typically, suicide means that one intentionally and deliberately kills oneself in order to obtain something. It could be to get rid of a life that is seen as meaningless and a mere burden. Or, it could be for some noble end. When some Buddhist monks in Vietnam set themselves on fire in an attempt to stop the US aggression against their country, they did indeed commit suicide. They intended their death. Only if they killed themselves intentionally and voluntarily, they believed, would the public opinion in the United States react against the war. Here it is reasonable to assume that the act was avoidable. A similar and more recent example is the event that sparked the Tunisian uprising in 2011:

> The unrest began about a month ago when Mohammed Bouazizi, a 26-year-old university graduate, set himself on fire in an act of protest. Unable to find steady work, Bouazizi often sold vegetables without the required permit. After the police confiscated his vegetable cart and he was unable to lodge a formal complaint, the desperate youth attempted suicide in order to bring his frustration to light.
>
> (*The Majalla*, 11 January 2011)

Some suicides are heroic in this way. However, there may also exist situations where people commit suicide for more mundane reasons. They may want not to put pressure upon their close ones in a situation of economic scarcity, for example. Hence they kill themselves intentionally and could have abstained from doing so.

Need we also claim that, in order for an act of killing oneself to count as suicide, it should also be an act of *active* killing? In my chapter on murder I assumed that intentional killing of an individual is not murder unless it is also active. I think our understanding of suicide should be more inclusive, however. The reason is that this is how we tend to speak.

Suppose I am standing on the tracks and see a trolley approaching me. I realize that, unless I leave the tracks, I will be killed. I could easily leave the tracks, but I don't. It so happens that I want to be dead rather than alive. With the intention of being killed, I stay on the tracks, even though I could have left them. Consequently, I am run over and killed by the trolley. Did I commit suicide?

I believe we should count this as suicide. It is the intended/merely foreseen distinction (which we know from the Sanctity-of-Life Doctrine), not the acts/omission distinction (which we know from the moral rights theory), that we should rely on here. Or, so I will do, at any rate, in *my* stipulated definition of what it means to commit suicide.

This stipulation means also that if you stop drinking and eating in order to put an end to your life, you commit suicide. Remember, however, that I have restricted my use of the term 'suicide' to situations outside what we usually call end-of-life decisions. Thus, when a terminally ill patient refuses to eat and drink, she is not committing suicide.

My stipulation does imply, however, that people who depend on a ventilator for their survival, and who could go on with their lives for an indefinite time, and who remove the ventilator, do commit suicide. The next chapter on assisted death has more on such cases. In a similar vein, those who for political reasons starve themselves to death, *do* commit suicide.

Does all this mean that Jesus committed suicide? One could argue like this. He could have escaped his fate, but, eventually, he decided not to. He allowed the Roman authorities to kill him, for what he believed to be a noble cause. He wanted to save the rest of us. And he saw his *death* as crucial to his mission. Merely *seeming* dead would not have been enough. My intuition is that he did not commit suicide. One could compare this, however, to the case with the person who stays on the tracks and allows the trolley to kill him. He does commit suicide, I argued. So where is the difference? Why did Jesus not commit suicide? The analogy is not close enough, however. The fact that an *agent*, and not a trolley, killed Jesus means that *he* did not kill himself and, hence, he did not commit suicide. In a similar vein, if a doctor removes the ventilator and the patient who could have gone on with her life for an indefinite period of time dies, then this is not suicide on the part of the patient, and hence not assisted suicide on the part of the medical doctor. Here the doctor *kills* the patient, if only by allowing death to come when the ventilator is withdrawn.

To commit suicide, then, is intentionally to kill oneself (for whatever reason) when one could have abstained from doing so; one's killing of oneself was either active or passive; the killing happened in a situation where one could have gone on with one's life for an indefinite time.

3. LUDWIG WITTGENSTEIN ON SUICIDE

In this book, I use suicide as one example of killing among others. One may wonder, however, whether suicide is special. The Austrian philosopher Ludwig Wittgenstein did indeed find suicide special. He was in his life surrounded by people, many of them his family, who committed suicide. Moreover, suicide seems always to have been a live option for him.[3] He famously made the following comment on the subject:

3. See Ray Monk, *Ludwig Wittgenstein: The Duty of Genius.*

> If suicide is allowed then everything is allowed. If anything is not allowed then suicide is not allowed. This throws a light on the nature of ethics, for suicide is, so to speak, the elementary sin. And when one investigates it it is like investigating mercury vapours in order to investigate the nature of vapours.[4]

This oft-quoted passage is usually taken as a statement to the effect that suicide is wrong, but one need only read through it carefully to note that this is not so. No stand is taken on the issue by Wittgenstein. I suppose the best way of understanding the quoted passage is as follows. What Wittgenstein wants to claim is that, if *any* conventional type of action (like murder, suicide, abortion, and so forth) is absolutely prohibited (there are no permitted instances of it), then suicide is one such absolutely prohibited action. If there are morally permitted instances of suicide, then there must also be morally permitted instances of *all* other conventional types of actions, such as murder or abortion.

Wittgenstein may be right about this, but in order to find out if he is, we need to proceed in a piecemeal manner—as I have often insisted in this book. We must work through *all* the putative candidates of suspect action types here and cannot just focus on suicide. But suicide is the subject of this chapter, so let us now turn to the three theories under scrutiny and investigate their implications for the morality of suicide.

4. DEONTOLOGY

On deontology the matter is simple. Suicide means the intentional killing of an innocent human (rational) being and it is hence wrong. A possible exception comes to mind. What if a murderer commits suicide? He is not innocent. On the Kantian, retributivist, understanding of the deontology discussed in the previous chapter, the

4. Concluding paragraphs—Wittgenstein, L. *Notebooks* 1914–1916.

murderer deserves to be killed. Does that mean that he has a right to kill himself? My guess is that most adherents of the theory would say no. Only someone authorized to punish the murderer has the right (and obligation) to kill him. By killing himself, the murderer cowardly *avoids* the punishment he deserves.

4.1. Kant on Suicide

Only when necessary, I distinguish in this book between the Sanctity-of-Life Doctrine as such, and a Kantian deontology, delivering the same verdict on intentional killing of innocent human beings. I made such a distinction in the previous chapter where I focused on the retributivist, Kantian aspect of the doctrine. There may be reason to do so also in this chapter. This is why.

One may wonder *why* the Sanctity-of-Life Doctrine should put the killing of others and the killing of oneself on a par; is it not worse to kill another person, one may wonder? Of course, a defining characteristic of the Sanctity-of-Life Doctrine is that it makes no difference here. It is the killing of an innocent human being that is wrong. What about Kant? He, too, treats suicide as no better than murder. Could he perhaps provide some kind of *rationale* behind such a strict view of suicide? This is what he has to say, explicitly, about suicide:

> To annihilate the subject of morality in one's person is to root out the existence of morality itself from the world as far as one can, even though morality is an end in itself. Consequently, disposing of oneself as a mere means to some discretionary end is debasing humanity in one's person. . .[5]

The first part of the quoted passage can perhaps be understood on a metaethical constructivist view of morality—of the kind defended for example Christine Korsgaard.[6] However, the addition made by

5. I. Kant, *Metaphysics of Morals*, p. 423.
6. See, for example, Christine M. Korsgaard, *The Sources of Normativity*.

Kant that 'morality is an end in itself' counts against such an interpretation. Yet, let us accept it for the sake of argument. Then, if I kill myself, this means that no morality exists 'for me'. If everyone were to do the same, there would be no such thing as a morality at all, one could add. This does not strike me as an argument in its own right, however. Who, then, would there be to complain? If morality is a construction, then there seems to be no *need* for it if there are no moral agents.

The second part of the quoted passage, therefore, must be the part that is intended to carry the substantial moral argumentative burden. But it, too, may seem to be hard to accept. Even if we accept that we should not 'debase' humanity in ourselves, why does suicide mean that we do that? Furthermore, why does killing oneself mean that one uses oneself as a mere means to a discretionary end? Let us focus on this latter question.

First of all, what are we to say about the 'discretionary' part of the argument? What if the end is a noble one? What if I commit suicide in order to save humanity? That could hardly count as a 'discretionary' end. In a sense all ends are 'discretionary', of course. When I act, I choose the end for which I act. However, in the passage Kant must mean that the end is not only chosen, but also somehow *arbitrary*. He seems to think that the person who commits suicide must act out of a whim, capriciously, or something of the kind.

But if I kill myself in order to spark a revolution, in the manner the young Mohammed Bouazizi did in Tunisia in 2010, then the end is all but arbitrary. Even Kant would admit, I suppose, that it was an end for which it made sense to make *some* sacrifices. Why not an end for which it would be reasonable to sacrifice ones life? Most people tend to admire Mohammed Bouazizi, I believe. Should they not also be allowed to say that, bravely, he did the *right* thing?

I think Kant could admit that Bouazizi acted for a noble cause. Or, perhaps I am too optimistic with regard to Kant's readiness to support revolution. His political philosophy was, after all, terribly conservative.[7]

7. Lisa Hecht has reminded me of this.

Anyway, Kant *should* have seen Bouazizi's act as admirable, it seems to me. And yet, regardless of how he would have viewed Bouazizi's *cause*, he would have objected to his *act*. He would have objected to it on principled grounds. The grounds are that, not even for a noble end are we allowed to violate the dignity in ourselves, which is what we do when we commit suicide We use ourselves, our humanity, and hence also our dignity, as a mere means, when we sacrifice our rationality, and this is something we are not allowed to do, not even for a noble end. This is no different from how he conceives of murder, then. We are not allowed to murder, i.e. to destroy dignity, in order to save lives. In a similar vein, we are not allowed to kill ourselves in order to save lives, let alone, of course, in order to enhance the quality of our own lives. His stand on suicide is, thus, consistent and comprehensible.

5. THE MORAL RIGHTS THEORY

The implications of the moral rights theory with respect to suicide are straightforward and at variance with what people in Russia and the United States believe. Since we own ourselves, we are free to do whatever we see fit with ourselves, so long as this does not mean that we violate any negative rights of anyone else. And no one owns me, unless I have sold myself as a slave, so I can kill myself without any regard for bad side effects of my action for others.

It is true that John Locke thought otherwise. I have already quoted him, in Chapter 2, when I presented the moral rights theory. This is what he had to say about suicide:

> But though this be a State of Liberty, yet it is not a State of Licence, though Man in that State have an uncontrollable Liberty, to dispose of his Person ... yet he has not Liberty to destroy himself.[8]

8. John Locke, *The Second Treatise of Government*, Chapter 2:311.

I took this to be a lack of consistency in his libertarian moral rights theory, however. This was probably just an attempt to be 'politically correct'. If doesn't fit with his general theory.

6. UTILITARIANISM

It might be thought that the crucial question to the utilitarian treatment of suicide is the general idea about how well people fare. If you are extremely pessimistic in your assessment of how our lives go, if you believe that everyone is, as a matter of fact, living a life not worth living (with a net surplus of pain over pleasure), then we should all kill ourselves. On the other hand, if we all live lives (remember, we are not discussing typical end-of-life situations) that are considered worth experiencing (they contain a net surplus of pleasure over pain), then suicide is wrong. In particular, and more precisely, one may think that the typical utilitarian view of suicide would be that it is right to commit suicide if and only if *the rest* of your life will provide you with more pain than pleasure. It is not as simple as that, however. The reason it is more complicated is that utilitarianism takes seriously 'external' effects of a practice such as suicide.

6.1. Should We All Kill Ourselves?

I suppose it is correct to say that, if Schopenhauer is right, if life is never worth living, then according to utilitarianism we should *all* commit suicide and put an end to humanity. But this does not mean that *each* of us should commit suicide. I commented on this in Chapter 2 when I presented the idea that utilitarianism should be applied not only to individual actions but to collective actions as well.

It is a well-known fact that people rarely commit suicide. Some even claim that no one who is mentally sound commits suicide. Could that be taken as evidence for the claim that people live lives worth living? That would be rash. Many people are not utilitarians. They may avoid suicide because they believe that it is morally wrong to kill oneself. It is also a possibility that, even if people lead lives not worth living, they believe they do. And some may believe that although their lives, up to now, have not been worth living, their *future* lives will be better. They may be mistaken about this, holding false expectations about the future.

From the point of view of evolutionary biology, it is natural to assume that people should rarely commit suicide. If we set old age to one side, it has poor survival value (of one's genes) to kill oneself. Thus, it should be expected that it is difficult for ordinary people to kill themselves. But then theories about cognitive dissonance, known from psychology, should warn us that we may come to believe that we live better lives than we do.

My strong belief is that most of us live lives worth living. However, I do believe that our lives are close to the point where they stop being worth living. But then it is at least not very far-fetched to think that they may be not worth living after all. My assessment may be too optimistic.

Let us just for the sake of the argument *assume* that our lives are not worth living, and let us accept that, if this is so, utilitarianism implies we should all kill ourselves. As I noted above, this does not answer the question of what, according to utilitarianism, we should do, each one of us. My conjecture is that we should not commit suicide. The utilitarian explanation is simple. If I kill myself, many people will suffer. Here is a rough explanation of how this will happen:

> suicide 'survivors' confront a complex array of feelings. Various forms of guilt are quite common, such as that arising from (a) the belief that one contributed to the suicidal person's anguish, or (b) the failure to recognize that anguish, or (c) the inability to prevent the suicidal act itself. Suicide also leads to rage, loneliness, and awareness of vulnerability

> in those left behind. Indeed, the sense that suicide is an essentially selfish act dominates many popular perceptions of suicide.[9]

The fact that all our lives lack meaning, if they do, does not imply that others will follow my example. They will go on with their lives and their false expectations—at least for a while devastated because of my suicide. But then I have an obligation, according to utilitarianism, for *their* sake, to go on with *my* life. It is highly likely that, by committing suicide, I create more suffering (in their lives) than I avoid (in my life).

Going on with my life in spite of the fact that it lacks meaning (contains a net surplus of pain over happiness) is not such a big deal. Even if the net balance of the rest of my life does consist of pain rather than happiness, this is something I am already used to. I have strategies to cope with it. These strategies are not perfect—after all, given the hypothesis in this section, my net balance will be negative. However, this is a sacrifice, not too heavy, I should make in the best interest of my dear ones. This seems to be what utilitarianism requires from me.

6.2. Suicide in Individual Cases

Up to now I have conducted the discussion in very broad and general terms. Are our lives in general worth experiencing or not? If not, we ought all to kill ourselves, but each and every one ought to go on with her own life, I have concluded from utilitarianism. If our lives are worth living, we ought all to go on with our lives. And this applies to each and every one of us as well. However, there may exist exceptions from these general rules.

Suppose there are some people who lead terrible lives, even if they are not suffering from identifiable diseases that would qualify them for assisted death (to be discussed in the next chapter); should

9. See Michael Cholbi, entry on 'suicide' in *The Stanford Encyclopedia of Philosophy*.

they not kill themselves, if we assess the matter from the point of view of utilitarianism? Certainly, when they commit suicide, they cause suffering among their close ones. However, if their suffering is terrible, would it not still be permissible for them to kill themselves?

To the extent that they have communicated to their close ones how terrible their lives are, and to the extent that they have convinced their close ones about the fact that there is nothing that could be done to improve the quality of their lives, they could very well kill themselves. Their close ones, too, may see a point in their suicide. So, perhaps, on balance, there will be no bad side effects if they kill themselves. Their close ones will be sad, of course, but will no more have to suffer from the knowledge that their loved ones are living terrible and irreparable lives. They have put an end to their suffering, the only end available.

It strikes me as plausible to conclude here, that these people, if such people exist, have a right, according to utilitarianism, to kill themselves. In fact, if there is really no way of making their lives better, this is what they *ought* to do. This seems to be the message sent from utilitarianism about suicide.[10]

Finally, there may exist rare historical situations where, by committing suicide, you may turn history into a better direction. Then it might well be your utilitarian duty to commit suicide. This may well have been true of the Buddhist monks in Vietnam during the war, and it may well have been true of Mohammed Bouazizi, who sparked the Tunisian revolution in 2011 with his suicide.

7. A TENTATIVE CONCLUSION

We have seen that the cultural variations are important when it comes to suicide. So here we should not rely on our gut feelings. We should try to transcend our narrow cultural horizon when we

10. See Victor Cosculluela, *The Ethics of Suicide*, pp. 76–81, about our obligation to commit suicide.

contemplate the matter. Here are some preliminary results, when *I* attempt to do so.

The moral rights theory strikes me as clearly wrong. The fact that it doesn't count external effects of acts of suicide as morally relevant, unless they constitute boundary-crossings, is not acceptable.

Deontology may well be close to the mark in its verdict that suicide is always wrong. It is close to the mark, if all lives are, as a matter of fact, worth living (setting end-of-life decisions and altruistic suicides to one side). However, it is yet too strict, as I see it. While the general permission issued from the moral rights theory is insensitive to possible bad external effects of suicides, deontology is insensitive to possible good external effects. There seem to be actual cases of altruistic (other regarding) suicides that are not only right, but praiseworthy and courageous as well. The ban on such suicides, issued by deontology, therefore counts heavily against this doctrine. Moreover, it is also insensitive to the possibility that there are cases where people just happen to lead *very* bad lives, and where it strikes me as cruel not to allow them a possibility to escape from their plight through suicide. It doesn't matter whether there are, in fact, such cases. The mere possibility of such cases, and the strict verdict from deontology, is enough to cast doubt upon it.

It may well be that actions performed from the motive resented by deontologists are most of them wrong. When you intentionally destroy your own rationality, your action is likely to produce misery. This is so even if you do not kill yourself, but merely destroy your rational capacities by, say, yielding to a craving for drugs. However, it is not the motive as such that *makes* such actions wrong. Remember a similar discussion on the role of our motives in the chapter on murder. In such situations where life is unbearable, it seems to me, it is morally all right to use oneself (one's dignity, and humanity, and rationality) as a mere means to a better total life—to put an end to one's suffering.

The fact that neither deontology nor the moral rights theory concurs in the utilitarian verdict that we should all commit suicide if it would surface that we all lead lives worth not living, is also a problem for these theories, even if this matter may be seen as of little *practical* importance. It counts in favour of the moral rights theory that it *allows* all of us to kill ourselves in such a situation. Many may feel that this is a *more* plausible stance than the utilitarian verdict that, in such situations, we are under a moral *obligation* to commit a collective suicide.

Chapter 7

Assisted Death

Should a person who suffers from an incurable fatal disease and who doesn't want to live any more have the right to request and receive a lethal injection which terminates his or her life?

	China	Russia	United States
Yes	85%	75%	65%
No	13%	19%	35%
Don't know	3%	5%	3%

Real death—in real life

On April 21, 2011, 38-year-old Jia Zhengwu helped to "euthanatize" his seriously ill wife by pushing her off the Yellow River bank after she thought about committing suicide after the paraplegia caused by rheumatic arthritis and ankylosing spondylitis became intolerable.

The defense lawyer asked the court to give probation to Jia, arguing that he had no intentional criminal motive and substantially helped his wife to attain a dignified death.

The lawyer said that Jia "euthanatized" his seriously ill wife just to relieve her from the physical and spiritual pain even though the action is not allowed by China's criminal law.

However, the court ruled that Jia's action has constituted a criminal offence and sentenced him to five years in jail for intentional homicide.

Jia was given a lenient treatment because he had fulfilled his duty to look after his wife before he "killed" her, the court said.

(Sino-US.com http://www.sino-us.com/11/0943397918.html, accessed on 14 January 2013.)

1. ASSISTED DEATH

Assisted death, even if the term is relatively new, is an old phenomenon, and the extant discussion about it is to some extent merely an aspect of the discussion about suicide. However, the advance of modern medicine, rendering it possible for physicians to keep their terminal patients lingering on for long time, together with a shift towards respect, in general, of autonomous decisions made by patients, has recently given rise to intense public discussion about the issue. This discussion pertains to problems that are related to, but different from, the problems related to suicide, at least as the notion of suicide has been defined in the previous chapter. I have no intention in this chapter to account for this recent discussion on assisted death in its entirety, but I do intend to tease out—as far as possible—the implications from deontology, the moral rights theory, and utilitarianism, for assisted death. However, where these implications depend on difficult empirical questions, I will not try to find out about them in detail. The question is, rather, whether each theory identifies what kind of empirical facts are the relevant ones in a plausible way.

By 'assisted death' one may mean many different things. I will here use the term to cover cases of active and intentional killing of a person suffering from a terminal and painful disease in order to spare this person further suffering. It hence includes what is usually called euthanasia, where a doctor actively and intentionally kills a patient in order to spare this person further suffering, and also what is usually called physician-assisted suicide, where a medical doctor provides the means but where the patient performs the final active and intentional killing of herself. It should be noted, however, that there are cases of what is called euthanasia in the Netherlands that are not examples of assisted death as I understand the notion. I think of cases where the patient who is killed suffers from incurable and unbearable suffering but not from any *terminal* disease. I make my restricted use of the term 'assisted death' in order to capture something that should at least on the face of it appear less controversial than suicide. Moreover, on my strict definition of 'suicide', made in the previous chapter, according to which a person who is in a terminal state and who kills herself does not commit suicide, physician-assisted 'suicide' is, strictly speaking, a misnomer.

The use of the term 'euthanasia' in the Netherlands is, then, broader in one respect than mine. In another respect, however, it is narrower. In the Netherlands a person is only euthanized if she is killed at her own request. I will also allow for the possible existence of non-voluntary euthanasia—active and intentional killing of a patient in order to save him from incurable and unbearable suffering *without* his request—and I will include such cases of euthanasia in the notion of assisted death. As we will see, this may mean that it is easier, not more difficult, to find a rationale behind legalisation of assisted death.

There is also logical space open for involuntary euthanasia, where the killing of a patient in order to save him from incurable and unbearable suffering caused by a terminal disease takes place *against* the express wish of the patient. However, since this kind of euthanasia is murder, I will not include it in my notion of assisted death, and I will not discuss it in the present chapter. I have already discussed it in the chapter on murder.

In ordinary language we often meet with the claim that not intended, but merely foreseen, hastening of the death of terminal patients exemplify assisted death. This is not how I use the term in the present chapter. In order to count as a case of assisted death the patient must have been actively and intentionally killed, either by herself or by a physician. It is also crucial that the act takes place within a health-care setting. I will not discuss cases where a person who is not a medical doctor kills a friend at request and out of mercy. Thus, the example with Jia Zhengwu, described at the opening of this chapter, is, strictly speaking, not an example of assisted death. Furthermore, my main focus will be on cases where a medical doctor is the person who performs the act of killing, not on cases where the patient kills herself. When the patients are allowed to choose between these two options, as they are permitted to do, for example, in the Netherlands, most seem to prefer that the medical doctor, not they themselves, performs the act of killing. I suppose they tend to argue that it is the doctor, not they themselves, who possesses the expertise in this field.

2. THE TYPICAL LEGAL SITUATION

If we borrow from the moral rights theory the distinction between active and passive killing (acts and omissions) and from the Sanctity-of-Life Doctrine the distinction between intentional and merely foreseen killing, then we can roughly characterize the legal situation in most Western countries as well as in China and Russia in the manner illustrated in Figure 7.1:

It now transpires that active and intentional killing of a terminal patient, even at his request, and in order to save him from incurable and unbearable suffering, is forbidden in most countries. This is what I have characterized as euthanasia and a form of assisted

killing	death intended	death merely foreseen
active killing	forbidden	permitted
passive killing	permitted	permitted

Figure 7.1. The Standard Legal Situation

death. However, in a few countries (the Netherlands, Belgium, and Luxemburg), such killing is sometimes allowed. In those countries physicians are permitted to kill patients at their request, provided the patients suffer from an incurable and unbearable suffering. This is the exception, however. And even if there exist in many countries opinions to the effect that assisted death should be legalized, the rule is still that this field is closed.

Active killing of patients, if death is merely foreseen, is sometimes accepted even in countries where assisted death is forbidden. A painkiller that kills not only the pain but the patient as well is legally accepted if the death of the patient was only a foreseen side effect of the intervention, if the patient was dying anyway (the requirement of proportionality is satisfied), and if there was no better way to kill the pain. This may seem quite liberal, but as a matter of fact, it may have come to be the exception rather than the rule that it is not possible to achieve the good effect (to kill the pain) without killing the patient. Of course, this is a rule that is often bent in actual medical practice. However, it may be rare that palliation that hastens death needs to take place if the intention is to relieve suffering only. According to Susan Fohr, 'the correct use of morphine is more likely to prolong a patient's life . . . because he is more rested and pain-free'.[1]

Hastening death intentionally but passively, by not continuing with life support, at the request of a patient, such as when a ventilator is removed and the patient dies, is often controversial, but such cases nevertheless seem to take place all over the medical world now and then.

Let us now look more closely into the two distinctions, between acts and omissions, and between intended and merely foreseen effects, which both seem to play a role in medical practice and which

1. Susan Andersson Fohr, 'The Double Effect in Pain Medication: Separating Myth from Reality'. I have the quotation from Wayne Sumner, *Assisted Death*. The claim is contested, however. See Peter Allmark et al., 'Is the Doctrine of Double Effect Irrelevant in End-of-Life Decision Making?'.

each of them plays a crucial role in the moral rights theory and in the Sanctity-of-Life Doctrine, respectively.

2.1. Acts and Omissions

Is it active killing to give an injection that kills the patient, when death is not intended? As far as I can see, it is. This is not a book on metaphysics, and I only touch now and then on deep metaphysical problems. The distinction between acts and omissions, between active and passive killing, depends on the solution of difficult metaphysical problems, of course. However, since I will not hold it against the moral rights theory that it relies on the distinction, and since it is upheld in common sense thinking, I will be brief here. This does not mean, of course, that I claim that the distinction is morally relevant. This is another discussion to which I will soon turn. My assumption is only that it makes sense.

It is true that there are no particular actions that are either acts or omissions. All particular actions are active under some description and passive under some other description. I am now actively typing this sentence. At the same time I omit some of my duties to my students. And I allow that poor people in the Third World die. I could right now have sent all my money to OXFAM in order to save as many as possible among them. The very same act is active (typing) and an omission (to supervise my students and to help people in distress). However, in relation to a *result*, we may classify acts as active and passive (instances of the relevant type). To inject a painkiller that kills the patient is active *killing*. Not to treat a patient, who therefore dies from his disease, is passive *killing* (the *allowing* of death to come).

The distinction is somewhat vague. The idea behind it is that sometimes we initiate, or maintain, a causal chain, leading up to the death of the patient. Then we kill the patient actively. Sometimes we allow a causal chain to unfold, leading to the death of the patient. We then allow that the patient dies. A problematic case is when we take a patient off a ventilator. Is this active or passive killing? On my understanding of the action it is passive killing. We allow the patient to die. This is so regardless of whether our *disconnecting the ventilator* is active or passive. In ordinary circumstances it is active. We *remove* the ventilator. However, if the ventilator is connected to a timer, and we *omit to press a button* with the consequence that the ventilator stops functioning, then we disconnect the ventilator passively. In any case, our *killing* is passive. We allow the patient to die. We do not block the causal chain any more that leads to the patient's death (provided the patient cannot breathe on his own). We stop keeping him alive. I am here in agreement with Philippa Foot's treatment of the subject.[2]

I here assume that death is in the interest of the patient. What if it is not? Then it is objectionable of a physician to stop keeping the patient on the ventilator even according to the moral rights theory, of course. But this is not because not providing the ventilator any more means active killing; it is wrong because the physician has undertaken to provide this kind of aid for the patient. If this were not the case, and if the ventilator belongs to the physician, not the patient, then the removal of it is not active killing and, according to the moral rights theory, morally all right.

Jeff McMahan has suggested that it is of importance to the doing/allowing distinction if the one removing the ventilator is the same person who first provided this kind of life support.[3] I do not think that this is of importance for the question of whether the killing is active or merely an instance of allowing death to come, however. The removal of the ventilator means that the patient is allowed to die, regardless of who it was who put it there in the first place. And the moral status of the removal, according to the moral rights theory, depends, rather, on who owns the ventilator, and what kind of contract exists between physician and patient.

The same can be said about another factor that McMahan stresses. If the life support is self-sustaining, the removal of it

2. Philippa Foot, 'Morality, Action and Outcome'.

3. Jeff McMahan, 'Killing, Letting Die, and Withdrawing Aid', pp. 256–258.

means that the patient is actively harmed, he suggests. I do not share this intuition either. Whether it is right or wrong to remove the ventilator, on the moral rights theory, depends on the relation between patient and physician and on who owns the ventilator; however, the removal of the ventilator means, even if the ventilator is self-sustaining, that the patient is allowed to die. The patient is not actively killed when the ventilator is removed.

As earlier noted, I will not go deeply into this problem. Let me just observe that there are two influential attempts to make sense of the active/passive distinction, one made by Jonathan Bennett (who doesn't believe that it is morally relevant) and one made by Alan Donagan (who does believe that it is morally relevant).[4] The intuitive view I rely on here, with its stress on the initiation and maintenance of causal chains, is clearly closer to Donagan's theory than it is to Bennett's. The reason for this choice is that Bennett's theory (which draws roughly upon a distinction between how many versions there are of a certain action type) seems to deliver the wrong answer in many situations, for example the situation where we take a patient off a ventilator. This is active killing, on Bennett's view (there are only a few ways in which we can perform this action as compared, say, to a case where we do not give medication to a patient). On Donagan's view, if we distinguish between relevant and irrelevant causal chains, we can make sense of the claim that it is passive killing (we allow that nature takes its course and hence, we allow that the patient dies).

Of course, since we are not God (or Aristotle's immobile mover), when we initiate a causal chain we also break a causal chain. However, when we initiate one, through an act of ours, we, according to the moral rights theory, assume responsibility for it. Suppose a person is standing on the pier at Brighton. I approach her. She cannot swim. Yet, she jumps into the water. She wants to see if I am prepared to make an effort to save her. I don't. She drowns. Am I responsible for her death? If we assess the matter from the point of view of the moral rights theory, which relies on the active/passive

4. Jonathan Bennett, *The Act Itself* and Alan Donagan, *The Theory of Morality*.

distinction, I am not; it is true that she would not have jumped had I not been present and, yet, she, and not I, is responsible for her death. When she jumped into the water, she initiated a causal chain ending with her death.

Had I instead scared her with my appearance, so that she had fallen into the water, then I would have been causally responsible. Even if I had inadvertently caused her to fall into the water, I caused her plight. So, on the moral rights theory, I would be under an obligation, if possible, to save her. Or, that may be a bit rash. What if she is extremely jumpy? Could we not then say that she has placed herself in harms way? *She* is then responsible for her plight when she falls into the water. That seems to be a reasonable assessment.

Admittedly, it is not quite clear in detail how to distinguish between relevant and irrelevant causal chains; it might even take a moral assessment to draw the line. In that case, the moral rights theory must pay a high intellectual price for the distinction, of course. I leave that problem for some other occasion.

This classification of a case where we no longer keep a patient on a ventilator as passive killing, as a case of having nature taking its course, is in accordance with received wisdom and helps us to understand the legal situation in those countries where assisted death is prohibited but other kinds of hastening of the death of patients are yet allowed.

2.2. Intended and Merely Foreseen Death

The Sanctity-of-Life Doctrine, if it is taken literally, for example with reference to authoritative statements of it,[5] operates with a very liberal notion of what you merely foresee rather than intend. Some have argued that it is *too* liberal. In the chapter on the trolley cases, I discussed this kind of criticism made against the principle. I then concluded that, once we keep in mind that an action can still be wrong, according to deontological thinking, even if it is not

5. *New Catholic Encyclopedia*.

wrong because the motive behind it is of the wrong sort, and once we keep in mind that rightness and wrongness are absolute notions (an action is either right, i.e., permitted, or wrong, i.e., forbidden), we may stick to the liberal interpretation of the principle. It is indeed wrong to act on the wrong motive, but it is also wrong to act on a good motive when the bad side effects you foresee are out of proportion when compared to the good thing you aspire to. To accept such a liberal understanding of the principle is to make best sense of it.

There are, of course, situations where we allow patients to die, but where there is no intention to hasten their death. This is true when a dying patient with pneumonia is not given another penicillin cure. Are there also situations where there is an intention to hasten their death, but where this is achieved by passive measures, and hence allowed? There are such cases in most countries where assisted death is prohibited, I have claimed. They are often controversial, however, so it makes sense to elaborate on this question. An obvious example of this on which we may focus is when a patient has been diagnosed as being in a permanent vegetative state. This means that, if the diagnosis is correct, then the patient is not only in a *persistent* vegetative state, but the situation is *irreversible*. The patient's cortex is destroyed. Consequently, she has no consciousness; this does not mean, however, that she is brain dead (the rest of her brain is functioning). She is sometimes awake, sometimes asleep. She can breathe without help but she must be given food through a tube. Physicians sometimes[6] stop feeding patients in a permanent vegetative state. But this means that, *intentionally*, these patients are starved to death.

3. THE SANCTITY-OF-LIFE DOCTRINE

As I have here understood the Sanctity-of-Life Doctrine, it operates with the distinction between intended and merely foreseen

6. See, for example, Grubb, Andrew et al., 'Survey of British clinicians' views on management of patients in persistent vegetative state'.

death but not with the distinction between acts and omissions. Even to deprive a patient in a permanent vegetative state of food in order to hasten his death is forbidden according to the doctrine. What happened in the so-called Bland case bears witness to this.[7] In this case it was decided that a patient in a persistent vegetative state should not be artificially fed or hydrated any more. It is *obvious* that the intention behind the action (of not feeding or hydrating the patient) was to hasten death. Similar cases are easily found in most other Western countries, including Sweden. And they are all legally tolerated. However, advocates of the Sanctity-of-Life Doctrine have—and should have—moral problems with such cases. The Sanctity-of-Life Doctrine is at variance with standard medical thinking. This is what one advocate of the doctrine, Luke Gormally, has to say about the Bland case (in relation to something I had written about it):

> Tännsjö refers to the *Bland* case as offering clear evidence of the purchase of 'standard thinking' on the courts. But what did the three Law Lords, who explicitly stated that the proposal to withhold tubefeeding from Anthony Bland was intended to hasten his death, themselves think of the distinction on which they relied between intentionally killing someone by a positive act and doing so by planned omission? It was 'a distinction without a difference' according to Lord Lowry; it was a 'morally and intellectually dubious distinction' according to Lord Mustill. And Lord Browne-Wilkinson confessed that 'the conclusion I have reached will appear to some to be almost irrational . . . I find it difficult to find a moral answer'.[8] What cases like *Bland* show is not the intellectual merits of Tännsjö's 'standard thinking' but rather the willingness of the judiciary to accommodate what doctors want to do. The lesson is sociological not ethical.[9]

7. Airedale NHS *Trust v. Bland* (1993).

8. See [1993] 2 *Weekly Law Reports* at p. 379 (Lord Lowry), p. 399 (Lord Mustill), p. 387 (Lord Browne-Wilkinson).

9. 'Terminal Sedation and the Sanctity of Life', p. 82.

Now, since my point was sociological and not ethical (I described the existing legal situation), I do not see that Gormally disproves the point I made about standard medical thinking. However, it is clear that, on his understanding of the Sanctity-of-Life Doctrine, the doctrine does not condone when people are intentionally but passively allowed to die. The Sanctity-of-Life Doctrine *is* at variance with medical practice in many Western countries. And this clearly is also Luke Gormally's view.

Something similar to the Bland case happened in 2009 in Italy. The pope and conservative politicians such as Berlusconi attempted (in vain) to interfere with the action (or rather omission) of the physician caring for a patient, Eluana Englaro, diagnosed as being in a permanent vegetative state, when her parents convinced him to stop feeding their daughter. Before the Pope and Berlusconi could intervene, the girl died. The pope declared that, the 'true response cannot be to give death, even if it is seemingly more soothing, but to show the love that can help people face pain and agony in a human way'. This seems to be the conclusion we must draw, if we want to rely on the Sanctity-of-Life Doctrine.

3.1. The Sanctity-of-Life Doctrine and the Objection from Heavy Demands

There is an interesting implication of the rejection of the acts and omission distinction in the Sanctity-of-Life Doctrine. It is sometimes thought that utilitarianism makes too heavy a demand on us. We are not allowed to live high and let die and provide, as a rationale for this behaviour, that we only *allow* poor people to die, we do not actively kill them. According to utilitarianism, the distinction between acts and omissions is morally irrelevant. When the Sanctity-of-Life Doctrine concurs in giving up on the moral relevance of the common sense acts and omission doctrine this means that it, too, has very strict implications for us. We are not allowed to live high and let die. It is of no avail to claim that, when I purchase a new car rather than send my money to OXFAM, I merely foresee the death of people in need, I do not intend it. This may well be true, but note that there is also a requirement of proportionality to be observed. The negative effects I merely foresee must stand in some reasonable proportion to the positive effects I intend to bring about. But that requirement of proportionality is never fulfilled in relation to trifle things we allow ourselves instead of saving lives.

This aspect of the doctrine can be seen either as a weakness or as a strength of it. In my view it adds to its plausibility. I can't help feeling, however, that its very strict prohibition against euthanasia is a problem for it. In particular, it is a problem that it cannot accommodate the legal situation even in countries where assisted death is prohibited.

4. THE MORAL RIGHTS THEORY

On the moral rights theory, there is no problem in accepting all sorts of hastening of death, only provided they take place at the request of the patient. Not only passive killing of the patients, or active killing where death is merely foreseen, but also active and intentional killing is acceptable. The legal situation in exceptional countries like the Netherlands, Belgium, and Luxemburg is acceptable. As a matter of fact, according to this doctrine the legislation should be much more liberal. Anyone who wishes to be killed, for whatever reason, should have a right to assistance, if she could find someone who was prepared to do the actual killing. All who adhere to the doctrine do not accept it in such a strong version, however. This may well be true of Dan W. Brock. Here is an expression of the view, however, given by him, where no qualifications are explicitly made (though they may well be there implicitly):

> The form of moral view ... of why killing persons is morally wrong will be rights-based. It posits that persons have a moral right not to be killed, but that right, like other rights, is theirs to use as they see fit so long as they are competent to do so;

> specifically, persons can waive their right not to be killed when they judge that their future is not on balance a good to them, and so its loss will not constitute a harm. In such cases, when they waive their right not to be killed by refusing life support, or by requesting terminal sedation, physician assisted suicide, or voluntary active euthanasia, these actions taken by their physicians (or others) will not wrong them by taking from them without their consent what is rightfully theirs, that is will not violate their right not to be killed.[10]

One may think that there could exist negative external effects of a system where killing at request is allowed. And such effects could obtain even without any boundary-crossings taking place. Should the feelings for the person who has been killed at his request count for nothing? They should indeed count for nothing, according to the theory. I own myself and I am free to do as I like with myself. My children and grandchildren do not own me. When I have myself killed I do not cross their boundaries. So they should have no say.

5. UTILITARIANISM

A utilitarian who accepts that the distinctions between active and passive killing (acts and omissions) and between intended and merely foreseen killing make sense (not all do) must yet claim that these distinctions are morally *irrelevant*. In order to show that the active/passive distinction is morally irrelevant, they are likely to gesture at James Rachels's famous thought experiment.[11] In the thought experiment a person is intentionally killed in two ways, each one ascertaining that the killer is due to inherit that person's fortune. In one version the killer is prepared to press the head of his victim down under the water where he happens to be drowning; however,

10. Dan W. Brock, 'From the moral rights' perspective', p. 74.
11. James Rachels in 'Active and Passive Euthanasia'.

the victim drowns, all by himself, so the killer need not intervene actively. He merely allows—with the intention to inherit—the victim to drown (although he could easily have saved him). In the other case, he needs to intervene actively; for a short while he holds his hand on the head of the victim until the victim has drowned. In both cases he collects his inheritance.

The reader is invited to share the intuition with the author that it is no better when the killer allows the victim to drown than it is when he actively stops him from escaping from the water. Note that the intention is the same in both cases. The killer intends the victim to die so that he can collect the inheritance. However, the argument can be, and has been, criticized. First of all, some (who adhere to a moral rights theory) may claim that they do see a moral difference between the two cases. As a matter of fact, this is what they *must* say, if they want to stick to their guns and defend their favoured theory. Moreover, it has been claimed that the argument is invalid. It rests on what has been called an 'additive' fallacy.[12] Even if the two killers are both doing the wrong thing, and even if they are equally blameworthy because of what they have done, the distinction between active and passive killing may play a function in *other* circumstances, such as when people are killed not for bad reasons, as in the example, but for good reasons (such as in euthanasia).

As I have insisted over and over again in this book, I do not think that any simple argument such as this one can settle the question about the relative merits of competing moral theories. We have to try out their implications in many different situations, and see whether the implications are plausible or not. So here it should suffice to say that according to utilitarianism, neither the acts/omission distinction nor the intended/merely foreseen distinction carries any moral weight. This may be seen as a strength in the present context, at least when utilitarianism is compared with the Sanctity-of-Life Doctrine. Both theories allow that sometimes the life of a patient is shortened. However, according to utilitarianism,

12. See Shelly Kagan, 'The Additive Fallacy'.

once a decision has been reached to the effect that we are allowed to treat a patient in a manner that shortens the patient's life, all sorts of means are available to the utilitarian, some of which are not available to the adherent of the Sanctity-of-Life Doctrine. This means that, from the point of view of the patient, there is always a risk that the caution to keep to the rules stipulated by the Sanctity-of-Life Doctrine means that death will be more painful than it need be, if it comes through the most efficient methods sanctioned only by utilitarianism. But I suppose the adherent of the Sanctity-of-Life Doctrine will then say that, what the utilitarian claims is 'unnecessary' suffering is no such thing. It is (morally speaking) *necessary* suffering.

Utilitarians are likely to argue that there are cases where euthanasia, in the form of the active and intentional killing of a patient in order to spare him suffering, are morally required. This is so if there are no bad side effects of the action and no better alternatives available. It does not create suffering and pain in the patient's close ones, for example, and it would be worse merely to allow the patient to die (for both the patient and the patient's close ones). Jia Zhengwu's wife in the introduction to this chapter may have been an example of this. I feel certain when I claim that this would have been true of my own father (see my preface to the book).

However, even if it is clear that there must be cases where, according to utilitarianism, it is right actively and intentionally to kill a patient in order to spare him suffering, this does not mean that assisted death in general and let alone euthanasia even at the patient's request should be legally permitted. It should be legally permitted, according to utilitarianism, if this is part of the legislation, governing end-of-life decisions, which has the best consequences. Many utilitarians believe this to be a fact (the present author included), but it is not easy to *show* that this is so. And if it is not, then a utilitarian must also concede that there exists morally necessary suffering (when some patients are denied euthanasia, in spite of the fact that they need it, only in order to keep people at large at ease).

5.1. The Legal Issue from the Point of View of Utilitarianism

It is of note that much of the discussion about whether euthanasia should be legalized has been conducted in utilitarian terms. Arguments against legalisation often point to possible bad side effects of such a legal practice. Here are some examples.

If we legalize euthanasia, euthanasia will be seen as an alternative rather than as a complement to good palliative care. Hence, such good palliative care will not be developed. This is bad, since most patients would prefer good palliative care to euthanasia.[13]

If we legalize euthanasia, and do so in a restrictive and responsible manner, we will not be able to keep our restrictive and responsible legislation and legal practice. We will soon find that we are on a 'slippery slope', where inevitably we will end up with a terrible legislation and legal practice. So we had best not take the first step. This is not the place to assess arguments such as these, at least not to the extent that they are based on empirical claims.[14] However, it is of importance to be clear about the forms they take.

Here a rough overview of the possibilities alluded to in the argument from a slippery slope will have to suffice. The argument comes in many versions. In one version is the idea that in order to avoid inconsistent or arbitrary decision, once we have legalized euthanasia, we will have to pass from a practice where euthanasia is given at the patient's request to a situation where it is up to the doctor

13. Could we not have both? According to the argument, we can't. However, there exists an interesting report on the situation in Belgium, indicating not only that both a good palliative care and a system of euthanasia is possible, but that it is also actual. See J. I. Bernheim and A. Mullie, 'Euthanasia and Palliative Care in Belgium: Legitimate Concerns and Unsubstantial Grievances'.

14. For a critical review of them, see Rietjens, Judith A. C., Paul J. van der Maas, Bregje D. Onwuteaka-Philipsen, Johannes J. M. van Delden, och Agnes van der Heide, 'Two Decades of Research on Euthanasia from the Netherlands. What Have We Learnt and What Questions Remain?'.

to decide. This argument has been put forward by John Keown. He invites us to consider the following case:

> Imagine two patients of Dr. A: X and his brother Y. They are identical twins, with an identically painful terminal illness and suffering to an identical degree. They lie, side by side, in hospital. X, who is competent, pleads with A for a lethal injection of potassium chloride because the 'suffering is unbearable'. Dr. A agrees that death would indeed be a benefit for X and agrees to administer the injection to give him a 'merciful release'. X requests the same for his brother Y, who is incompetent, on the grounds that he, too, must be experiencing 'unbearable and useless' suffering. Is Dr. A to deny Y the same benefit he has agreed to confer on X? If so, what has become of the doctor's duty to act in the best interests of his patient?[15]

According to Keown, this presents us with a kind of dilemma. When we ponder the example, we realize—this is, I think, the best way of reading him—that no sound moral rationale exists behind a restricted system of euthanasia. If the competent patient is provided euthanasia, why should not also his brother have the same service? After all, he has the same need. If we deny him what he needs, with the argument that he has not made any request for euthanasia, then we show that we have to provide euthanasia to anyone who asks for it, for whatever reason. So either we end down at the end of the slippery slope in situations where the doctors decide about euthanasia (basing their decisions on their assessment of the patients' needs) or euthanasia is provided at the patient's request (irrespective of needs).

I admit that the argument poses a challenge. However, first of all, it is not clear that a rationale behind the legislation *must* be provided. I will return to this when I discuss the ethics of war. Let me here just note that at least no rationale behind the legislation

15. Keown, *Euthanasia, Ethics and Public Policy*, p. 78.

need be incorporated in the legislation as such. We can look upon the actual legislation as a political compromise or a mere result of a democratic *procedure*. Why, then, can it not be stable?

Secondly, it is not clear that it would be bad to have a system where euthanasia is provided at request. This is what is recommended by the moral rights theory. So it is at least not obvious that, at this end of the slippery slope, a truly terrible situation is awaiting us.

Finally, and more importantly, from the point of view of utilitarianism there may very well exist a rationale behind a legislation according to which both a request and a need is required in order for euthanasia to be legally acceptable. After all, this kind of legislation may be optimal. Then it *is* sanctioned by utilitarianism. If simple pragmatic considerations provide the rationale behind the legislation, this would be a natural move to make. In that case, there is no inconsistency in denying euthanasia to the incompetent patient.[16]

Or, if we find this cruel, we may add that non-voluntary euthanasia is also an option for some incompetent patients, but not at the discretion of a physician. Instead it could be made available to incompetent patients with a need for euthanasia, only provided that a *proxy* of a kind has made a request for it (the brother, say, in Keown's example).

In a second version, the slippery slope argument claims that, once we legalize euthanasia, giving physicians the right to kill patients at their request, provided certain conditions are fulfilled, there will be a growing misuse. Physicians will also kill patients in situations where the conditions stipulated in the law are not met.

In a third version of the argument, it is claimed that, if there is a legal right to euthanasia, giving some people what they want, this will mean that other people, who do not really want euthanasia, will come to request it, only in order not to be a burden to their close ones or to society.

16. For a thorough criticism of Keown's argument, see Hallvard Lillehammer, 'Voluntary Euthanasia and the Logical Slippery Slope Argument'.

In a fourth version, it is society that seizes the opportunity to save scarce medical resources by starting to put pressure on patients who are costly to keep alive. Even people with various kinds of disabilities may come to be targeted by such campaigns.

Again, this is not the place to try to find out if there is any truth in these empirical arguments. Those utilitarians who defend the claim that euthanasia should be legal also question these empirical arguments, of course. The discussion has been mainly over the correct interpretation of statistics and reported experiences gathered from The Netherlands. Here it must suffice to note that, if utilitarianism is true, then these are the kinds of considerations that should be allowed to decide the matter. However, neither on the Sanctity-of-Life Doctrine nor on the hard-core libertarian version of the moral rights theory are these considerations of any relevance at all. And it is of note that so much of the discussion pro and con legalisation of euthanasia is indeed conducted in utilitarian terms. Doesn't this count in favour of utilitarianism, one may ask?

6. A PRELIMINARY CONCLUSION

The Sanctity-of-Life Doctrine, which is the version of deontology that has been developed in order to deal systematically with the problem of euthanasia, is at variance with the intuitions among the Chinese, the Russians, and the Americans. I believe this is a problem for the doctrine. Even if it is less strict in its view of end-of-life decision than what first meets the eye—it does allow for merely foreseen hastening of death in some instances—it is still far too restrictive. If we abide by it, it means that we inflict suffering on patients, and I cannot help believing that this is unnecessary suffering. Note also that, while I have focused in my discussion of assisted death on the euthanasia aspect of the phenomenon, the Sanctity-of-Life Doctrine (as well as the Kantian version of deontology) is equally restrictive in its view of physician-assisted suicide. It is no better, according to this theory, when one kills oneself than if a doctor performs the killing. Many people will have problems with this assessment in particular, I submit. Pace Ludwig Wittgenstein, quoted on suicide in the previous chapter, they find this moral symmetry problematic. If anything is morally problematic here, they will claim, it is the killing of another person rather than the killing of oneself.

The moral rights theory may be seen to be not only in harmony with a majority view, but also in a position where the limits for the practice of euthanasia are put exactly where they should be put. Euthanasia is acceptable if, and only if, it takes place at the patient's informed and voluntary request. And the physician should not be compelled to provide the service; she is only allowed to do so when she sees fit.

However, a problem with the moral rights theory, in my opinion, is that it doesn't take seriously what could be called negative externalities of a legalisation of euthanasia.

Perhaps there are no such negative externalities associated with a legalisation, but the fact that such externalities, should they obtain, would, according to the moral rights theory, be morally irrelevant, since they would not constitute any boundary-crossings, strikes me as implausible.

Utilitarianism, on the other hand, is very much sensitive to these possible negative externalities. This counts in favour of utilitarianism, it seems to me. As I have already noted, it is also a striking fact that so much of the discussion pro and con legalisation of euthanasia has been conducted in utilitarian terms.

However, as we have seen in the chapter on murder, utilitarianism can, in extreme circumstances, justify not only non-voluntary but involuntary euthanasia as well. Many would find this counterintuitive. I have confessed that I have some problem with this implication myself. So there is need to return to the question—in the concluding chapter of this book.

Chapter 8

Abortion

If a woman feels that she doesn't want to take care of her expected child, is it then morally permissible for her to have an abortion?

	China	*Russia*	*United States*
Yes	36%	61%	34%
No	58%	33%	62%
Don't know	6%	6%	4%

1. INTRODUCTION

Few issues relating to the ethics of killing raise such strong feelings as discussions of abortion. While some women claim that it is their right to terminate the pregnancy they carry, others (often male activists) are prepared to kill physicians who perform abortions in order to see to it that justice is done. Here the rationale behind both these stances, as well as others, will be discussed when I examine deontology, the moral rights theory, and utilitarianism in relation to abortion. We will also see that new aspects of these theories surface once we have a look into what has been called population ethics, a field we cannot avoid in our discussion about their application to the issue of abortion.

I suspect that if some of the people who believe that abortion is a permissible solution to rather trivial practical problems would come to read this book on the ethics of killing, they would not feel comfortable stumbling upon a chapter on abortion in it. They tend

DOCTOR KILLED DURING ABORTION PROTEST

By William Booth Washington Post Staff Writer Thursday, March 11, 1993; Page A01

PENSACOLA, FLA., MARCH 10—A doctor was shot to death outside his abortion clinic here today when a man who prayed for the physician's soul stepped forward from a group of antiabortion protesters and opened fire, according to police and witnesses.

David Gunn, 47, was shot three times in the back after he got out of his car at the Pensacola Women's Medical Services clinic, according to Pensacola police. He died during surgery at a local hospital.

This morning, police initially were called to simply squelch an antiabortion protest at the clinic. When they arrived, police said, Michael Frederick Griffin, 31, of Pensacola told them he had just shot Gunn.

Griffin, dressed in a grey suit, quietly surrendered to police, who said they took his .38-caliber snub-nosed revolver. Griffin was arrested and charged with murder and is being held in Escambia County jail.

Don Treshman, head of the antiabortion group Rescue America in Houston, told the Associated Press that Griffin yelled 'Don't kill any more babies,' just before the shooting this morning.

not to think of abortion as (morally permissible) killing, let alone as (morally permissible) deliberate killing of innocent human beings. Rather, they prefer to describe abortion differently, in a manner allowing that there is no mention of killing at all. And yet, for reasons to be explained, the chapter does deserve to appear in the book. It is not at all far-fetched to speak of abortion as intentional killing of (innocent) human beings. It should be noted, however, that the classification of abortion as killing of innocent human beings does not settle the moral matter. Some think that abortion is wrong in principle. Are they right? In order to find out we need to determine whether the principle upon which they base their judgement is true or not. Some argue that abortion is sometimes right (permissible killing), sometimes wrong (wrongful killing). They owe us an answer to the question *when* it is right and *why*, in such cases, it is right. And, correspondingly, to when and why it is wrong.

Again, I turn to the three by-now well-known families of theories, in search of answers to these questions.

It should be noted that our intuitive responses to a phenomenon such as abortion are likely to be heavily influenced by our cultural background. Almost two-thirds of the surveyed Russians see abortion as a legitimate solution for a woman who feels that she doesn't want to take care of her expected child, while only one-third (roughly) of the Americans and the Chinese make the same judgement. I have earlier results for Sweden indicating that among Swedes, 83 percent see abortion in situations such as these as acceptable (among Swedes who vote for the Christian Democratic Party, the morally speaking most conservative party in Sweden, 75 percent gave the same answer!). The present author, then, has grown up in a, in its view on abortion, *very* liberal culture.

2. THE SANCTITY-OF-LIFE DOCTRINE

In relation to abortion, the two versions of deontology, Kantianism and the Sanctity-of-Life Doctrine, part company. According to Kant, it is wrong to kill innocent *rational* beings. Foetuses are not among them. There is no indication that Kant would have objected on any principled grounds to abortion. He has not explicitly discussed the subject, however, so I will say no more of Kantianism in this chapter. According to the Sanctity-of-Life Doctrine, however, it is wrong (absolutely) intentionally to kill an innocent *human* being.

This idea invites the question: when does human life begin? A standard answer among recent advocates of this theory is: at conception. It used to be different. Traditionally, Roman Catholics abided by the verdict by Aristotle and claimed that the foetus received its soul (or form) during pregnancy (with a difference between male and female foetuses: at forty days and ninety days for males and females, respectively). I see the recent version of the doctrine as an improvement (informed by biological thinking) on the earlier version, and I will hence speak no more of the earlier one. We should not hold it *against* the advocates of the theory that they have shown capable of learning from the progress of science.

However, the question remains to be answered as to whether this is a *plausible* response. Does human life begin at conception? I think it does. It means that I who write this have been a just fertilized egg, an embryo, and a foetus—before I became a philosopher. I have not been an egg or a sperm, however. At conception a new organism started its life, with its own genome (or 'form', as Aristotle would have said), responsible for much of its development, from beginning until death. I am that organism.

2.1. Human Metaphysics

There are several ways of making sense of the answer that human life begins at conception. Here some distinctions are helpful. Some people (let us call them human essentialists) believe that there is a true answer to the question as to what kind of creatures we humans are. Others (let us call them human nominalists) think that there is no fact of the matter in this regard; there is nothing to be right and wrong about, when the question is posed. We may choose to speak about this in the manner we like. Human being, according to them, is not a natural kind. My being human is not like water's being H_2O. Human essentialists, on the other hand, believe that our being human *is* similar to water's being H_2O.

Human essentialists and nominalists may hold roughly two kinds of views about what it means to be human (even if it reflects, among the nominalists, only a manner of speaking). They may hold that humans are organisms (animalism) or they may hold that humans are spiritual or psychological entities. Given the answers to these questions we may also pose further questions about human (personal) identity. When are two instances of a human being instances of the same human being? The answer to this question depends on the answer to the former question, about our 'nature'.

As far as I can see, only an essentialist answer to the questions of what we are—to the effect that, basically, we are psychological (spiritual) entities, or at least entities held together by mental traits, such as memories—poses a threat to the Sanctity-of-Life Doctrine. Such a view is inconsistent with the claim that I have been an embryo. The embryo had no psychological traits at all. So it cannot, on this view, have been a human entity at all. And since it had no mental traits, I share no mental traits with it whatever. Hence, I am not identical to it.

However, this view is doubly problematic. It is problematic in being essentialist and it is problematic in having the content it has. So there are two ways for the adherent of the Sanctity-of-Life Doctrine to defend the claim that human life begins at conception against this view. One is to reject human essentialism and argue that this is just the way the adherents of the view are using the words (when putting forward their moral view). When *they* speak of innocent human beings, *they* refer to human organisms, period.[1] Or, they may claim that, essentially, we human beings *are* organisms.[2] Many philosophers would grant them either of these premises, and very few would question both of them, so I will not quarrel with the Sanctity-of-Life Doctrine on this account. Metaphysically speaking the doctrine makes good sense. That's why I am prepared to concede that *my* life started at conception.

1. It seems correct to classify Derek Parfit, in his *Reasons and Persons*, as a human (person) nominalist. The same is true of the present author. See my 'Morality and Personal Identity'.

2. Well-known representatives of animal essentialism are Erik Olson, *The Human Animal*, and Jens Johansson, 'What Is Animalism?'.

Having said this, some caveats must be made. First of all, not *all* human beings need to begin their life at conception. Human reproductive cloning is a possibility today. What if a human being is constructed through reproductive cloning—when does *it* begin its human life? At cloning, the adherent of the Sanctity-of-Life Doctrine should claim. When the egg has been provided with its new genome and starts dividing, *then* a human being has come into existence.

Here is another caveat. Some embryos divide. The result is twins. When does the life of each twin begin? At twinning, the advocate of the Sanctity-of-Life Doctrine should say (and often says). This means that the original organism has ceased to exist (in the same manner that the egg and the sperm cease to exist at fertilization). Twinning is the end of one human organism and the beginning of two new ones. All this makes good metaphysical sense.

Finally, we have the placenta. It is genetically identical to the foetus. Does this mean that it is a part of the foetus? I think the advocates of the Sanctity-of-Life Doctrine should claim that it is indeed a part of the foetus, a part the foetus/child loses when it has no use for it any more (at birth).

2.2. The Sanctity of Human Life

It makes sense to claim, then, that human beings are organisms (animalism). But the Sanctity-of-Life Doctrine makes the further claim that being human (being a human organism) means that you possess a certain value or dignity. Your life is sacred. No one is allowed intentionally to kill you—for whatever reason. How can this theory be defended?

Some religious advocates of the Sanctity-of-Life Doctrine may have argued in the following way:

(1) Man is created in the image of God
(2) Whatever is created in the image of God has—for this very reason—a special value or dignity
(3) Hence, man has a special value or dignity

Even if valid, this is not a sound argument. Each one of the premises of it is false (I would claim). Moreover, I think many adherents of the Sanctity-of-Life Doctrine would reject it. Many would reject the first premise. Even if they are religious believers, they take ideas such as the one expressed in (1) in a metaphorical sense. And many who believe in the Sanctity-of-Life Doctrine are not religious believers at all. They believe that (1) is false. They still hold on to (3). Moreover, some who accept (1) and (3) may still believe that (2) is false. They may see (2) as an expression of wishful thinking. Thus, I do not think it wise for adherents of the Sanctity-of-Life Doctrine to rely at all on this argument.

Others have defended the idea that we humans possess a certain value or dignity, and hence immunity against being killed, with reference either to our typically human mental capacities, or else with reference to our *potentiality* for developing such capacities (possessed also by embryos and foetuses).[3] The idea is that, if an entity has a potential for developing a mental state like ours, then it must not be killed.

Does this also include couples of eggs and sperm? It does not. They can provide *material* for entities with an ordinary human mental life, but they cannot *develop* into such entities. The egg and the sperm are lost in the process when a foetus is created. The foetus, on the other hand, develops, under appropriate circumstances, into a grown-up human being.

But what are we then to say of human embryos or foetuses that, for genetic reasons, will never develop these capacities? Should we say that we are allowed to kill them? This is what is implied by this theory. Moreover, if our moral status, and our immunity to being killed, is given by the fact that we are entities (organisms) with a potential for rational thought, then it is also permissible to kill *adults* lacking this potential. This is clearly not a typical version of

3. See, in particular, Don Marquis, 'Why Abortion Is Immoral', and most recently in 'Abortion and Death'.

the Sanctity-of-Life Doctrine, and in the present context I will skip over it.

2.3. Who Is Human?

Given an animalist understanding of what it means to be human, it is in many cases very easy to settle whether a certain individual (be it an embryo, a foetus, or a grown-up) is human or not. We know roughly how to distinguish members of the human species from members of other species. This may have been more difficult in earlier times, however, when Homo sapiens walked the earth together with other closely related species such as the Neanderthal. As a matter of fact, while writing this, I stumbled upon the following in *The New York Times*:

> Neanderthals mated with some modern humans after all and left their imprint in the human genome, a team of biologists has reported in the first detailed analysis of the Neanderthal genetic sequence.
>
> The biologists, led by Svante Paabo of the Max Planck Institute for Evolutionary Anthropology in Leipzig, Germany, have been slowly reconstructing the genome of Neanderthals, the stocky hunters that dominated Europe until 30,000 years ago, by extracting the fragments of DNA that still exist in their fossil bones. Just last year, when the biologists first announced that they had decoded the Neanderthal genome, they reported no significant evidence of interbreeding. (6 May 2010)

Is this, according to the Sanctity-of-Life Doctrine, a threat to our moral standing? Moreover, future experiments with genetic engineering may put even harder stress on the theory. Today we often resort to the notion of transhumanism in our discussion of bioethics. The day may not be so far when transhumans walk the earth. I think of creatures who are smarter than we, endowed with senses we lack, yet similar to us in many ways, but not of our species. And what are the adherents of the theory to say of seemingly human individuals who differ genetically from the rest of us, for example by having an extra chromosome? Are people with Down's syndrome human beings? No, Martin Luther would have answered. Yes, most contemporary advocates of the doctrine tend to argue. But how are we to settle such a dispute?

Here is a final problem with reference to our human species. Our classification of species seems to allow that two individuals who are qualitatively indiscernible belong to different species (which have developed independently of each other in different places in space). In order to belong to the same species, we need to have common ancestors. But could such an extrinsic historical fact be of moral relevance, one may wonder?[4]

It is clear that the *vagueness* of the doctrine in this respect poses a problem for it. If we want to claim that the doctrine gives the *best* explanation of the content of our considered particular intuitions in some field, it must count against this claim that the doctrine lacks precision. It is also problematic that it grants moral importance to a notion that is extrinsic in the manner just mentioned.

2.4. Abortion

Given the answer to the question when human life begins, the implications from the Sanctity-of-Life Doctrine for abortion are straightforward. To the extent that abortion means the intentional killing of the foetus, it is wrong. It is no better than murder. It is murder. And the same is true of the intentional destruction of embryos at the IVF clinic.

There is some room for abortion, however, with reference to the principle of double effect. If the uterus of a pregnant woman is removed in order to save her life, the death of the foetus (in the uterus)

4. See Fred Feldman, 'Death and the Disintegration of Personality', p. 63, about this.

that results can be viewed as a merely foreseen side effect. Even in rare cases where the foetus's head is crushed (craniotomy) in order to save the mother's life is it reasonable to claim that the death of the foetus is not intended, but merely foreseen.[5]

This does not in itself settle the question of whether the procedure was morally permissible, however. The foreseen bad side effect (the death of the foetus) must stand in a reasonable proportion to the good intended effect (the saving of the life of the woman). The doctrine has no clear answer to offer in this regard and this, again, is a problem if we want to argue that it gives the best explanation of the content of our considered intuitions in some field.

It should be noted—and it has often been noted—that the doctrine implies that abortion is wrong, even in the case where the pregnancy is the result of rape. The foetus is an innocent human being, and hence it must not be killed. It is not responsible for being in the woman's womb in the first place. When the pregnancy is the result of rape, the rapist should be punished, not the foetus.

It goes without saying that the advocate of the Sanctity-of-Life Doctrine does not only hold that abortion is immoral (murder). As we know, they want abortion to be prohibited by law (in the way that murder is prohibited by law).

2.5. A Soft Version of the Doctrine

Some have had problems with the implication of the Sanctity-of-Life Doctrine that abortion is just as bad as murder (that it *is* murder). Could one not claim that, even if foetuses should not be killed, it is worse to kill an adult than a foetus?

Ronald Dworkin has, somewhat unexpectedly, defended such a soft version of the doctrine. Now, Dworkin is a well-known advocate of a moral rights theory, so one may wonder why he is defending the Sanctity-of-Life Doctrine in the first place. As a matter of fact,

5. See L. Geddes, 'On the Intrinsic Wrongness of Killing Innocent People', about this.

I am not quite certain how serious his defence (of a revised version of it) is. In his argument it is combined with a moral rights theory. Hence, there are two kinds of reasons why we should not commit murder: one of them has to do with the fact that we violate the rights of an autonomous individual if we kill him (against his wish), the other has to do with the fact that his life has a special value. The first kind of reason does not apply to abortion, since foetuses are not persons. The second does, however, but to a reduced degree. This has to do with the fact that the special value, on Dworkin's account, varies among different individuals. The life of a foetus is less valuable than the life of a grown-up person. This is how he explains his idea:

> We believe . . . that a successful human life has a certain natural course. It starts in mere biological development—conception, fetal development, and infancy—but it then extends into childhood, adolescence, and adult life in ways that are determined not just by biological formation but by social and individual training and choice, and that culminates in satisfying relationships and achievements of different kinds. It ends, after a normal life span, in a natural death. It is a waste of the natural and human creative investments that make up the story of a normal life when this normal progression is frustrated by premature death or in other ways. But how bad this is—how great the frustration—depends on the stage of life in which it occurs, because the frustration is greater if it takes place after rather than before the person has made a significant personal investment in his own life, and less if it occurs after any investment has been substantially fulfilled, or as substantially fulfilled as is anyway likely.[6]

Dworkin uses this idea in a suggestion as to how pro-life people and libertarians should be able to find a political compromise. I have

6. Ronald Dworkin, *Life's Dominion*, 1994, p. 88.

discussed his idea elsewhere, and will not repeat my argument to the effect that this suggestion must be a non-starter.[7] The interesting question here is whether Dworkin's soft version of the Sanctity-of-Life Doctrine means an improvement on the standard (hardcore) version. I doubt this. The adherents of the standard doctrine take pride in the fact that they make no distinctions *within* the human species. This is why the doctrine can serve as an antidote against all sorts of racist, or sexist, or otherwise discriminatory practice among human beings. This aspect is jeopardized by the idea that we gain in value or dignity by making 'investments' in our lives. My guess is that, adherents of the Sanctity-of-Life Doctrine, who do not share Dworkin's idea that there is also a right to life, would simply reject his modification of the theory. They would not see it as an improvement. Quite to the contrary, they would see his weakening of the prohibition against killing as something that makes it less, not more, attractive.

3. THE MORAL RIGHTS THEORY

According to the Sanctity-of-Life Doctrine, human beings have a special moral standing. A related claim made by moral rights theorists is that *persons* or *moral agents* have a special moral standing. So even if adherents of the Sanctity-of-Life Doctrine and adherents of the moral rights theory hold different views about the moral implications of having moral standing, they share a concern in answering this question: who has moral standing?

3.1. Personhood

In a discussion about abortion, just as in a discussion about animal ethics (to be pursued in a later chapter), it is crucial to know what exactly it means to be a person (a moral agent) and who exhibits this

7. Torbjörn Tännsjö, 'Why No Compromise is Possible'.

characteristic. There is no unanimity among adherents of the moral rights theory as to how this question should best be answered, however. This means that there is little point in going into details here. I will assume that embryos and foetuses in their early development (at least during the first trimester of the pregnancy) are not persons (moral agents). They are human organisms, but they lack the characteristics necessary for personhood. They have no memory of their past, they have no idea about their future, they do not see themselves as entities existing over time. Hence, they possess no rights. They do not own themselves, and they have no right not to be killed.

These creatures should not be *injured*, however. If a pregnant woman is using drugs in a manner that leads to disease in her future child, then she violates the rights, not of her foetus, but of her future child. The act that violates the rights of the child takes place during pregnancy, before the foetus has developed a personality, but the harm done to the child surfaces only later, when the child has been born and begins to suffer from the condition caused by the mother.

3.2. Do Mothers Own Their Children?

An alleged problem for the moral rights theory is that, on its account of original acquisition, the parents (the mothers, really) become the owner of their children, who, hence, start out their lives as slaves. In this book, I have not gone into any details about the idea of original acquisition of property; I glanced over it in Chapter 2, where I first presented the theory, since it has little importance in a book on the ethics of killing. In the present chapter, it is of some relevance, however. Irrespective of how one can legitimately acquire property, it is hard to see why the *creation* of something should not be included. What I create myself I do own. So there seems to be a genuine problem for the theory to handle here. This is how Susan Moller Okin in her 1989 book *Justice, Gender, and the Family* puts the problem:

> Anyone who subscribes to Nozick's principle of acquisition must explain how and why it is that persons come to own

> themselves, rather than being owned, as other things are, by whoever made them.[8]

If correct, this would be devastating to the theory, of course. For not only would my mother own me, she would in turn be owned by her mother, and so on. But the fact that she was owned would mean that she did not own me, after all. The first human couple would own all their descendants!

The most straightforward solution to the problem is to say that an individual gains ownership in herself once she has developed a personality. She can then *sell* herself as a slave, but she does not *start out her personal life* as slave.[9]

3.3. Abortion of Foetuses Who Have Developed into Persons

To kill a foetus, which has not yet developed personhood, is not prohibited by the moral rights theory, then. It is also permissible to get rid of a foetus, which has not been invited to a mother's womb, even if this means that the foetus will die. This is so even if the foetus *has* developed into a person (a controversial assumption; some adherents of the doctrine would deny that this ever happens). This is the message of Judith Jarvis Thomson's famous thought experiment:

> You wake up in the morning and find yourself back to back in bed with an unconscious violinist. A famous unconscious violinist. He has been found to have a fatal kidney ailment, and the Society of Music Lovers has canvassed all the available medical records and found that you alone have the right blood type to help. They have therefore kidnapped you, and last night the violinist's circulatory system was plugged into yours, so that your

8. *Justice, Gender and the Family*, p. 79.

9. This is the solution suggested by Nozick himself in *Anarchy, State, and Utopia*, p. 38. For a discussion of this and similar problems, see Hillel Steiner, *An Essay on Rights* and Anna-Karin Andersson, *Libertarianism and Potential Agents*.

> kidneys can be used to extract poisons from his blood as well as your own. The director of the hospital now tells you, 'Look, we're sorry the Society of Music Lovers did this to you—we would never have permitted it if we had known. But still, they did it, and the violinist is now plugged into you. To unplug you would be to kill him. But never mind, it's only for nine months. By then he will have recovered from his ailment, and can safely be unplugged from you.' Is it morally incumbent on you to accede to this situation? No doubt it would be very nice of you if you did, a great kindness. But do you have to accede to it? What if it were not nine months, but nine years? Or longer still? What if the director of the hospital says. 'Tough luck. I agree, but now you've got to stay in bed, with the violinist plugged into you, for the rest of your life.'[10]

Thomson's conclusion in relation to the thought experiment is that you have a right to unplug the violinist. This conclusion is congenial with the moral rights theory. To the extent that the foetus can be seen as an aggressor who has invaded your body, you have a right to remove it, even if (a controversial assumption, we remember) it has developed into a person. This is a right to self-defence you hold, even against *innocent* threats to your life and integrity. The doctrine doesn't really deal in any notion of guilt and hence not really in any deep moral notion of innocence. You have a right to defend yourself against all sorts of threats to your life and integrity. But you have only a right to *remove* the foetus—a right to obviate the threat. You have no right to *kill* the foetus (if it can survive outside your body).

> I am not arguing for the right to secure the death of the unborn child. It is easy to confuse these two things in that up to a certain point in the life of the fetus it is not able to survive outside the mother's body; hence removing it from her body guarantees its death. But they are importantly different. I have argued that

10. Judith Jarvis Thomson, 'A Defense of Abortion', p. 37.

> you are not morally required to spend nine months in bed, sustaining the life of that violinist, but to say this is by no means to say that if, when you unplug yourself, there is a miracle and he survives, you then have a right to turn round and slit his throat. You may detach yourself even if this costs him his life; you have no right to be guaranteed his death, by some other means, if unplugging yourself does not kill him.[11]

Furthermore, in many cases it could be plausibly argued that, even if you have not invited the foetus to be in your womb, you have taken on responsibility for it. Thus, according to the moral rights theory, you have no right to remove it in a manner that means that it dies. One may argue, for example, that if you did not abort it *before* it became a person, if you had a legal right to do so, then you have tacitly and implicitly undertaken to care for it. You are in a position in relation to it similar to the position of the lifeguard in relation to a drowning person. You have undertaken to save him.

With regard to legal matters all advocates of the moral rights theory tend to argue that at least early abortions should be permitted. But if early abortions are permitted (in the way they are in the United States, for example), this prepares the room for the argument that women who do not abort their foetuses early in their pregnancy, when it is legal to do so, do assume responsibility for them.

3.4. Infanticide

I noted that it is controversial whether foetuses ever develop into persons. Judith Jarvis Thomson granted that they did, but merely for the sake of the argument. Other defenders of a moral rights theory have explicitly claimed that they don't. This means that, at least from the point of view of the moral rights theory alone, there are no principled arguments against infanticide. Infanticide can be seen as nasty, and a completely superfluous practice, at least in a modern

11. 'A Defense of Abortion', pp. 44–45.

developed society with access to contraceptives and safe abortion methods. And yet, if foetuses are not persons, then it is *all right* for us to kill them, if we see fit to do so. The Canadian-born moral rights philosopher Michael Tooley has famously defended infanticide and based this claim on the view that neonates do not possess the capacities necessary for personhood and a serious right to life (these two notions somewhat unexpectedly come to the same, on his account). This is how he puts his point:

> My approach will be to set out and defend a basic moral principle specifying a condition an organism must satisfy if it is to have a serious right to life. It will be seen that this condition is not satisfied by human fetuses and infants, and thus that they do not have a right to life. So unless there are other substantial objections to abortion and infanticide, one is forced to conclude that these practices are morally acceptable ones.[12]

In his argument he relies on the following moral assumption, congenial to the moral rights theory:

> An organism possesses a serious right to life only if it possesses the concept of a self as a continuing subject of experience and other mental states, and believes that it is itself such a continuing entity.[13]

Like most moral rights theorists, he believes that, as a matter of fact, both foetuses and neonates lack the required capacity.

4. UTILITARIANISM

According to utilitarianism, an abortion is right if and only if there was nothing else that could have been done that would have

12. Michael Tooley, 'Abortion and Infanticide'.
13. Ibid., p. 24.

produced a better outcome. How often is this requirement fulfilled? If we look at actual abortions, do they fulfil the criterion? Are they morally acceptable? If we think of all those merely possible abortions that never take place, is it morally acceptable that they don't take place? Or, should those foetuses have been aborted?

4.1. Actual and Possible Abortions

It is not possible to answer these questions with any confidence. To the extent that a utilitarian relies on a method of decision making urging her to maximize, not actual happiness, but expected happiness, the answer must vary with the person pondering each question. It is highly likely, however, that while some actual abortions are wrong, and some abortions that never take place should have taken place, it is also true that, some abortions that take place are right and some abortions that do not take place should not have taken place. There are cases where an abortion solves a pressing problem. There are cases where an abortion means that a child, who would have had a terrible life, is replaced by a child who leads a good life, and so forth. However, when this is said, it should be noted that utilitarianism is, or so it strikes me, at any rate, much less abortion-friendly than expected. It is clear that some actual abortions are wrong, if utilitarianism is true. For a person brought up in an abortion-friendly culture, with a leaning towards utilitarianism, this comes as a surprise. According to utilitarianism, it is normally wrong to abort a foetus, which would have developed into a happy individual, who could lead his or her happy life at the expense of no one else. This argument applies with equal strength to the *conception* of happy children, of course. If I can conceive a happy child, and don't, it is highly likely that my (lack of) action is wrong.

4.2. Legislation

Does utilitarianism have any implications for how we should legislate abortion? Obviously, there are no straightforward such implications. Most utilitarians tend to argue that a legal right to abortion should be granted to pregnant women, at least up to something like the second trimester, however. They may be right about this, but it is difficult to tell. The consequences of various different possible schemes of legislation are difficult to assess.

5. POPULATION ETHICS

If we want to make an inference to the best explanation (provided by a moral theory) of the content of our basic intuitions in a field, the theory had better be a general one. Otherwise it does not present us with the *best* explanation of our 'data'. A claim we often meet, however, is that *no* moral theory can handle problems in population ethics—problems where we compare outcomes with different individuals and different numbers of individuals.[14] Such problems arise in the discussion about abortion. Now, if this is so, if our moral theories are not applicable in population ethics (including important aspects of the ethics of abortion), moral philosophy is in deep trouble. Or, are we allowed to bracket this domain and stay satisfied with theories that can account for the rest of our moral life? In an anthology published by the present author and Jesper Ryberg, Derek Parfit has suggested that this might be an option:

> The reasoning in this anthology shows how hard it is to form acceptable theories in cases that involve different numbers of people. That's highly important. And it gives us ground for worry about our appeal to particular theories in the other two kinds of case: those which involve the same numbers, in the different outcomes, though these are not all the same people, and those which do involve all and only the same people. But there is still a clear distinction between these three kinds of case. And

14. See Gustaf Arrhenius, *Population Ethics*.

> there may be some hope of 'quarantining' the impossibility, and the resulting scepticism, to Different Number Choices.[15]

The idea of quarantine is problematic, however. Problems in population ethics are mundane in nature. We often come across them, and we typically do in our discussion about abortion. Moreover, unless our theories deliver satisfactory answers in this sphere, we pay an *intellectual* price when we rely on them in our moral explanations. So a choice among deontology, the moral rights theory, and utilitarianism *should* take into account how they handle problems in population ethics.

An alleged problem with utilitarianism is that it leads to what Derek Parfit has nicknamed the 'repugnant' conclusion. If this is so, and if this is problematic, it is problematic not only for utilitarians, but for adherents of deontology as well. For, according to the theory, in its Kantian version, we have at least an imperfect (utilitarian) duty to make the world a better place (an imperfect duty of beneficence). To this is added the (perfect) duty that this may never be done in a manner that means that we intentionally kill innocent rational beings. But the utilitarian duty is still there. Furthermore, the Sanctity-of-Life Doctrine comes with the principle of double effect and its requirement of proportionality. This invites utilitarian considerations of a similar nature as the ones posed to a Kantian deontologist. So let me begin my discussion of population ethics with a discussion about the repugnant conclusion.

5.1. The Repugnant Conclusion

The alleged 'repugnant' conclusion is the conclusion that a world with ten billion extremely happy people (the A-world) is worse than a world (the Z-world) where many people (many enough) live lives barely worth living. Is this counterintuitive? Some think it is. Is there a way of challenging their intuition? I think there is. I will be

15. Derek Parfit, 'Postscript'.

brief here, since I have in so many contexts argued that we should be suspicious about our intuition, if we have it, that the A-world must be better than the Z-world.

There is a problem with large numbers. It is difficult to get a grasp of the Z-world. But a way of thinking of it is, of course, as the idea that civilisation goes on for many thousands of years—while the A-world represents the happy ending of civilization. But then, is it so obvious that the A-world is better? Moreover, the graph usually used to represent the option between the A-world and the Z-world is in itself misleading. Figure 8.1 illustrates how this usually looks:

Note that the Z-world has been represented by dotted lines. The reason is that it is impossible to squeeze it into a sheet of paper like the one you are now looking at. If you could really see and take in its breadth, knowing that the breadth represents a number of people living lives worth living, you would perhaps react differently to it.

We may hold a much too gloomy picture of the Z-world. But the way people live there may be similar to the way we live. There are ups and downs in our lives. Perhaps a typical human life often ends up with only a few hedons as its net sum. Perhaps many lives end up with a negative sum. But then, is the Z-world so bad as one may at first have thought? Those who think of people living in abject poverty and misery, when they look at the representation of the Z-world, may have misunderstood completely what the Z-world really looks like.

It is difficult to imagine what it would be like to live an extremely happy life, containing much more happiness than our lives do now. Or, a way of conceiving of this, of course, is to take such a life to be like an ordinary life, only that it goes on for, say, a thousand years. But then, is the A-world really better than the Z-world?

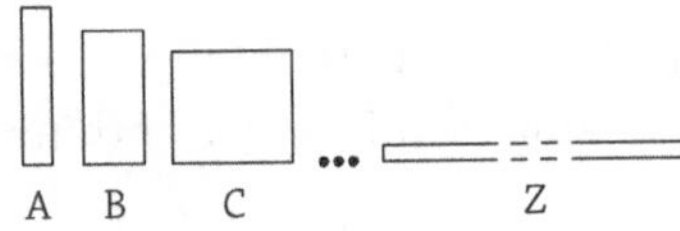

Figure 8.1. The Repugnant Conclusion

We must make sure we do not ask ourselves, in which world would I like to live? Of course, the answer is, in the A-world. But that question is irrelevant to the moral comparison between the two worlds.

Considerations such as these should either make the intuition that the A-world is (clearly) better than the Z-world go away or, at least, they should give us pause if we want to use the intuition as *evidence* against utilitarianism. This does not mean that there should surface an intuition to the effect that the Z-world is better than the A-world, that should be taken as evidence *for* utilitarianism. To the extent that some people believe that the Z-world is better than the A-world, this is probably a conclusion they have *derived* from utilitarianism. It is not an independent moral intuition. Thus, it should not be counted as independent evidence for utilitarianism. My claim is only that there is no evidence to be found either way here. This is like the Footbridge case in our discussion of the Trolley cases, then.

But if our intuitions with regard to the comparison between the A-world and the Z-world are unreliable, then we must ask whether there is any evidence to be found elsewhere. And there is. The following idea was alluded to already by Derek Parfit in *Reasons and Persons*, and I have used it as an argument to the effect that the Z-world is better than the A-world.[16] A somewhat similar argument has later been adopted by Michael Huemer, who has given it a nice name. He speaks of it as an argument from 'benign' addition.[17] The argument (at least in my own more elaborate version of it) trades on the possibility of moving from the A-world to the Z-world in a series of steps that are clearly, each one of them, an improvement of the situation. My idea is simple. It is shown in Figure 8.2. We start with the A-world. We move to a A^{+}-world where those who inhibit the A-world are still with us. By this move we improve their situation. At the same time we add a large number of people with lives worth living,

16. Torbjörn Tännsjö, 'Why We Ought to Accept the Repugnant Conclusion'. Parfit discusses this possible move in *Reasons and Persons*, sections 148–149.

17. Michael Huemer, 'In Defence of Repugnance'.

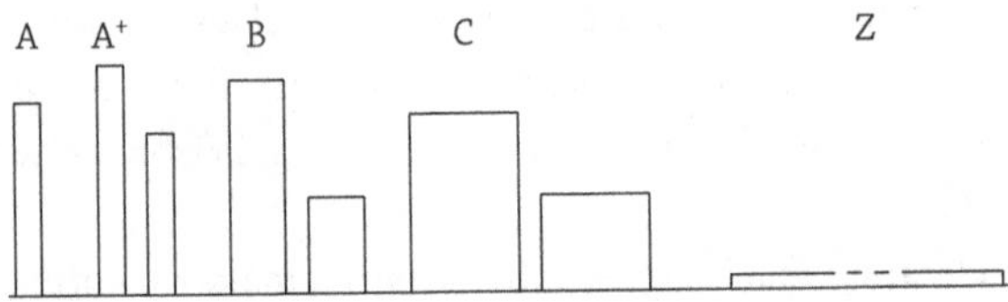

Figure 8.2. The Argument in Defence of the Repugnant Conclusion

even if they are not as happy as the original people. In the next step leading us to a B-world we level out differences between people in the A⁺-world in a manner that means that each one among those who are best off loses less than anyone among those who are worst off gains (there is an equal number of each category); at the same time, we add a large number of people, living lives worth living but not as good as the lives lived by the rest (the added people are just as many as the existing ones; this is again benign addition, then). And we do this over and over again until we have reached something close to the Z-world. Here we can see that each step means an improvement, and we can see this without *presupposing* utilitarianism. Each step is intuitively *very* plausible.

It should be noted that Parfit himself does not share my intuitions here. He claims that at least sometimes when we compare different number cases, we introduce an element of imprecision in our assessments. The more extra people we add, the more imprecision. So even if each of the steps I make in the argument when we get far down along the moral alphabet are not steps for the worse, according to Parfit, they are not steps for the better, either. The worlds I successively compare are imprecisely equally good. They are better in one respect but not better all things considered.[18] As I have indicated, my intuition is different. The idea that different numbers bring with them imprecision strikes me as ad hoc. Nothing is more precise than a natural number. Moreover, even on Parfit's recent account it seems as though we are at least permitted, through successive pairwise choices (made, perhaps by different people in different times and places, when only two options are

18. Unpublished material and conversation.

available in each case), to move from the A-world all the way down to the Z-world. After all, if two outcomes are imprecisely equally good (or bad), then we can opt in each case for either one of them, without making any moral mistake.[19]

5.2. The Moral Rights Theory and Population Ethics

In its most plausible interpretation, the moral rights theory is *actualist*. Only actual individuals have rights. We have not done anything wrong, unless there is an *actual* person who has a legitimate complaint to make against our action. This means that, if I do not create a happy individual, even if I can do so, I do nothing wrong. A merely hypothetical individual has no legitimate complaint to make. I suppose I do something wrong, however, if I create an unhappy individual. For example, I violate the rights of a person if I put him into a miserable existence, caused by a congenital disease, where there is nothing he can do to improve his situation. Now he has an actual and legitimate complaint to make against me. I should not have brought him into existence. The moral rights theory caters for the intuition, if we have it, that there is a moral asymmetry between our *obligation* not to create suffering individuals (who are hence harmed by coming into existence) and a general *permission* to do as we see fit in reproductive matters; in particular, there is no obligation to procreate, not even if those who we could bring into existence would lead happy lives. As long as we do not create miserable individuals, we may do as we like, when making reproductive choices.

It is noteworthy that the moral rights theory does not *block* the moves from the A-world down to the Z-world. If these moves are,

19. There are other aspects to Parfit's argument, mainly to do with lexical superiority, allowing him to claim the Z-world is, all things considered, worse than the A-world. I do not share his ideas in this regard either, but the discussion of them will be left for another occasion.

as a matter of fact, undertaken, we end up with a population (the Z-population) where everyone is leading a life worth living. There is no room for any complaint, then. So we haven't done anything wrong. This is similar to the moves mentioned in relation to Parfit's new ideas about imprecision. On the other hand, if we just avoid making these moves, if, as it were, we stay satisfied with the A-world (we who inhabit the A-world opt for a happy ending of humanity), we make no moral mistake either, according to the moral rights theory. Again, there is no one who has any legitimate complaint to make because of our decision.

I can't help finding all this problematic. According to the moral rights theory, Adam and Eve may refrain from having children, even if, had they decided differently, billions of billions of happy persons would have been around!

Here is another consequence of the theory. Suppose I can either create Adam or I can create Eve. If I go for Adam he will have a short life just worth living. If I go for Eve, she will have a long, happy, and fulfilling life. I go for Adam. Did I do anything wrong? I did not, on the moral rights theory. There is no one there to complain about what I did. Adam is, after all, happy to be around. By creating him, I did not violate his rights. And Eve does not exist, so she has no complaint. But this cannot be right. If these are the options I have, I ought to create Eve. The 'asymmetry' has to go.

There is also a general theoretical problem with actualism as such. Suppose I can either give life to a person, Sarah, who will lead a terrible life, if I do. Or, I can give life to Hagar, who will lead an even worse life. Suppose, as a matter of fact, I give life to Sarah. Now, this is clearly wrong, according to the moral rights theory. Sarah has a legitimate complaint against my decision. So my decision was wrong. But what if instead I had given Hagar life? Would not that have been even worse? It would, but since Hagar, given my actual decision, is a merely possible person, there is no complaint she can make.

If, instead, as a matter of fact, I give life to Hagar, then, of course, Hagar has a legitimate complaint. So, once again, my decision is wrong.

It seems as though, whatever decision I make, I act wrongly. This does not amount to any outright contradiction,[20] but it means that the normative status of my action is dependent on what I actually do, and this is indeed strange. I think we must count this against the moral rights theory, if we want to use it in something we claim gives the *best* explanation of the content of *any* of our considered intuitions.

6. CONCLUSION

With respect to abortion the deontology in the form of the Sanctity-of-Life Doctrine is in trouble. The conclusion that abortion is *always* wrong cannot be right. It might be thought that deontology in its Kantian version fares better. It allows the killing of human organisms that have not developed a personality.

The moral rights theory may seem to square with common sense thinking about abortion. Like Kantianism, it allows that we kill human organisms that have not developed a personality. It differs from Kantian deontology, however, in that it does not incorporate any imperfect duty to maximize happiness. This, too, may seem to be in line with standard thinking about abortion. We should not give life to miserable individuals, but we have no obligation to create happy individuals. And yet, this seems to me the wrong conclusion to draw about abortion. The problematic aspect of the moral rights theory, it appears to me, is that according to it, it is all right for very casual reasons to abort a foetus, not yet developed into a person, who would have come to lead a good life had she not been aborted.

Utilitarianism gives a subtle and nuanced verdict on abortion. Abortion is sometimes right, sometimes wrong, and it is problematic not to allow a foetus to develop into a happy person. It should

20. Derek Parfit in *Reasons and Persons*, p. 395, discusses an example of this kind and claims that it leads to contradiction, but this means that he overstates the (real) problem with the view.

be noted that, if Kantianism is taken to imply the repugnant conclusion (at least as an imperfect duty), Kantianism and utilitarianism give the same answer to the problem of abortion. These moral theories are extensionally equivalent in their assessment of the morality of abortion.

All three theories have problems in what has been called population ethics. However, while utilitarianism and deontology (with its imperfect duty of beneficence) has to struggle with the repugnant conclusion, the moral rights theory has additional problems. It *allows* the repugnant conclusion, and gives rise to other and even more problematic implications as well. It implies that it is permissible for Adam and Eve to have no children even if this would block the entire development of a happy humanity; it allows a couple to conceive a moderately happy child rather than an extremely happy child; and it leads to strange implications where we have to choose between two bad lives. This counts heavily against it when it comes to explaining the content of our considered moral intuitions.

Chapter 9

Survival Lotteries

Some people are stranded on a desert island. They have no food. In order to survive they arrange a lottery. Everyone agrees to take part in the lottery. The person who draws the winning ticket is killed and eaten by the rest. Half of the group survives because of the lottery. Was it morally permissible to arrange and take part in the lottery?

	China	*Russia*	*United States*
Yes	10%	17%	38%
No	86%	80%	58%
Don't know	4%	3%	4%

Stranded

Uruguayan Air Force Flight 571, also known as the Andes flight disaster, and in South America as Miracle in the Andes (El Milagro de los Andes) was a chartered flight carrying 45 people, including a rugby team and their friends and family and associates that crashed in the Andes on October 13, 1972. More than a quarter of the passengers died in the crash, and several more quickly succumbed to cold and injury. Of the twenty-nine who were alive a few days after the accident, another eight were killed by an avalanche that swept over their shelter in the wreckage. The last of the 16 survivors were rescued on December 23, 1972.

The survivors had little food and no source of heat in the harsh conditions, at over 3,600 metres (11,800 ft) altitude. Faced with starvation and radio news reports that the search for them had been abandoned, the survivors fed on the dead passengers who had been preserved in the snow.

(Wikipedia)

1. INTRODUCTION

In my survey, as is shown above, I asked the Chinese, the Russians, and the Americans about a rather drastic case, where people in a planned and regulated fashion kill and eat each other, in order to survive. My idea was to question them about something that could in principle have happened, but only in extraordinary circumstances, where we need not bother with side effects of any established *practice*. I was inspired by a real but less radical event, also reported above from Wikipedia, the air crash in the Andes in 1972. However, reality is not as drastic (at least not if we judge from the reports about it) as I wanted it to be, and hence I had to revise it. It is crucial that people in the kind of survival lottery I want to discuss *kill* one another in order to survive. However, a problem with my example, inspired by the real event in the Andes, is that it involves cannibalism. I realize now, in particular when I see how people have reacted to my example, that much of their reluctance to accept it may have something to do with a dislike, not for a survival lottery as such, but for cannibalism. There seems to exist a widespread taboo against cannibalism that may have distorted the reactions to my example. Judging from the reactions, this taboo is much stronger in China than in the United States.

1.1. John Harris's Organ Lottery

The idea of a survival lottery is not new, of course. John Harris has famously suggested that one could have a lottery as the basis of the distribution of organs for transplant purposes.[1] The idea is that those who draw the winning ticket in the lottery are killed and their organs distributed among people in vital need of organs. Since one donor of organs can serve many recipients, such a lottery, if agreed upon, could be to the advantage of most people. In particular, the

1. John Harris, 'The Survival Lottery'.

expected utility for those who enter the lottery may be higher than the expected utility for those who don't, at least if we judge the matter exclusively from the point of view of the survival value of the lottery. I will discuss this kind of lottery as well. It is superior to the cannibalistic lottery in that it avoids all sorts of food taboos, but it has another drawback as compared to the cannibalism example; it presupposes a new and never heard of social institution. Harris's lottery is taken to be, not exceptional, but as part and parcel of how we live together in a society. Here the best move is perhaps to try to abstract from the problem we have of imagining *us* arranging such a lottery, as Harris does. Instead, we are invited to say what we think of such a system assuming that it is in place somewhere else in space and has been established on a voluntary basis by those who take part in it. This is also how Harris describes this possibility:

> Suppose that inter-planetary travel revealed a world of people like ourselves, but who organized their society according to this scheme . . . In such a world a man who attempted to escape when his number was up or who resisted on the grounds that no one had a right to take his life, might well be regarded as a murderer. We might or might not prefer to live in such a world, but the morality of its inhabitants would surely be one that we could respect.[2]

Under such circumstances, what, if anything, is wrong with the lottery? Is it worthy of our 'respect'? It may be difficult to imagine this, however. We are likely to think that, while we could adjust to the fact that one of our children dies because of heart failure (and a lack of a suitable heart for transplant purposes), we could never adjust to the fact that one of our children draws the winning ticket in the survival lottery and is killed. In order to assess the lottery in a fair manner, we *must* accept the assumption that this is the way we behave, however. Perhaps it is easier

2. Ibid., p. 401.

to do this if we think of Harris's extraterrestrial case. Note also that the lottery may be voluntary. Some may have chosen to stay out of it. They receive no organ if one of their own fails, of course, but they do not risk having to sacrifice their lives to save the lives of others. Under *this* assumption, what would be wrong with the lottery?

1.2. John Taurek's Rescue Lottery

Let me also note that in the philosophy literature there exists another and related survival lottery, the one described and (weakly) recommended by John Taurek.[3] This lottery is different. It concerns the saving of lives, rather than killing. And yet, it deserves a place in a book on killing since, even if it is framed in terms of how many lives we save, it could equally be framed in terms of how many lives we sacrifice. Moreover, how the theories under scrutiny in this book treat it will throw some further light on them. Here the idea is not that we arrange a lottery where those who draw the winning ticket are killed. On the contrary, here we arrange a lottery where those who draw the winning ticket are saved (and those who don't are *allowed* to die). The idea is that for practical reasons we can only save one of two competing groups of people, either a small group (one person in the limiting case) or a larger group (typically something like three to five persons). In Taurek's favoured example six people need a certain medicine to survive. Five of them could share it between them, and yet survive, since they need only one fifth of the available amount. The sixth person can only survive if he gets all of it. According to Taurek, if all things are equal, and no special obligations exist, the right thing to do would be to construct a survival lottery of a very simple nature: we should toss a coin and give the medication to the five on one outcome (heads, say), and to the single individual on the other outcome (tails, say), giving an

3. John Taurek, 'Should the Numbers Count?'.

equal survival chance to each *individual*. Is he right about this? Does he get any support for this idea from any of the theories under scrutiny?

2. DEONTOLOGY

Let us here focus on a somewhat more detailed and elaborated description of a survival lottery of the kind about which I asked the Chinese, the Russians, and the Americans. A broadcasting company is casting a reality TV show. The intention is to transport sixteen people, together with the host of the show, to a small island in the Pacific Ocean. The members of the expedition will gather for successive tribal councils and cast their votes. One by one the members of the expedition will be voted off the island. Whoever is eventually left at the end of the show with the host is the 'Survivor' and wins a fortune. On their way to the island, however, the plane they are travelling in develops a technical problem. After an emergency landing on the water in the middle of nowhere the plane soon sinks, taking the crew with it into the deep water. The members of the expedition, together with the host of the show, however, succeed in swimming to a nearby island. Here they find themselves on wasteland. They possess one sharp knife and a functioning lighter, they find a well that provides them with fresh water, and they can make a fire using driftwood they collect on the shore, but there is nothing for them to eat: no fish, no game, no roots or vegetables. They wait for help but none arrives. After two weeks they realize that they will all probably starve to death. They gather for their first tribal council and agree to arrange a survival lottery. The 'winner' of the lottery will be held down by the rest, killed with the sharp knife, roasted over the fire, and then consumed. One person a week will be killed in accordance with the rules of the lottery. Two members of the expedition declare that they are Kantians. They are not willing to take part in the lottery, and this is accepted by the rest. After several weeks five persons have been killed and eaten. The two Kantians have meanwhile died from starvation and have been buried according to their wishes. Then a ship arrives and the nine survivors are rescued at last.[4]

2.1. The Air-Crash Case

I will discuss this version of the case in this and the following sections. It might seem that it should be more palatable to adherents of deontology than the short version. After all, those who do not want to take part in it are allowed to stay out of it. However, from the point of view of the doctrine, this makes no difference. It is wrong to arrange the lottery, it is wrong to take part in it. Those who do are no better than murderers. It is clear that they intentionally kill innocent human beings. The fact that this killing is voluntary and life-saving doesn't make it right. As a matter of fact, if they stick to the Kantian, retributivist version of the doctrine, discussed in the chapter above on capital punishment, those who survive deserve to die for what they have done.

This is indeed what Kant should say about cases such as this one, given his retributivist view on capital punishment. He may have hesitated, however, when it comes to the actual *execution* of the death penalty in cases such as these. In a comment on a similar case, where one person kills another one on a life raft in order to save his own life, Kant defends 'law professors' and claims that they are:

> quite consistent in making legal allowance for such emergency acts. For the authorities can't attach any punishment to this injunction, because that punishment would have to be death, and it would be an absurd law that threatened death to one who refuses to die voluntarily in a dangerous situation.[5]

4. This is the description I give of the case in my book *Understanding Ethics*.

5. Immanuel Kant, *On the Old Saw: That May Be Right in Theory But It Won't Work in Practice*, p. 68n.

Yet for all this lenience shown by Kant, there is no doubt about the fact that, according to his deontological theory, the survivors did the wrong thing. The right thing would have been to accept to die in this situation.

2.2. John Harris's Organ Lottery

John Harris's survival lottery is no better from the point of view of deontology. Here innocent (rational) people are intentionally killed. Or, should we rely here on the principle of double effect and say that there is really no intent here to kill them? When we take the organs from a person, we 'merely wish to use a couple of his organs, and if he cannot live without them ... *tant pis*!'—as Harris puts it.[6] This seems fair enough on the liberal reading of the principle of double effect I have abided by in this book, and I will return further down in the chapter to this possibility. Let us just, for the time being, *stipulate* that the persons whose organs are being harvested are killed before their organs are removed.

Furthermore, let us suppose that people have deliberately and freely entered the lottery, in order to enhance their survival chances. Suppose they willingly give up their lives, when they have drawn their ticket. Those who stay out of the lottery receive no organs when they suffer from organ failure. They are allowed to die. Is there, then, any moral problem with what they do? From the point of view of deontology, in both its Kantian and its Thomistic version (the Sanctity-of-Life Doctrine), there is certainly still a problem. Those who are killed are indeed killed intentionally and they are indeed innocent, so this is wrong. It would be of no avail if they were to kill themselves. Suicide is no better than murder. It is not right to kill an innocent human being even to save many lives.

Harris's case is also different from the air-crash case in that when people arrange the lottery, they are not in a situation of any

6. Ibid., p. 402.

emergency. They do it just to enhance slightly their expected survival chances. Most people who take part in the lottery will neither need any organs themselves nor have to contribute any organs to others. This means, I suppose, that in this case Kant would not have hesitated. Those who killed the 'winners' in the lottery are not only murderers; they deserve the death penalty for what they have done.

2.3. Taurek's Case

Let us finally consider Taurek's case. The case concerns the saving of lives, not killing. This means that, irrespective of whether I save the many or the few, or toss a coin, I will not violate any perfect duties (constraints) specified by the doctrine. I do not kill intentionally, I do not treat anyone as mere means to the rescue of another, and so forth.

However, we can also see the lottery as deciding whom I should allow to die. And now the principle of double effect kicks in. If I save the sole person I can claim that the death of the other five is merely a sad foreseen side effect of what I do. Thus, I violate no moral constraint by saving the sole person. But this is not the end of the matter. We must also query whether the requirement of proportionality is satisfied. The criterion is a bit vague, of course, but it strikes me as obvious that it is *not* satisfied if I save one life and foresee the loss of five. Consequently, what I should do, according to the Sanctity-of-Life Doctrine, is to save the many. From a Kantian point of view we reach the same conclusion, it seems to me. The perfect obligation not to kill is not violated regardless of what I do. However, I also have an imperfect obligation to make the world a better place, to the extent that I can do so without violating any perfect duty. But then I should save the many rather than the sole person.

Or, is that assessment rash? After all, according to deontology, every human (rational) being has the same value; it is because of this inherent value or dignity or sanctity that no innocent human (rational) being may be intentionally killed. It also reasonably implies that every innocent human being should be treated with *equal* respect. Does this imply that, in Taurek's case, we should toss a coin?

Only if there is no other and *better* way of showing everyone equal respect. As we will see in the next section, such a better way exists.

3. THE MORAL RIGHTS THEORY

In the more refined description of the air-crash case, where the two Kantians are allowed to stay out of the lottery, and where it is clear, then, that everyone who enters it does so deliberately and freely, there is no moral problem with the lottery, according to the moral rights theory. We own ourselves and are free to enter lotteries such as these if we wish. Moreover, it seems rational to do so. The same is true of Harris's lottery, of course, should it ever be adopted. The problem with Harris's lottery, however, is that it is hard to see that ordinary people would enter it. This has to do with the fact that we would find it terrible to be killed in the manner described by Harris. In particular, it would be terrible to know that a dear member of one's family would be killed like that, even if her death would save several lives. But this is not an objection to Harris's case. If we treat it as an extraterrestrial phenomenon or mere thought experiment, we can conclude that those who enter it do nothing wrong. They are perfectly rational, moreover, when they enhance their survival chances by entering (given that they are capable of looking upon the prospect of being killed as no worse than the similar prospect of dying from an organ failure).

3.1. Taurek's Case

What is a moral rights theorist to say about Taurek's case? As a matter of fact, there is much in Taurek's own presentation of it that presupposes that he himself adopts a moral rights theory.

His discussion concerns six individuals who need a certain medication to survive. As we remember, one of them needs all the medicine to survive, while the other five can survive on one-fifth each of the available stock. This means that if the medication is given to those five, they will survive, and the one who needs all the medication will die. If, instead, the medication is given to the one who needs all of it, he will survive, but the rest will die.

Taurek claims, first of all, that if the person who needs all the medication *owns* it, he has a right to use it. He need not share it with the five. This is what follows from the moral rights theory, of course.

Moreover, Taurek claims, if *I* own the medication, I may give it either to the five or to the single individual. If I happen to know the single individual, who needs all the medication, I am free to give it to him. Again, this is what the moral rights theory seems to imply in those circumstances.

Need I give it to anyone at all, if I own it? I suppose not, on a strict understanding of the moral rights theory. If I own it, I may destroy it and let all six die. Taurek does not address this possibility.

What if I have not contracted to give the medication to anyone in particular, and what if, furthermore, I have no special relation to any one of them, but I still want to save lives. Whose life should I save? Should I save the single person who needs all the medication or should I save the five who need each only one-fifth of it? Here is Taurek's answer to the question:

> So what do I think one should do in . . . a situation in the absence of any special concern for any of the parties involved?
>
> First, let me suggest what I would do in many such cases. Here are six human beings. I can empathize with each of them. I would not like to see any of them die. But I cannot save everyone. Why not give each person an equal chance to survive? Perhaps I could flip a coin. Heads, I give my drug to these five. Tails, I give it to this one. In this way I give each of the six persons a fifty-fifty chance of surviving. Where such an option is open to me it would seem to best express my equal concern and

> respect for each person. Who among them could complain that I have done wrong? And on what grounds?[7]

This is a strange claim. It has no rationale in the moral rights theory. According to the moral rights theory I can do as I see fit. But I suppose Taurek may here think of some kind of addition to the hard (negative) core of the theory. He seems to acknowledge at least a *weak* positive right to life. Each one among the six people facing me holds this right. How should I, given that I am prepared to do anything about their plight in the first place, best satisfy their demands on me? Taurek's answer is: toss a coin.

This answer strikes me as the right one in a choice between two people (all other things being equal). Perhaps some of this credibility spreads over to cases where the choice is between one person and only a few other persons. But Taurek's point is more radical:

> Yet I can imagine it will still be said, despite everything, 'But surely the numbers must count for something.' I can hear the incredulous tones: 'Would you flip a coin were it a question of saving fifty persons or saving one?' 'Surely in situations where the numbers are this disproportionate you must admit that one ought to save the many rather than the few or the one.'
>
> I would flip a coin even in such a case, special considerations apart.[8]

Since this is just a description of Taurek's own disposition to act, it may very well be true. However, if understood as a recommendation, it doesn't strike me as at all plausible. And it is indeed less plausible, the greater the difference is in numbers. Moreover, if we take into account the probability that our rescuing mission will

7. John Taurek, 'Should the Numbers Count?', p. 303.
8. John Taurek, 'Should the Numbers Count?', p. 306.

succeed, even more problematic implications follow, as Katharina Berndt Rasmussen has shown.[9] Suppose I am on a mission where I can save lives. I can either save five people (and here success is certain), or try to save a solitary person. I cannot do both. Suppose the chance that I will succeed, if I attempt to save the solitary person, is 1 percent. Now, if I want to give equal chances of survival to each individual, I am not allowed to toss a coin any more. This would give a 50-percent chance of survival to the five, but only a 0.5-percent chance of survival for the solitary person. So instead I must arrange a lottery with 101 tickets; if any of the tickets between numbers 1 and 100 is randomly drawn, then I go for the solitary person, and only if the ticket 101 is randomly drawn do I go for the five. This means that all have an equal chance to survive, slightly less than 1 percent (1/101). It also means that, almost certainly, I will embark on a mission, which almost certainly will fail.

If we find this conclusion 'awkward' (which Berndt Rasmussen does), then we should instead distance ourselves from the actual case at hand, and adopt as a general method of decision making to save the many rather than the few when the chances that we succeed are the same, and to save the largest expected number of lives when we have access to probabilities that we can take into account. If we all abide by this method of decision making, this means that we all stand a better chance on the whole of being saved, if we happen to need to be saved. For statistical reasons, it is more likely that we end up among the many than among the few!

As a matter of fact, Taurek concedes this, and concedes that, if people for prudential reasons agree about a practice where the many are saved rather than the few, then they have a right to abide by it.

This is pure moral rights talk, of course. But it means that we may abide by *any* principle we may come up with, if only we agree to do so.

However, the case here discussed by Taurek seems to be different. He appears to consider a positive right held by the people I can

9. Katharina Berndt Rasmussen, 'Should the Probabilities Count?'.

save—even if a very weak one. This weak positive right exists irrespective of any agreement. But then it is not a good idea to give an equal chance to everyone in the situation to survive. A better idea is that, quite generally, everyone should be given an equal *maximum* chance of being saved. And this could be thought of as a completely general rule.

According to this rule we ought to save the many rather than the few. And I suppose that, if we have an obligation to save lives at all, that is *not* grounded in the core of the moral rights theory (we have agreed about it, contracted to do so, and so forth), but which comes as an addition to the theory in the form of an idea of a *positive* right to life held by everyone, it would best be spelled out as a positive right to an equal *maximum* chance of being saved. And this means that we should be saved if we are among the many rather than among the few.

The idea that we have a positive right to an equal maximal chance of being saved has credibility in its own right. It makes sense, moreover, to abide by it as a utilitarian rule of thumb.

Does this rule mean that we ought to arrange survival lotteries of the kind where some are killed in order to save the lives of others? This does not follow, of course. The principle can be added to either deontology or a strict libertarian moral rights theory. On both theories we are forbidden to kill innocent people unless they agree to this. On the former we are forbidden to do so even if they agree to it.

4. UTILITARIANISM

Utilitarianism has no problem with the survival lotteries here described, either in the air-crash version, or in Harris's version, where people deliberately and freely enter the lotteries in order to survive (the air-crash case) or to enhance their survival chances (Harris's lottery). However, utilitarianism is very liberal in its verdict on the air-crash and organ lottery cases. This may be seen as a weakness or a strength. In the modified version of the air-crash case, there are two Kantians who stay outside the lottery. They are allowed to do so and when they die they are buried, according to their wishes. This is good news if it is assessed from the moral rights point of view. In a situation as special as this one, where we are free to assume that there are no bad side effects to our actions (we may even keep it secret, if necessary—perhaps this is what happened in the Andes!), it is nevertheless reasonable to suppose that an implication of utilitarianism is that it was *wrong* to bury the Kantians. Perhaps one more life could have been saved if their bodies had been consumed as well. They should have been told that they should not be eaten, but, even so, *after* their death, they should have been eaten. Very likely, it was wrong, according to utilitarianism, to bury them.

Does utilitarianism imply that Harris's survival lottery should be made obligatory? It does not. The problem with the lottery is that we can only have it on an institutional basis, and because of our reluctance to accept to be killed, even in order to save lives, the establishment of the system would create terror among us. However, if it could (and this is a mere thought experiment) be established secretly, with no bad side effects, then, according to utilitarianism, it ought to be established. After all, with the system, more lives would be saved than if we did not have it.

4.1. Harman's More Realistic Example

It is hard to imagine how Harris's lottery could be established systematically and secretly. But think instead of a thought experiment devised by Gilbert Harman:

> You have five patients in the hospital who are dying, each in need of a separate organ. One needs a kidney, another a lung, a third a heart, and so forth. You can save all five if you take a single healthy person and remove his heart, lungs, kidneys, and so forth, to distribute to these five patients. Just such a healthy person is in room 306. He is in hospital for routine tests. Having seen his test results, you know that he is perfectly healthy and

> of the right tissue compatibility. If you do nothing he will survive without incident; the other patients will die, however. The other five patients can be saved only if the person in Room 306 is cut up and his organs distributed. In that case, there would be one dead but five saved.[10]

Again, it is hard to believe that the killing of one in order to save the five could take place secretly. But let us *assume* that, in some rare situation, it would be possible for the physician to be absolutely and correctly sure that if he would do so, no one would ever come to know about it. Let us ponder the case cast in the third person. Here it is possible to think that, if the doctor kills the one and saves the five, this could happen without *any* bad side effects. In particular, the public support of the health-care system would not be jeopardized. If this was so, if he did cut up the healthy patient, and if there were indeed no bad side effects, what he did would be the right thing according to utilitarianism. In fact, it would have been wrong for him *not* to kill the healthy patient in Room 306 in order to save the needy ones. In this verdict the Sanctity-of-Life Doctrine, combined with the principle of double effect, must concur. When the doctor cuts up the patient in Room 306, the intention need not be to *kill* him. The idea is just to use his organs to save lives. If the doctor could take the organs without killing the patient, then he would do so. From a Kantian perspective, however, what he does is wrong. He uses the patient as a mere means.

It is of note that this situation seems similar to the Footbridge case in the discussion about the trolley cases. Does this mean that the same heuristic device, providing us with the answer that this kind of killing is wrong, is operative even here? It is hard to deny that this must be so. The doctor must exercise physical force when he removes the organs from the healthy patient and treats him as a mere means to the rescue of the other ones. But then we should be

10. Gilbert Harman, *The Nature of Morality*, pp. 3–4.

suspicious of our intuitive response. We should not treat the content of our intuition, if we have it, as evidence.

In Harman's example, there is, as I have stressed, no need to assume that any intentional killing takes place when the organs are removed. However, Peter Singer and Katarzyna de Lazari-Radek have presented a version of the example where such an intention to kill is part of it. They invite us to think of a surgeon who, when operating on a person's brain, can easily *kill* the patient, hence making the patient an organ donor—and get away with it.[11] Do we find this example worse than Harman's one? If the intention is what matters, this should indeed be the case. If the hypothesis that our strong reaction in Harman's case (if we have such reaction) is based on the heuristic device described by Greene et al. is correct, on the other hand, then we should find the example where the killing is intentional but involves less force *more* acceptable than in Harman's case. Compare the force it takes to remove all the organs of the patient to a slight movement of the lancet in the other case! Together with a colleague, I have tested this hypothesis.[12]

We allowed 150 freshmen psychology students to give their verdicts on two versions of Harman's case, first where it was explicitly stated that the doctor who removed the organs of the patient had no wish to see the patient dead, and then where it was supposed that the doctor *intentionally* allowed (without exercising *any* force) a patient to die, by not resuscitating him in time, in order to make him an organ donor. Both cases were cast in the third person and we stressed that the cases were exceptional ones; we asked our respondents to assume that there were no bad side effects. In the original Harman case we also stressed that the doctor did not want to see his patient dead, but merely foresaw the death of the patient when he took away the organs. In the

11. *The Point of View of the Universe*, pp. 297–298.

12. Henry Montgomery and Torbjörn Tännsjö, 'Why Are We Reluctant to Push the Big Man Off the Footbridge?'.

other scenario, where the doctor allowed the patient to die, we stressed that the death of the patient was intended (otherwise he could not become an organ donor). The students assessed both scenarios, and the order in which they considered them turned out to be of importance.

Even if the difference was not statistically significant, more students were prepared to accept intentional killing if it happened without the exercise of any force (through a mere omission to resuscitate the patient) than merely foreseen killing through the exercise of personal force. Moreover, if the respondents first confronted Harman's original example and then our example of intentional killing without the exercise of force, the difference was statistically strongly significant. Thus, when making comparisons *within* the same participants, more participants accepted or endorsed using the single patient's life to the benefit of the other five patients in the scenario with no force but with an intention to kill, than in the scenario with use of personal force but with no intention to kill.

It is clear, then, that it is not the intention to kill that makes people react to Harman's example (even if some may mistakenly believe that there must be an intention to kill in it, unless it is pointed out that no such intention is present). Still, a majority found it wrong to kill in order to save lives in *both* scenarios. How do we explain this? My conjecture is that the main explanation has to do with the health-care setting in which the experiment is devised. Even if we urged the respondents to imagine that there were no bad side effects, it is unlikely that we managed to convey that message to them. In this the case is strikingly different from the trolley one.

4.2. Utilitarianism on Taurek's Case

Finally, what is a utilitarian to say about Taurek's case? Taurek himself has articulated the answer. He assumes that David, who needs all the medication, also owns the medication and that the utilitarian should provide David with a reason to give away what he owns. David asks *why* he should give it away:

> I think David's question deserves an answer. What could there be about these strangers that might induce David to think it worth giving up his life so that they might continue to live theirs? The usual sort of utilitarian reasoning would be comical if it were not so outrageous. Imagine any one of these five entreating David, 'Look here David. Here I am but one person. If you give me one-fifth of your drug I will continue to live. I am confident that I will garner over the long haul a net balance of pleasure over pain, happiness over misery. Admittedly, if this were all that would be realized by your death I should not expect that you would give up your life for it. I mean, it may not be unreasonable to think that you yourself, were you to continue to live, might succeed in realizing at least as favourable a balance of happiness. But here, don't you see, is a second person. If he continues to live he too will accumulate a nice balance of pleasure over pain. And here is yet a third, a fourth, and finally a fifth person. Now, we should not ask you to die to make possible the net happiness realized in the life of any one of us five. For you might well suppose that you could realize as much in your own lifetime. But it would be most unreasonable for you to think that you could realize in your one lifetime anything like as much happiness as we get when we add together our five distinct favourable balances.'[13]

This captures nicely the utilitarian reasoning. It should be noted in passing that, according to utilitarianism, the numbers do not count, at least not directly. It is the sum total of happiness produced that counts. In the quoted passage, in contradistinction to other passages of his paper, Taurek caters for this. Taurek himself does not find this argument convincing. He even finds it outrageous. But

13. John Taurek, 'Should the Numbers Count?', p. 300.

what better argument could be put forward to David? David may retort, of course, that the sum total of happiness realized if the five are given the medication is not felt by anyone. This is a standard objection to utilitarianism, of course. But a standard answer to it exists as well. The standard answer is that, even if the sum is not felt or experienced by anyone, it is a sum *of* felt or experienced happiness. Note that it is true also that the net balance of pleasure over pain within a single life—referred to by the person confronting David in the quotation above—is not anything that this person or anyone else ever experiences. And yet, we find that it has the utmost importance to us. Again, it is a net balance of experienced pleasure over experienced pain.

5. CONCLUSION

The survival lottery I presented to the Chinese, the Russians, and the Americans was not very popular. This is true in particular of the Chinese and the Russians, but even among the Americans there was a strong majority condemning it. This may be seen as good news for deontology; it is the only theory discussed in this chapter that concurs in the majority verdict. However, my own intuitions are quite different. Furthermore, I tend to believe that an important reason why people dislike the survival lottery I have presented to them has to do with aesthetics rather than ethics. These people have a strong inhibition against cannibalism. Their gut feelings tell them that it is wrong to consume human flesh. They may be right about this, as a general rule, but their gut feelings lead them astray in the case presented to them. Or, so I would be prepared to argue, anyway.

Would I have obtained a different result if instead I had presented John Harris's survival lottery to them? I doubt it. As I have noted, since in his example killing is done on a regular basis, I believe most people would choose not to join in. The lottery would enhance our chance to survive slightly, but it would not maximize happiness (because of our irrationality). So the right way of assessing Harris's example is to see it as a mere thought experiment. Again, it might be difficult to get people in a survey such as this one to accept this assumption. Anyway, surveys such as these are extremely costly, so it is not possible for a philosopher to raise funding for any experimenting with them. My survey was indeed a single shot.

Yet for all that, there seems to be a good reason to accept, in principle, the idea that we arrange survival lotteries, in particular if this not only enhances our chances of survival but also maximizes the sum total of happiness among us. This is what happens in the example I presented in my survey and this is what would happen if rational people were to organize Harris's kind of lottery. You may even imagine here that people who draw the winning ticket in the lottery suffer less than a person who has to accept that he will die because there is no organ available for him. Those who draw the winning ticket in the lottery, if perfectly rational, can comfort themselves with the thought that *their* death is not in vain. When they accept to be killed, they know that they save many lives.

If I am correct in this assessment, then this spells a problem for deontology. The implications of deontology are at variance with the idea that it is defensible to save lives in the manner described in the examples. But I find it hard to see anything wrong, at least in principle, with such lotteries.

However, both utilitarianism and the moral rights theory are compatible with this judgement. They both imply that it *is* defensible to save one's life in the manner described in the example. You could say that they both explain this observation. Which theory gives the *best* explanation of it?

Some may find it counts against utilitarianism that not only does it sanction the lottery as it has here been described in the air-crash case, but it also sanctions that those who stay outside the lottery are consumed for food, once they are dead. And it may be thought that it counts even heavier against utilitarianism that it would sanction the physician in Harman's thought experiment who secretly uses the patient's organs to save several other patients—and gets away with it. This is certainly Harman's own intuition (although *I* have argued that we should debunk it). The moral rights theory seems, on the other hand, to draw the line where it should be drawn. The lottery is acceptable if and only if those who voluntarily join into it in fact accept it. Harman's physician does the wrong thing, according to the moral rights theory. It is of note that *both* utilitarianism and the Sanctity-of-Life Doctrine (with its reliance on the principle of double effect) condone it.

However, we have seen in relation to Taurek's case that the moral rights theory has an implication that many may find equally objectionable. On the moral rights theory, we need not save lives, even if we can do so easily. We need not share our medicine with others, provided we own it, even if this means that they die, and we need not make any efforts at all to save people in need; after all, we own ourselves, and we can do as we see fit with our physical and mental capacities, so far as we do not violate any negative rights.

I leave the final verdict of these theories to the concluding chapter of this book.

Chapter 10

Killing in War

If our country were offered guarantees for its safety and sovereignty by the United Nations, now equipped with military forces of its own, would it then be in order if our government decided to disarm completely, only offering some restricted military resources to the United Nations, to keep the peace in the world?

	China	*Russia*	*United States*
Yes	22%	15%	31%
No	68%	79%	63%
Don't know	10%	6%	6%

1. INTRODUCTION

After each one of the twentieth century's two terrible world wars, attempts were made to obviate war altogether through international organizations, first the League of Nations and then the United Nations. These attempts have not yet come to fruition. However, this does not mean that this kind of approach to the problem must be a dead end. Some people still strive to establish a global democracy where there is no more war (or global injustices, or environmental disaster).[1] One out of five Chinese citizens, and almost one out of three Americans, are prepared to give up the national defence, if only the UN provides guarantees. I find that *extremely* hopeful,

1. See my *Global Democracy. The Case for a World Government* for both an argument to this effect and for references.

considering that this is an idea that has hardly been discussed among people at large. However, we still live in a world with wars, even if we happen to live at a comparatively peaceful time.[2] And yet, many bloody wars are in progress while I write this. Moreover, so long as we do not have a world government with a monopoly on the use of armed force, the situation could easily worsen—something that seems to be happening right now. Hence, an approach to war other than simply abolishing them has also been tried out. Rather than to obviate wars, this approach intends to render them less prominent and less brutal. During the last century a lot of rules, with their roots in an old moral (philosophical) tradition about just and unjust wars, have been established in international law, codified in the Laws of Armed Conflict (LOAC).[3] They specify both when war is legitimate, *jus ad bellum*, and how a war should be conducted, irrespective of whether it is just or unjust, *jus in bello*. The focus in this chapter is on this attempt and, in particular, on the legal idea of *jus in bello*. How do the three theories put to test deal with the question of killing in war? In particular, what kind of legislation would we endorse on each of the three theories: deontology, the moral rights theory, and utilitarianism?

2. ACTUAL RULES

War is regulated by the LOAC. In today's world, there is a widely shared view that there are just and unjust wars. The ones that are unjust are the 'aggressive' ones. The ones that are just are those

2. This has been true ever since the end of the Cold War and roughly up to 2008. Since then the situation may have deteriorated somewhat again. See The Human Security Report on this, http://hsrgroup.org/human-security-reports/human-security-report.aspx/.

3. The extent to which these rules have roots in the philosophical tradition may sometimes have been overemphasized in the present discussion. For an interesting argument to the effect that much of the philosophical tradition has questioned the idea of moral symmetry between just and unjust combatants, see Gregory M. Reichberg, 'Just War and Regular War: Competing Paradigms'.

fought in 'self-defence'. Perhaps there are also just wars fought on humanitarian grounds.[4] Here the LOAC is less clear. It is also part of the LOAC that wars, irrespective of whether they are just or unjust, can be fought in a just or unjust manner. In international positive law these two distinctions are thought of as independent of one another. *Jus ad bellum* is one thing, *jus in bello* quite another thing. What will interest me here are both, but my main focus will be on *jus in bello*. Can we make *moral* sense of roughly the legal rules that exist? In particular, can we make sense of the idea that *jus in bello* can be understood as independent of *jus ad bellum*?

I will not go into any detail in the description of the rules themselves. It should suffice to note here that among them are rules to the effect that it is illegal to target civilian bystanders—that even if military actions directed at the enemy soldiers may 'spill over' as direct harm done to civilian bystanders, this should never be the aim of the attack. All sorts of measures should be taken to minimize harm to civilian bystanders and, if there is no reasonable proportionality between the aim of harming the enemy and the damage done to civilian bystanders, then a military action is criminal. There are also rules about how prisoners of war should be treated. It is prohibited to punish them once they have surrendered. To kill them is no better than to commit murder. The idea is that international courts should punish violations of rules such as these when possible.

Does a moral principled rationale behind rules such as these exist? In order to find this out it is crucial to look at very basic moral ideas and try to apply them to the problem at hand. This is what I will attempt to do in the present chapter, where I dig into deontology, the moral rights theory, and utilitarianism. This approach, in this application of it, has proved to be controversial, however.

4. With regard to humanitarian wars I tend to think in analogy with Gandhi who when he was asked by a reporter what he thought of Western civilization answered that it sounded like a good idea.

2.1. Moral Methodology

In the preface to his seminal work on the ethics of war, which inaugurated the recent philosophical interest in the subject, Michael Walzer claims that it is pointless to move bottom up from the most basic moral ideas to the more practical precepts we know in our ordinary moral discussions about war as well as in positive international law. If we were to start our discussion, as I do in this book, and as I plan to do in this chapter, with the basic moral principles, we would 'probably never get beyond them', he writes.[5] In this chapter I will try to show him wrong on this count. It should also be noted that, in his rejection of such an approach, he is not quite consistent. After all, he claims that he *is* basing his argument on a moral rights theory. 'The morality I shall expound is in its philosophical form a doctrine of human rights'.[6]

I suppose what Walzer means to say is that he doesn't stick to any very *precise* theory of rights. Moreover, he is not trying to *apply* it. Rather, he adheres to a more intuitive method, where the theory is moulded while his argument is developed. My idea is, as we have seen in this book, that we can do better if we apply different theories to the problem and see our enterprise as a kind of crucial test. Which one of them can best explain our data? And the datum to be explained in this chapter, more exactly, is the intuition that existing rules of law are roughly as they should be. The ideal would be if we could obviate war altogether, but as long as we have not done that, we had better regulate war. Furthermore, the actual regulations are *roughly* as they should be. This is *my* firm belief. Theories that cannot explain this datum are in trouble. The theory that best explains it gains support—through an inference to the best explanation.

5. Michael Walzer, *Just and Unjust Wars. A Moral Argument with Historical Illustrations*, p. xv.

6. Ibid., p. xvi.

2.2. Three Different Approaches

In this chapter I will again look at the three basic moral views I have discussed thus far in this book, in order to investigate their implications for the problem at hand: a deontological theory, both in its Kantian retributivist form and in the form of the Sanctity-of-Life Doctrine—of which the principle of double effect is a part—a libertarian moral rights theory, and utilitarianism. I will try out these basic moral approaches to the problem and attempt to find whether they can provide us with a rationale behind existing positive international law. To the extent that they cannot, I will hold this against them, not against positive existing international law.

I should caution the reader that, even if these three traditions, in my description of them, are clear and distinct, this does not mean that thinkers fall neatly into them. It is very common that actual historical thinkers incorporate elements from more than one of these traditions in their thinking. This is true in particular in the discussion about just and unjust wars. I consider this bad intellectual habit, but it is a fact.

3. DEONTOLOGY

As I understand deontology here, it is taken to include a strict prohibition against the killing of innocent human (rational) beings. According to the theory, there is also an imperfect (utilitarian) duty to promote happiness in the world. It is not quite clear what it means to say that this is an imperfect duty, but this is of no importance in the present context. Here it suffices to note that if much is at stake, if important values are threatened, there is a need to do something about this. However, it is never permissible to violate any perfect duty in the attempt to fulfil an imperfect one. It is not permissible to kill intentionally even in order to save lives. I do not assume that an adherent of deontology must think that all immoral actions should be prohibited. For example, it is natural to think that an adherent of the theory is prepared to live with a legal system not forbidding lying, at least not forbidding lying in all sorts of circumstances. It does seem, though, as if most adherents of the theory would argue that serious kinds of wrongdoing, such as murder, must be kept illegal. In particular, Kantianism typically goes together with a retributivist theory of crime and punishment. It is important that those who intentionally perform immoral actions, such as murder, should be punished. But then it is crucial to have such actions criminalized. Now, since this will turn out to be a problem with the theory in the present context, I will also discuss whether the theory can be relaxed in this respect. More about that later.

3.1. Deontology and Pacifism

If life is sacred, should one *ever* kill? On one plausible reading, pacifism is the logical conclusion that follows from deontology. But that might be a bit simplistic. Could not a war in defence of important values such as national independence, democracy, and welfare, render war legitimate? I think there are two promising lines of argument to this effect available for the adherent of the doctrine.

First of all, it is possible to argue that even if one aims at the attacking combatants in a defensive war, the intention is not really to kill them. At least this is so if war is fought without anger, and only as a means to saving important values. You rely, then, on the principle of double effect, which forms part of the version of deontology I have called the Sanctity-of-Life Doctrine.

It is true that weapons kill, but it is possible to fight a defensive war with the following intention. I throw my deadly weapons at the enemy in order to incapacitate him, foreseeing his death, but not intending it; had it been possible to incapacitate him without killing him (putting him to sleep for a week, say), I would have done so. If this is the case, on the traditional understanding of the principle of double effect, the death of the enemy combatants is merely a foreseen, and not an intended, effect; the intention was to defend important values such as national independence, democracy, and a happy life for all. The Augustinian view that wars should be fought with the right attitude seems to reflect this kind of thought:

> The passion for inflicting harm, the cruel thirst for vengeance, an implacable and relentless spirit, the fever of revolt, the lust of power, and such like things, all these are rightly condemned in war.[7]

It is true that, on the principle of double effect, a requirement of proportionality (between the good you intend and the bad you merely foresee) should also be satisfied. Is it satisfied in defensive war? It is at least arguable that sometimes it is. If important values are at stake and no killing performed by the just combatants is intentional, then this may well be true. It is true if there is reasonable hope of success in the defensive attempt.

The other line of argument is different. You then refer to the necessity of capital punishment insisted on by Kant. Many adherents of deontology have also thought that there exists a strict obligation to execute murderers. They adhere to a retributivist theory of crime and punishment. This was, as we remember from the chapter on capital punishment, Kant's view. If those who attack you are no better than murderers (to the extent that they succeed in their attempt, they *are* murderers), they deserve to die. This means that you are allowed to *intend* their death. On this reading, *only* losses among civilians on the aggressive side of the war count morally against your actions. But then it is quite plausible that the requirement of proportionality can sometimes be satisfied.

The idea that war could be seen as just (deserved) *punishment* was often alluded to in the medieval writings about just and unjust wars.

7. *Contra Faustum* (XXII, 74). I have the quote from Gregory M. Reichberg, 'Just War and Regular War: Competing Paradigms', p. 198.

Those 'who are attacked should be attacked because they deserve it on account of some fault', as Aquinas wrote.[8] And the unjust combatants are 'guilty of strife and commit sin'.[9]

One may argue, of course, that many who fight on the unjust side never kill anyone. How, then, can they all be legitimate targets? I suppose the answer to this question is that they are complicit in the killing that goes on by simply being a member of the army responsible for it. To show this is no small intellectual task, but I will here just assume that the adherents of deontology can somehow handle it in a satisfactory manner.

3.2. Just Warfare

All this means that, in deontology, if interpreted in a charitable manner, there is room for defensive war. Deontology makes room also for a requirement of restraint when a defensive war is fought, roughly in the manner it is defined in international law. The just combatants should respect the immunity of innocent bystanders on the aggressive side. And even if they foresee in some circumstances that their actions targeted at the enemy combatants spill over on innocent bystanders, their action may still be morally permissible. The crucial thing is that they do not aim at the bystanders. If they do, they act as murderers. The requirement of proportionality should furthermore be respected. Finally, of course, they shall do what they can to minimize the harm done to innocent bystanders, when such harm is inevitable.

Michael Walzer is critical of the principle of double effect and proportionality. It is too permissive, he thinks. It is not enough to see to it that the requirement of proportionality is met and to see to it that you do not intend the death of civilians. You must also be

8. Thomas Aquinas, *Summa theologiae* II-II, q. 40, a.19.

9. Ibid., q. 41.a.1, reply to obj.3. I also have the quotes from Aquinas from Gregory M. Reichenberg, op. cit., p. 198.

prepared to pay a price yourself in order to lower the costs among civilians. Or at least you need to take some 'extra' risks:

> if saving civilian lives means risking soldier's [sic] lives, the risk must be accepted.[10]

This seems to imply that you should be prepared to jeopardize victory on the just side in order to keep the costs among civilians on the unjust side low. If this is how he should be understood, then I do not share his intuition here. And I note that the Sanctity-of-Life Doctrine here seems to be in agreement with actual international legislation. Thus, it can provide a moral rationale behind it.

Literally understood, the principle of double effect urges a military commander to attack only combatants, even if they know that by doing so they will kill more innocent civilians than if they actually target only a few of these very same civilians. This is a congenial understanding of the principle, I submit, even if this has been questioned. It has been contested by Frances Kamm, who argues that:

> Being constrained by someone's right not to be treated in a certain way (e.g., terror killed rather than collaterally killed) may not have the same moral significance when it will not make a difference to whether he is harmed or terrorized as it has when it makes such a difference. This is an instance of what I call the Principle of Secondary Permissibility (PSP).[11]

Kamm speaks here about rights. I do not think a *deontologist* should accept the Principle of Secondary Permissibility, however. To do so would be to compromise the rationale behind deontological thinking. Those who went after the innocent bystanders would have the wrong kind of intention. We should here bear in mind Thomas Nagel's idea, quoted in Chapter 2, that the very essence of evil is that

10. Michael Walzer, *Just and Unjust Wars*, p. 156.
11. Frances Kamm, 'The Morality of Killing in War', p. 447.

it should repel us. So, if the intentional killing of innocent bystanders is an evil, we should not contemplate it, even in order to keep the number of innocent victims of war low.

If deontology can provide a rationale behind the international law regulating the actions of just combatants, it fails completely when it comes to unjust combatants, however. Even if they abide by the legal rules of *jus in bello*, and target no civilian bystanders, they are no better than murderers when they aim at the just combatants. Hence, they deserve to die, according to the retributivist version of the doctrine. And even setting retributivism to one side, they act wrongly. Even if murder need not be retributed in kind, it is still plain wrong.

If we accept deontology in its retributivist version, we have to accept the funny implication that prisoners of war, taken from the unjust side in the war, should be punished (executed). After the war, not only those who started the war, but all those who took part in it, should be punished. This flies in the face of international law. And this implication is a serious problem for the retributivist version of deontology.

3.3. Moral Symmetry

I have claimed that, typically, those who defend deontology are not prepared to allow that a serious crime such as murder goes unpunished, let alone that it is not rendered illegal. That's why the adherent of the doctrine needs to show that there is some moral symmetry between just and unjust combatants, otherwise there exists no rationale behind existing legislation. And they have gone to great length in order to show this. It seems to be a hopeless task, however.

One could try to argue that those who fight the unjust war (the unjust combatants) have often not chosen to do so. This is often not true. But even if in some cases it is true, this is of little avail from the point of view of this doctrine. For the prohibition against killing is strict. Not even if threatened at gunpoint are you allowed to kill an innocent person just in order to save your own neck.

It has also been noted in the recent discussion, for example by Jeff McMahan, that on this kind of theory, there is no way of meeting the proportionality requirement, when innocent bystanders are killed by unjust combatants. They do the wrong thing when they kill the just combatants. And they do even further wrongs when their actions spill over to the bystanders. So there is no moral room for *jus in bello* when you fight an unjust war, not even if the matter is assessed from the point of view of the Sanctity-of-Life-Doctrine, with its stress on the principle of double effect. The idea behind the requirement of proportionality is that the bad effects you merely foresee should be proportionate to the good effects you intend. But to intend to kill the just combatants is *evil*, not good.

> in order for the killing of innocent civilians not to be excessive in relation to the expected military advantage of an attack, military advantage must be *good*. Yet military advantage for those who are in the wrong and are fighting for the defeat of a just cause is, except perhaps in highly anomalous conditions, *bad*, impartially considered.[12]

It is no coincidence that Immanuel Kant had his plan for perpetual peace, rather than a philosophy of just war, and that the pope tends towards pacifism. From a deontological point of view, no support can be gained for existing international rules of just warfare. Deontology cannot sustain the idea of a legal symmetry between just and unjust combatants, since it cannot acknowledge any moral symmetry between them.

Could the adherent of deontology give up on the notion that murder should (always) be illegal? Could the adherent of the theory accept, on utilitarian grounds, that many murders (committed by unjust combatants) should be legal in the way they are legal in international law? This seems to be a high price to pay. I will discuss this possibility at the end of the chapter, however.

12. Jeff McMahan, *Killing in War*, p. 30.

4. THE MORAL RIGHTS THEORY

If deontology cannot provide a rationale behind existing international legislation, not even when interpreted as the Sanctity-of-Life Doctrine, with its reliance on the principle of double effect, it is tempting to follow Michael Walzer and turn to a moral rights theory. He has argued that from the perspective of a moral rights theory, it is possible to provide a rationale behind existing international law on *jus in bello* by showing that combatants on both sides are *morally* speaking equal. Here, as in the rest of this book, I will discuss the moral rights theory in its strict libertarian version, rendered famous by Robert Nozick in his *Anarchy, State, and Utopia*. There is no room for any idea of just (retributive) punishment in this theory, as we saw in the chapter on capital punishment. Nor is there any room for any 'positive' rights. No one is allowed actively to kill me, unless I consent to it, but I have no right to active assistance when my life just happens to be in danger.

4.1. Self-Defence

One important aspect of the moral rights theory is the idea that we have a right to self-defence. When my life is threatened, I have the right to kill in order to save my life. A third party has also a right to intervene and help me to defend my life against an aggressor. However, if she doesn't want to do this, she is at licence to abstain.

If the moral rights theory makes room for war at all, it is with reference to the idea of self-defence. A just war is a war fought in self-defence. A just war is fought in order to keep intruders off one's own territory, to avoid crossings of one's boundaries to which one has not consented. This defence is not without complication, however. Often, when my state is attacked, this does not mean that I am attacked. Can a libertarian moral rights theory allow that I see the defence of my state as self-defence?

This is not as straightforward as when I defend myself against someone attacking me. However, if the state is a minimal state,

I suppose I have a right to defend it. And even if it is not a minimal state—in real life it never is—it might be possible to argue that to the extent that it *contains* a minimal state (in the form of some basic legal structures, a police force, a military defence, and so forth), I may also be allowed to defend it. So let us grant the moral rights theorist the claim that defensive war is legitimate.

Can the moral rights theory defend the idea that innocents should be spared in a defensive war? It can, but here a qualification is in place. The moral rights theory doesn't operate with any idea of moral innocence (or guilt). The important thing is, rather, whether a person you kill poses a threat to you or not. And passive bystanders pose no threat to you. So you are simply not allowed to kill them. This spells trouble for the moral rights theory. Michael Walzer complained that the Sanctity-of-Life Doctrine, with its reference to double effect, was too permissive on this count. If he wants to be true to the moral rights theory, this is certainly so. The stress in this theory is against *active* killing (derived from the right of a self-owning individual not to be actively killed). There is no room in the theory for active killing even if death is merely foreseen. The principle of double effect is not part and parcel of this theory. So it seems that the only kind of defensive war acceptable to the moral rights theory is a war fought in the desert or at sea (or in outer space).

4.2. Moral Symmetry

Advocates of the theory have been eager to defend the idea that, as a combatant, you have a right to serve on the unjust side. As we will see, it is not quite clear *why* they have made this attempt. It is no doubt that they have made it, however. Michael Walzer thinks that those who serve on the unjust side have a right to do so and, hence, he takes it that they, too, kill in self-defence. After all, the just combatants threaten the lives of unjust combatants. Only the political leaders who initiate an unjust war are to be seen as criminals.

But how can it be that those who fight on the unjust side have a right to do so? How can it be that they have a right to kill the combatants who fight for a just cause? This is the kind of explanation Walzer provides:

> In our judgments of the fighting, we abstract from all consideration of the justice of the cause. We do this because the moral status of individual soldiers on both sides is very much the same: they are led to fight by their loyalty to their own states and by their lawful obedience. They are most likely to believe that their wars are just, and while the basis of that belief is not necessarily rational inquiry but, more often, a kind of unquestioning acceptance of the official propaganda, nevertheless they are not criminals; they face one another as moral equals.[13]

This is a strange statement to come from someone who believes in a moral rights theory. Robert Nozick thinks differently. He has insisted that 'it is a soldier's responsibility to determine if his side's cause is just'.[14] The implication of this is, of course, that if the war is not just, it is plain wrong to participate in it. Walzer quotes him and objects that those who don't refuse to take part are not *blameworthy*.[15] That is certainly so on the moral rights theory, which does not deal in blame and retribution. However, if they don't refuse, they risk becoming aggressors. And aggression is wrong, regardless of whether it is 'blameworthy' or not. How strange if it was not wrong; think of a case in which it was found out later that the victim of an attack was indeed innocent. If the attack on him had been all right only because it was undertaken in good faith, the victim would not have any right to restitution from the attacker, who had not committed any wrong. This is deeply unintuitive. The moral rights theorist should reject such an understanding of the theory.

Frances Kamm has recently defended the symmetry with a move similar to Walzer's. It is often reasonable to assume that the unjust

13. Michael Walzer, *Just and Unjust Wars*, p. 127.
14. Robert Nozick, *Anarchy, State, and Utopia*, p. 100.
15. Michael Walzer, *Just and Unjust Wars*, p. 40n.

combatants believe they are fighting on the just side. This is of no importance, according to Nozick. It is of the very last importance, according to Kamm, following Walzer. She stresses the point with the following analogy:

> suppose two people are debating an important issue to which no one yet knows the correct answer; they take opposite positions and one and only one of the positions is correct though no one yet knows who is correct. Are these debaters moral equals entitled to do the same things in the debate? We know that one of them must be defending an untruth (though he is not lying), and he may influence other people to believe in an untruth on an important matter. We would ordinarily think these debaters are moral equals and that it is permissible for each to do what the other does to defend his view and defeat his opponent in the debate.[16]

Is this not an utterly strange analogy? Do we not grant equal rights to those who debate, since we believe that this is helpful if we want to find out the truth about the matter at hand? And being defeated in a debate is not like being killed in a war, or is it?[17]

Could one find a better rationale behind the right on the part of the unjust combatants to kill just combatants, founded on the fact that combatants pose a threat to one another? This seems to be the standard rationale behind the idea of moral equality between combatants on the just and the unjust side of the war, but it does not stand up to reason, at least not if founded on a moral rights theory. Jeff McMahan has argued against this notion of moral symmetry with reference to the fact that a murderer has no right to kill a policeman in self-defence, and he makes references to both Pierino Belli and John Locke (who

16. Frances Kamm, 'The Morality of Killing in War', p. 439.

17. I have never been to a debate at Harvard, so I am open to the possibility that the analogy makes more sense there than it does in general.

belong, of course, to a moral rights tradition), who long ago made the same observation.

One would expect a defence of moral symmetry, in this theory, with a reference to consent. Could one argue that combatants, by becoming combatants, consent to being killed, regardless of whether they are on the just or the unjust side? One could compare this with participants to a boxing contest.

Walzer alludes to this and the idea has been defended by Thomas Hurka.[18] It is hard to believe, however, that it is true that those who engage in a modern defensive war consent, in the relevant sense, to being killed.

Walzer agrees about this and then resorts to the idea that combatants on both sides are like gladiators, who *have* to face one another in a deadly battle.

But is this true of those who enrol themselves only in order to defend their country when it is submitted to an unjust attack? This is hard to believe. They may well volunteer and they may well do so for a good reason. And very often the *unjust* combatants have joined the armed forces voluntarily, too, but for a bad reason. Moreover, on the moral rights theory, you are not allowed to attack bystanders who pose no threat to you even if you are coerced to do so. There are kinds of coercion you are supposed to resist, even at high risk on your own part. You are not allowed to kill a guard and rob a bank, only because some criminal told you that, unless you complied, he would punish you. Killing the guard and robbing the bank is still a violation of rights.

In one respect, the moral rights theory does provide a rationale behind the LOAC. Since it does not rely on any retributive ideas, it caters for the idea that prisoners of war should be treated in accordance with international conventions. After all, when they have surrendered, they pose no threat any more, so it would be wrong to kill them.

This rejection of retributive thinking may be seen as an intellectual resource in the present context. It is true that on the moral

18. Thomas Hurka, 'Liability and Just Cause'.

rights theory, you are doing the wrong thing when you fight on the unjust side. But there is no point in punishing you once war is over. Then you pose no threat any more to anyone. Thus, your moral crimes should go unpunished.

Does the idea leave room for punishment directed at those who started the unjust war? This is what is required by the LOAC. But if the moral rights theory has no room for retribution, how is it possible to defend such punishment? The obvious answer must be that people who have succeeded in starting unjust wars may do so again. They still pose a threat to the world. So we had better incapacitate them, either by executing them or by sending them off to something like a St. Helena, in our own defence.

The theory succeeds in providing a rationale behind existing legislation on some counts, but not all of them. It is very (much too) restrictive in its defence of civilian bystanders. And it cannot cater for the idea of equal treatment of combatants on both sides.

The reason moral rights theorists try to establish moral symmetry between just and unjust combatants is that they, like deontologists adhering to the Sanctity-of-Life Doctrine, want to keep serious wrongdoing (murder) illegal. I have hinted at the possibility that deontologists give up this ambition. Perhaps moral rights theorists can do so as well? In a way it may be easier for them than for deontologists to do so. They do not adhere to any retributivist theory of crime and punishment. I will return to this possibility below.

5. UTILITARIANISM

According to utilitarianism we ought to do what maximizes the sum total of happiness in the universe. This criterion applies to all actions, as well as to the adoption of international laws. We ought to adopt the laws that are optimal in the sense that having them, maximizes the sum total of happiness in the universe. It is likely that, for the time being, existing legal rules of just and unjust wars, the LOAC, are close to the optimal solution. But then we ought to stick to them. For a utilitarian it is as simple as that.

This is not to say that all acts condoned by these laws are right. According to utilitarianism, many of them are wrong. In particular, this is true of most actions performed by unjust combatants. Yet we should have them legally permitted since having them legally permitted has the best consequences. There are also, according to utilitarianism, actions that are right and even obligatory, but forbidden by the LOAC. There are *bound* to exist at least some situations where by violating the rules of *jus in bello* it is possible to hasten peace and, hence, making the world a better place. In such situations, according to utilitarianism, these actions are right (even obligatory). And yet, if the agent is found out, she should be punished. A utilitarian who has access to the notions of blameless wrongdoing (and blameful rightdoing) has no problem in acknowledging this.[19]

In my discussion of capital punishment I noted that there is logical space even in deontological thought for blameless wrongdoing. If the executioner has gone to all lengths to ascertain that the person she kills is guilty of the offence (murder) for which he has been convicted, her executing him, even if, *as a matter of fact*, he is innocent, may count as blameless wrongdoing. Could the same idea be applied in a defence of existing laws of just warfare? When people serve on the unjust side, their service should be seen as an instance of blameless wrongdoing? Is that a plausible view?

I think not. Even if there may exist *some* cases where *some* unjust worriers have done their best to ascertain that they are on the just side, but, alas, come to this conclusion mistakenly, this is the *exception* rather than the *rule*. In most cases, the unjust combatants did not bother to think about whether they served on the just or the unjust side. And in many cases, they actually *knew* that they served on the unjust side. They thought that, since everyone else complied, they could do so as well. However, according to deontology, this defence is not valid. They are *indeed* to blame for their

19. For my own contribution to this discussion, see 'Blameless Wrongdoing'.

complicity. They should have thought more carefully about their role in the war. And they should have protested, once they realized that they served on the unjust side, regardless of what the rest did. But the laws of armed conflict do not make any distinctions like these. *Everyone* who serves on the unjust side is immune against punishment for doing so. Hence, deontology cannot provide a moral rationale behind the laws of armed conflict. Utilitarianism, on the other hand, can.

Note that utilitarianism is flexible. The first explicit rule of warfare I know of is the one instituted by Solon in Athens to the effect that, after a civil war, no one should be punished for having fought on the losing side. People who had not taken part in the war, however, should be punished. I suppose the idea was that this was a way of making civil wars short and reducing resentment *post bellum*. If it worked, it could be supported from a utilitarian point of view. Perhaps there was a time when it was impossible to render war less terrible through legislation. In those times, there existed a utilitarian rationale for not having such a regulation. In today's world, with the UN, the International Criminal Court, the possibility of arranging international sanctions, and so forth, it seems wise to regulate warfare and to have explicit rules about how a war, just or unjust, can be fought in a just manner. Then this legislation has a utilitarian rationale. There may come a time when we do not need those rules any more. I alluded to this in the opening section of this chapter. It is of note that not only Immanuel Kant, but also Jeremy Bentham thought that it would be an easy task to do away with wars. According to Bentham, it was just a matter of establishing a free press, abolishing the secret diplomacy (in the way Wikileaks and Edward Snowden have managed today, I suppose), and having the colonial powers giving up on their colonial ambitions.[20] We know today that this was a bit naive. Actually, Bentham was even more naive than Kant. However, at least some utilitarians keep

20. Jeremy Bentham, *A Plan for a Universal and Perpetual Peace*, http://www.laits.utexas.edu/poltheory/bentham/pil/pil.e04.html

struggling to find a way of obviating, rather than regulating, war. My personal opinion is that this requires a world government and global democracy. If global democracy can indeed do the trick, it has a utilitarian rationale.

5.1. International Law

If the utilitarian solution to the problem here discussed is so simple, if utilitarianism can provide a rationale behind existing international legislation, why has utilitarianism so often been neglected in the present context? This has partly to do with a lack of understanding of utilitarianism, on the part of its critics. But it also has to do with how some utilitarians have themselves argued. This is true in particular of R. B. Brandt. It is a sad fact that this otherwise brilliant philosopher has brought the idea of a utilitarian defence of existing international rules of just war into disrepute. He has advocated the following rule, to be seen as an alternative to rules contained in existing international laws:

> a military action . . . is permissible only if the utility (broadly conceived, so that the maintenance of treaty obligations of international law could count as a utility) of victory to all concerned, multiplied by the increase in its probability if the action is executed, on the evidence (when the evidence is reasonably solid, considering the stakes), is greater than the possible disutility of the action to both sides multiplied by its probability.[21]

This is ridiculous. Who can believe that anything of this sort would work? Each party in a conflict would take advantage of the kind of license it gives them. As a matter of fact, this looks like a caricature of utilitarian thinking! Jonathan Glover is right when, politely, he observes that the 'reason why Brandt's rule is likely to be inadequate

21. R. B. Brandt, 'Utilitarianism and the Rules of War'.

as an instruction to appear in army manuals is that it leaves too much to the judgement of the soldier or strategist'.[22]

In comparison to Brandt's suggested rule, existing rules gain the upper hand. Perhaps they are not optimal. Perhaps there is some room for improvement. But Brandt's suggestion would not be an example of this.

When thinking of possible improvement, however, why not convict the unjust combatants? Their actions are, by and large, wrong, it is safe to assume. The fact that they often mistakenly believe they fight on the just side does not render their actions morally permissible. Two wrongs (one epistemic and one moral) do not make a right. In this the moral verdict from utilitarianism is no different than the verdicts from deontology or the moral rights theory. Furthermore, it is often true that the combatants on the unjust side could have developed more informed opinions about the war in which they were fighting, and it is then true that they should have done so. If they have to fear *post bellum* punishment, this should make them think more clearly before they enter the war.

And yet, there might exist very strong utilitarian reasons not to punish them afterwards. The reasons are fairly obvious.

First of all, it would be impossible to punish them all. They are too many. Also, it would be extremely costly. And to punish only some of them would invite the objection that it was unfair. It would be difficult to garner general acceptance of such a practice.

Secondly, it might be a good idea not to put this kind of pressure in international law on ordinary combatants, since this would mean that the governments who fight unjust wars would go to even greater length to cover up their bad intentions, to plant evidence in defence of their moves, and so forth, in order to convince the unjust combatants that they are on the just side.

Thirdly, as has been stressed by David Estlund,[23] at least in democratic countries it may be a good idea for ordinary citizens to

22. Jonathan Glover, *Causing Death and Saving Lives*, p. 277.
23. David Estlund, 'On Following Orders in an Unjust War'.

act on the assumption that the elected leaders make better political judgements than they are themselves capable of making. One could here also gesture at Condorcet's jury theorem, mentioned in Chapter 1 of this book, to the effect that the majority (if each member of it is right more often than not) is right more often than is any individual who makes up that majority. From a utilitarian point of view, this doesn't make it morally permissible to take part in an unjust war proclaimed by the democratically elected leaders. In this utilitarianism concurs with the verdict given by the Sanctity-of-Life Doctrine and the moral rights theory. It is still *wrong*—even if Estlund himself thinks otherwise. However, since the decision to join the unjust side was made with the aid of a method of decision making that a rational person would follow, it seems inappropriate to *punish* the person who used it. His wrongdoing was blameless (as even Walzer has claimed, we remember). The notions of blameless wrongdoing and of blameful rightdoing have a safe place in utilitarian thinking.

Finally, since it is difficult to see that any good consequences would ensue from an attempt to punish everyone who has fought on the unjust side in a war, such an attempt would certainly produce unnecessary suffering. But then it is wrong to make such an attempt, according to utilitarianism.

5.2. Legal Revision?

Or, is it after all a mistake to believe that it is a good thing to have such rules in place? When you start reading Jeff McMahan's important book you may think that this is how he reasons, at any rate:

> the idea that no one does wrong, or acts impermissibly, merely by fighting in a war that turns out to be unjust . . . lies at the core of the reigning theory of the just war and also informs the international law of war. Although the presence of this idea in the law is intended to have a restraining effect on the *conduct* of war, the widespread acceptance of this idea also makes it easier,

> even for independently minded people . . . to fight in war without qualms about whether the war might be unjust.[24]

When you read this you may get the impression that McMahan wants us to give up the idea that unjust warriors should go unpunished, but that is not his intention (you realize this when you read his entire book). He only wants us to give up the idea of a *moral* symmetry between combatants on both sides. He wants us to stick to the existing rules, at least for the time being. He shares my intuition that, roughly, the existing rules are as they should be. And he wants to continue to abide by them in spite of all the arguments he levels, mainly from a deontological (and a common sense) view to the effect that international law is morally mistaken.

Why should we then keep to existing rules? For purely utilitarian reasons, it seems! Or, at least, for broadly consequentialist reasons. Accordingly, it strikes a *utilitarian* reader, like the present one, that this concession should have given McMahan pause. Does this not imply that there is something *wrong* with the moral theories he has applied to the problem? If consequentialist reasoning gives us the correct answer to the question of what international laws we should adopt, should it not also give us the answer to the question of which actions we should take when conducting a war (irrespective of whether we are politicians deciding about it, generals planning it in detail, or combatants fighting it on the battlefield)?

5.3. Walzer on the Utilitarian Rationale

Not only McMahan but also Walzer recognizes the possibility that existing rules granting innocent bystanders protection in war may have a utilitarian rationale. However, while McMahan in the final analysis defends them on this count, Walzer objects to such a defence of them:

24. Jeff McMahan, *Killing in War*, p. 3.

> But no limit is accepted simply because it is thought that it will be useful. The war convention must first be morally plausible to large numbers of men and women; it must correspond to our sense of what is right. Only then will we recognize it as a serious obstacle to this or that military decision.[25]

But this is a *utilitarian* argument, not against having the laws we have, but against incorporating in the conventions a utilitarian rationale for them. This does not mean that utilitarianism cannot best *explain* why we should keep to existing rules. As I have argued and as McMahan has admitted, it can. But I think Walzer's observation is correct. It is correct on more general (utilitarian) grounds. It is *never* a good idea to incorporate into legislation any explicit or implicit reference to any particular moral rationale behind it. If we did, the support for them would wither.

This has to do with two facts. On the one hand, at least in democracies, legal regulations are in some cases the result of an *overlapping consensus*. People who hold very different basic moral outlooks find it possible to agree about the law as it appears. On the other hand, in many other cases, an existing law is the result of a *compromise*. Then it is highly likely that no rationale behind it exists at all. In either case, if any reference to one moral rationale in particular were included, the majority support of the law would be lost.

Walzer is therefore right when he insists that the rules of war should not refer, explicitly and even implicitly, to utilitarianism. But this is true of legislation in general. And yet, for all that, it seems as if utilitarianism can indeed provide a rationale behind them. As I have indicated, I count this in favour of the plausibility of utilitarianism.

Note furthermore that, in his comments on Nozick, even Walzer resorts to a distinction between wrongdoing and blameworthiness.

25. *Just and Unjust Wars*, p. 133.

A way of understanding him is as follows. The unjust combatants who kill their enemies are doing the wrong thing, but they are not blameworthy. We should not blame them. This move is clearly open to the utilitarian, but also, as we will see, to a moral rights theorist (even though Walzer for some reason resists it).

5.4. Some Utilitarian Implications

If it counts in favour of utilitarianism that it can provide a rationale behind existing laws on just warfare, does it not count against it that it has implications in individual cases at variance with these laws? Two examples come to mind.

First of all, international laws condemn terrorist acts, performed both by states and individuals. This is as it should be, if I have understood the implications of utilitarianism correctly. However, according to utilitarianism, there may well exist cases where individual acts of terror are morally obligatory; they may, for example, put a quick end to a terrible war. Does this count against utilitarianism?

Secondly, even the participation in an unjust war may have a utilitarian rationale. If I join the bad guys, this may mean a quick end to the war and a better peace than if I fight them. Then, according to utilitarianism, I ought to take part in the unjust war. Does this count against utilitarianism?

We know this kind of double utilitarian standards from many other contexts. As I have insisted, repeatedly, I see them as a sign of subtlety and strength in the utilitarian creed, not as a weakness. My strong intuition is that we *ought* to resort to terrorism, killing some innocent people, if there are no bad side effects (apart from the fact that these innocent people are being killed), and if by so doing we can put an end to a terrible war and hence save more lives than the ones we sacrifice. And my strong intuition is that it *is* right to take part in an unjust war, if this means a quick end to the war and a better peace than would otherwise be possible.

6. CONCLUSION

The problem with deontology is its idea about the role between the moral law and legal rules. It is not that it claims that all sorts of moral wrongdoing must be made illegal, but that it is adamant in the insistence that *serious* moral wrongdoing should *not* be left as a legally permitted option. In order to defend existing legislation, deontology needs the assumption that just and unjust combatants are on equal *moral* terms. But this cannot be shown, on deontology. Those who fight in support of an unjust cause, and kill those who defend a just cause, are murderers according to deontology. This means that there cannot be any way of defending the idea that unjust combatants should have a legal right to kill just combatants. This idea, however, is crucial to the entire system of international law about just and unjust wars.

Utilitarianism seems to get the upper hand in this contest. It doesn't need the assumption of moral equality. It can allow that legally, we condone moral wrongdoing, if the consequences of such legal rules are optimal. So long as there is war, utilitarianism can provide us with a moral rationale for roughly the kind of system of international law that is presently in place. The point in having this system is that it is difficult to ascertain whether a war is just or unjust, and even more difficult to obtain consensus about this. It is thus a good thing if, at least, those who have violated the rules of *jus in bello* can (sometimes) be persecuted and punished. Moreover, utilitarianism can allow for the kind of progress we all hope for, of course, with a world where there is no more war, where no rules about just and unjust wars, let alone rules about just and unjust ways of fighting wars, are needed.

But could not deontologists who defend the Sanctity-of-Life Doctrine, and libertarian moral rights theorists, give up their insistence that murder should (always) be illegal? Could they not—as Jeff McMahan seems to be prepared to do—rely on utilitarianism when deciding upon legislative measures, and rely on their own favoured theory only in private affairs?

This move is not open to a deontologist who accepts Kant's retributivism, of course. But those who rely merely on the moral prohibition against killing, tempered by the principle of double effect, could claim that, while their favoured moral theory instructs us about how to live our private lives, utilitarianism guides choices of legislation.

This move, however, invites the criticism I have levelled against McMahan: if utilitarianism is fine when it comes to legislative matters, why not apply it to problems of private morality as well?

To the moral rights theorists another possibility seems to exist, which, to my knowledge, has been neglected in the extant discussion. They can consistently claim that unjust combatants violate rights when they kill just combatants (they can give up the idea of a moral symmetry) and still allow that these rights violations may go unpunished. They stay, as it were, partly in a state of nature in this regard. Not making rights violations illegal does not mean that one violates any rights. If there are only negative rights, then those who have their rights violated when they are killed by unjust combatants in a war have no *right* to (legal) assistance. This is, I believe, how a moral rights theorist *should* argue, when facing the problem whether existing legislation is acceptable or not.

So, it seems at last, that the moral rights theory, even if it does not *imply* that current legislation *should* look roughly the way it does, is *consistent* with this legislation. It is *also* consistent with a legislation with a legal prohibition against unjust combatants killing just combatants and making it illegal for both to inadvertently kill civilians.

It is strange that the fact that the moral rights theory is at least compatible with current legislation has gone unnoticed by its adherents, who have therefore bent over backwards in an attempt to defend the (hopeless) moral symmetry thesis.

Chapter 11

The Killing of Animals

Is it morally permissible for us human beings to raise animals for food and clothing?

	China	*Russia*	*United States*
Yes	64%	63%	84%
No	31%	32%	14%
Don't know	5%	4%	2%

Anna Malpas, The Moscow Times

5:27PM BST 09 Oct 2009

Animal rights protesters posed in T-shirts printed with fake blood, several hiding their faces in surgical masks, outside the trial of a man accused of shooting pet dogs.

The trial could result in one of the country's first significant convictions for animal cruelty. It also provides a showcase for a new, more radical animal activism that is gaining popularity in Russia.

Dmitry Khudoyarov is on trial at Moscow's Cheryomushkinsky District Court on charges of killing a dog and permanently disabling a puppy by shooting them from his all-terrain vehicle.

He has pleaded guilty and could serve up to six months in jail, a year of community service, or pay a fine of up to 80,000 roubles ($2,580).

Activists standing outside the courthouse during a recent hearing wore T-shirts with splattered blood and the slogans, "Prison for the Slaughterer" and "Prison for the Serial Killer".

1. INTRODUCTION

Each year, human beings kill billions and billions of mammals and birds. These animals are raised, killed, and consumed for food and clothing, or they are used in medical experiments. More often than not, the treatment of these animals, at least during parts of their lives, is nothing but cruel. Many of them live their entire lives under miserable conditions; when death comes, it comes to liberate them from a fate much worse than death itself.

There exist long traditions of human cruelty towards non-human animals, both Western and Eastern. If moral rights theorists, of a kind to be discussed in this chapter, or utilitarians, adhering to the well-known hedonist version of their theory, are right, what has been, and what is being, done to animals is as bad as what happened to our fellow human beings in the Nazi concentration camps. And indeed, there is a growing movement arguing for animal welfare and rights based on such a radical stance. In modern times it started out in the West but we find recent examples of it also in a country such as Russia. If these movements are on the right track, one must ask: How could this cruelty go unnoticed for such a long time? How was it possible? How can we *do* this to sentient animals and get away with it?

There is one moral tradition, discussed in this book, the tradition of moral deontology, which can offer to explain why this is possible. According to this tradition, non-human animals lack moral standing. To the extent that people have adhered to this doctrine, it can explain how such cruelty has been, and is, possible. At least it poses no *moral* problem, if this tradition has it right. Which does not mean, of course, that those who adhere to it must, as a matter of fact, *act* in a cruel manner in their dealings with animals. But *if* they do, then this morality provides no moral reason for them to stop doing so.

Another explanation can be given with reference to the philosopher René Descartes. He believed that animals could not suffer. Hence, what may *seem* as cruelty towards them, is, strictly speaking, no such thing. He famously wrote:

> It is nature which acts in them according to the disposition of their organs, just as a clock, which is only composed of wheels and weights, is able to measure the time more correctly than we can with all our wisdom.[1]

It seems as the situation is changing, however. Few nowadays believe Descartes when he claims that animals cannot feel pain. According to received wisdom, at least it is obvious that mammals and birds can feel pain. More and more people begin to realize this, even if the thought may strike them as new and unexpected. Moreover, to many people animals in pain pose what they consider to be a *moral* problem. This means that human cruelty towards non-human animals is not any more seen as something natural. When exposed, and it gets exposed over and over again in modern media, there is a public reaction. The quote from *Moscow Times* at the opening of this chapter bears witness to the fact that it has even reached Russia. And this should not surprise us. In my survey, one-third among the Russians—as well as the Chinese—expressed that they did not accept that animals be raised for food and clothing.

But what reaction to cruelty towards animals is the *right* one? Granted that we owe them *something*, what *exactly* is it that we owe them? Once again, I will make no attempt to cover the entire discussion, but I will dig deeply into deontology (and in particular into the Sanctity-of-Life Doctrine), theories of moral rights, and utilitarianism.

2. DEONTOLOGY

There is a long Western tradition of anthropocentrism showing complete complacency with regard to the well-being of animals. According to this tradition, we are allowed to kill them, inflict pain

1. René Descartes, *Discourse on Method*; reprinted in Tom Regan and Peter Singer (eds.), *Animal Rights*, p. 62.

on them, and use them as mere means to our own purposes. At the heart of this tradition lies the assumption that animals lack moral standing. For Immanuel Kant this is made clear with something close to brutality:

> But so far as animals are concerned, we have no direct duties. Animals ... are there merely as means to an end. That end is man.[2]

Thomas Aquinas had earlier made the same point as follows, even though he admitted that it might tempt us to be cruel to one another if we allow ourselves to be cruel to animals:

> Hereby is refuted the error of those who said it is sinful for a man to kill dumb animals: for by divine providence they are intended for man's use in the natural order. Hence it is no wrong for a man to make use of them, either by killing them or in any other way whatever.[3]

2.1. Some Implications

Deontology, either in Kant's form or in form of the Sanctity-of-Life Doctrine, accepts the killing of animals. Regardless of whether the focus is on rational individuals (Kant) or human individuals (the Sanctity-of-Life Doctrine), it is clear that animals other than humans lack the required property that can grant moral standing. According to the doctrine, it is absolutely forbidden to intentionally kill human beings. There is, however, no similar restriction in our relation to nonhuman animals.

The Sanctity-of-Life Doctrine has not been clearly formulated until we have explained what it means to be a human individual. In a similar vein, to get a clear grasp of Kantianism, we need to decide

2. *Lectures on Ethics*, p. 239.
3. *Summa Theologica*, II, II, Q. 64, Art. 6.

what it means for an individual to be rational. The latter problem is not so important, however, in a discussion of animal ethics. Few if any nonhuman animals qualify on any reasonable account. But, of course, there are some human individuals who do not qualify (because of severe mental retardation, dementia, and so forth). I suppose Kant would have accepted that some human beings lack moral standing. So let us first focus on the Sanctity-of-Life Doctrine and its insistence that being human and possessing moral standing go hand in hand.

How do we distinguish human from non-human individuals, and when does an individual human life begin?

We met with this problem in the chapter on abortion. There we learned that the answer to the latter question is straightforward. A human life begins at conception. The answer to the former question, which is crucial in the present context, is less straightforward. How do we distinguish human organisms from non-human ones? Informed by modern science adherents of the doctrine tend to say, with a caveat to which I will return, that the crucial thing here is the genome. The human genome defines the human organism.

2.2. Difficulties with the Doctrine

The doctrine is often criticized on moral grounds. Granted that we ordinary human beings are biological organisms, what is so special with being *human*? If our genome defines us, what are we to say if we find other creatures, with a very different genome, that are intellectually and emotionally superior to us? Can we really claim that they lack moral standing? And what if we find that some—seemingly—human beings have a different genome from the rest of us, does that mean that we are allowed to kill them and eat them?

How different need they be, in order to lose their moral standing? What if they have just an extra chromosome—does this mean that they are not human?

The Oxford psychologist Richard Ryder has coined the expression 'speciesism'.[4] It has found a place in the Oxford English Dictionary, where it is defined as: 'discrimination against or exploitation of certain animal species by human beings, based on an assumption of mankind's superiority'.

Does the Sanctity-of-Life Doctrine amount to speciesism? I suppose it does. The doctrine makes a difference (discriminates) between human and non-human beings on the assumption of mankind's (moral) superiority. But this is just a characterization of the theory. What is *wrong* with speciesism? Here is an attempt to answer *this* question, made by Peter Singer:

> Why isn't species a legitimate reason? For essentially the same reason as we now exclude race or sex. The racist, sexist and speciesist are all saying: the boundary of my group also marks a difference of value. If you are a member of my group, you are more valuable than if you are not—no matter what other characteristics you may lack. Each of these positions is a form of group protectiveness, or group selfishness.[5]

This sounds problematic, if true. The idea seems to be that the relevant group is defined in an ostensive manner, by enumeration of the members. But is this true of the idea held by adherents of the Sanctity-of-Life Doctrine? Do they hold that they are special, whatever other characteristics (apart from being members of the group) they hold? Do they define the group to which they belong through a simple enumeration of its members?

I think not. Should it transpire, through some genetic test, that a typical adherent of the theory were not truly human, then her belief that she is special would wither; she would admit that she lacks

4. Richard D. Ryder, *Victims of Science: The Use of Animals in Research*.

5. Peter Singer, *Rethinking Life and Death. The Collapse of Our Traditional Ethics*, pp. 203–204.

special moral standing. Her life is not sacred. But then her view is not, in the *derogatory* sense given by Singer, 'speciesist'.

Yet for all that, she may be mistaken when she claims that being human grants a special moral standing. But this is true for all answers to the question of what it takes to have a special moral standing. They may all be mistaken. However, the mistake need not be as simple as the one characterized by Singer. And, once again, it is hard to believe that the mistake, if it is a mistake, can be exposed through a simple argument. We need here a more inductive approach.

The adherents of the doctrine have tried, in fact, to turn the objection upside down. It is a *strength* in the doctrine, they have claimed, that in order to obtain moral status, it is enough if you are one among us. You need not qualify in any stronger sense—you need not be smart, or be able to think or feel, in order to possess moral status. This means that the doctrine has provided a rationale exactly for those who oppose racism and sexism—among humans.

I noted that with a caveat, the Sanctity-of-Life-Doctrine takes the human genome to be definitive of what it means to be human. The caveat has already been mentioned earlier in this book. It has to do with the fact that two individuals, who are qualitatively similar, may still belong to different species, if their remote ancestors have developed independently of one another. This means that the Sanctity-of-Life Doctrine needs clarification. Is the genome really decisive, or is it only decisive together with the typical human evolutionary history? My guess is that most adherents of the theory would opt for the historical version. It is really membership of the human species that counts.

2.3. Non-Human Animals

It is remarkable that, while the metaphysical presuppositions of the Sanctity-of-Life Doctrine even in its standard version are animalist (we are essentially human *organisms* beginning to exist at conception), the doctrine grants no protection whatever to non-human animals. This does not mean that typical adherents of the doctrine are cruel to animals. Thomas Aquinas thought, as was mentioned, that it is a good idea not to be cruel towards animals, since those who are cruel towards animals tend to be cruel towards fellow human beings as well. Furthermore, an adherent of the doctrine may be kind towards animals out of mere *compassion*, and an adherent of the doctrine may even think badly of people who are cruel to animals, and decide not to socialize with them. Finally, an adherent of the doctrine may think that we have some moral obligations towards non-human animals and protest even on moral grounds against cruelty towards animals. However, to stay true to the rationale behind deontology, I suppose we must say that whenever there is a conflict between human and nonhuman life, between human and nonhuman suffering, and between human life and nonhuman suffering, the conflict must always be resolved in the interest of the human. Not even to avoid massive nonhuman animal pain are we allowed to kill one human being. Not even to avoid massive nonhuman animal pain are we allowed to inflict any amount of pain on a human being.

3. THE MORAL RIGHTS THEORY

Up to the present point I have discussed the moral rights theory based on self-ownership, mainly in the form it takes in Robert Nozick's statement of it (together with comments by contemporary philosophers such as Judith Jarvis Thomson and Dan W. Brock). Tom Regan is the philosopher who has most famously applied the theory to animals, however, and claimed that there are animal rights. He is the exception, though. Most adherents of the moral rights theory think that nonhuman animals lack moral standing. Here the exception is what will interest me, however. Can it help the moral rights theory to a plausible answer to the problems posed in animal ethics in general, and to the problem of killing of animals in particular?

3.1. Tom Regan on Animal Rights

According to the moral rights theory in general, there exist moral subjects who have moral rights by virtue of being the kind of creatures they are. Such moral subjects have certain rights, first and foremost to their own bodies, their own talents, and so forth. They 'own' themselves.

Some kind of reference to a capacity to function as a moral agent has often been made when it has been specified what it means to be a moral subject. A moral subject is an autonomous moral agent, a person, someone with an understanding of a subjective past, present, and future, someone who can make choices and view herself as responsible for the consequences of her actions; these are only examples of the way the notion of a moral subject has been delineated.

Traditionally the advocates of the moral rights theory, such as John Locke and Robert Nozick, have taken for granted that non-human animals lack moral standing. Or, at least they have thought that non-human animals lack moral rights. This is not because they are non-human—the doctrine is not speciesist—but because they are, even if sentient, typically not moral *agents*; they do not qualify as *persons*. Robert Nozick has suggested that perhaps utilitarianism applies to non-human animals, while most humans, those who are persons, have moral rights, but this is mere speculation on his part, and he has no definite answer to the question of how conflicts of interest between human and non-human animals are to be handled.[6] Again, to be true to the rationale behind his theory, I suppose the best answer would be that conflict should always be solved to the advantage of persons. The moral rights theorist Michael Tooley, as we remember from the chapter on abortion, has defended infanticide and claimed that neonates are not persons. Tom Regan thinks differently about this, however. He thinks that, not only neonates, but many animals, all mammals at

6. Robert Nozick, *Anarchy, State and Utopia*, pp. 35–47.

least a year of age, have moral rights. This is how he puts his most cautious claim:

> I adopt a conservative policy by asking whether a line can be drawn that minimizes otherwise endless disputation. The line I draw is "mentally normal mammals of a year or more."[7]

How can he defend such a position? Perhaps some great apes are persons, but what about the rest of the mammals? Can they assume responsibility for their actions?

Regan believes, just like Nozick, that moral agents, persons, have moral standing and rights. The reason they have rights is complicated, however. It has to do with the fact that they possess *inherent value*. Why do they possess inherent value? The idea is not, as it is in classical moral rights theory, that they possess inherent value (a notion we rarely come across in this theory) and hence rights (the notion we do meet with) *because* they are moral agents (persons). The explanation is different, and the explanation allows that not only moral agents, but also what Regan calls moral *patients*, have moral standing (rights). This means that there is a separation between two kinds of moral rights holders, on the one hand the moral agents, who can assume moral responsibility for their actions and, on the other hand, (mere) moral patients, who cannot do so but who are yet protected by strict moral rights.

3.2. Moral Patients

In order to possess moral standing, it is not necessary, then, to be a moral agent. Rather, it is sufficient if you pass what Regan calls *the subject-of-a-life criterion*. If you do, you possess inherent moral value. This value is equal for anyone who possesses it.

7. See his Preface to the 2004 edition of Tom Regan, *The Case for Animal Rights*, p. xvi.

I am not sure that we really need the category of inherent value, in our understanding of Regan's theory; as I noted, we rarely meet with this notion in the moral rights tradition. It strikes me as satisfactory if we grant that passing the subject-of-a-life criterion is sufficient for having rights. We may skip over the talk of inherent value. Be that as it may, this is how he characterizes what it means to be a subject of a life:

> To be the subject-of-a-life, in the sense in which this expression will be used, involves more than merely being alive and more than merely being conscious ... individuals are subjects-of-a-life if they have beliefs and desires; perception, memory, and a sense of the future, including their own future; an emotional life together with feelings of pleasure and pain; preference- and welfare-interests; the ability to initiate action in pursuit of their desires and goals; a psychophysical identity over time; and an individual welfare in the sense that their experiential life fares well or ill for them, logically independently of their utility for others and logically independent of their being the object of anyone else's interests.[8]

Are there really individuals who pass this test without being moral subjects? And is it true that all mammals pass the test, as Regan claims? It strikes me as very implausible that most mammals have 'a sense of the future, including their own future', but I will assume, for the sake of argument, that he is right about this and merely ponder the moral implications of his view.

3.3. On the Nature of Moral Rights

According to Nozick, moral rights are strict side-constraints upon our actions. We should never violate any rights, they are absolute. Regan prefers to speak of prima facie rights. Such rights are not

8. Tom Regan, *The Case for Animal Rights*, p. 243.

absolute; they can be violated, when much is at stake. If there is a conflict of rights, it is necessary to make a decision. Whose rights will gain the upper hand?

But is it possible for rights to conflict? Not on Nozick's negative interpretation of the notion. Nozick's rights are rights not to be interfered with. There is always a way of respecting them all. Regan's rights are partly negative, but also positive. In particular, all moral agents are obliged to assist and *prevent violations of rights*. This is a positive right to assistance, then. So there can be cases where, in order to fulfil our obligations, we have to kill innocent bystanders in order to avoid murder.

3.4. Consequences for the Treatment of Animals

If Regan is right, then it is forbidden to raise, slaughter, and eat mammals (moral patients). This is wrong in the same manner that it would be wrong to raise, slaughter, and eat fellow human beings (moral agents). It would be wrong because they pass the subject-of-a-life test and it is impermissible to kill anyone who passes this test.

In a similar vein, we are not allowed to use animals as mere means to our purposes, for example in animal experiments. We are not allowed to hunt them down just for the fun of it. We are not allowed to inflict pain on them at all. Moreover, we have an obligation, if we can, to stop those who do violate the rights of animals. If a human being attacks a sheep, we have an obligation to stop him.

But what if a *wolf* attacks a sheep? Do we have an obligation to save the sheep? We have not. Our duty to assist moral patients in need doesn't extend to this kind of case, since, when the wolf attacks the sheep, no violation of any right takes place. A wolf is not a moral agent and cannot, hence, violate any rights:

> wolves in particular and moral patients generally cannot *themselves* meaningfully be said to have duties to anyone, nor, therefore, the particular duty to respect the rights possessed by

> other animals. In claiming that we have a prima facie duty to assist those animals *whose rights are violated*, therefore, we are not claiming that we have a duty to assist the sheep against the attack of the wolf, since the wolf neither can nor does violate anyone's rights.
>
> (Ibid., p. 285)

This seems to have the radical implication that, even if we are allowed to do so, we have no moral obligation to save a human being who is attacked by a wolf. The theory also seems to imply that we have no right to kill an animal in order to save human lives. Think of the switch in the discussion of the trolley cases. If an animal is on the side-track, we have no right to divert a trolley into it, even in order to save the five people further down the track. Or, can Regan find a way to avoid this conclusion? Here, a much-discussed thought experiment devised by Regan is of importance:

> Imagine five survivors are on a lifeboat. Because of limits of size, the boat can only support four. All weigh approximately the same and would take up approximately the same amount of space. Four of the five are normal adult human beings. The fifth is a dog. One must be thrown overboard or else all will perish. Who should it be? If all have an equal right to be treated respectfully, must we draw straws? Would it not be unjust, given the rights theory, to choose to sacrifice the dog in preference to one of the humans? And doesn't this mean that the rights theory, because it authorizes appeals to considered beliefs as a legitimate way to test moral principle, dies at its own hands, so to speak? For no reasonable person would suppose that the dog has a "right to life" that is equal to the humans' or that the animal should be given an equal chance in the lottery for survival.[9]

9. Ibid., pp. 285–286.

Regan postpones the discussion of the example to a later section of the book, where he sides with the common sense view that the dog should be thrown overboard.

> Death for the dog, in short, though a harm, is not comparable to the harm that death would be for any of the humans.[10]

Regan arrives at this conclusion in a fallacious manner, it seems to me. He appears to conceive of the situation as a situation where different rights *conflict*. And he has devised solutions to such problems (innocent shields, and so forth). However, in the situation at hand—just as in the case where the wolf attacks a human being—there is no conflict of rights. If we allow the wolf to kill the human, no violation of any rights has taken place. The same could be said about his thought experiment. There are many ways of solving the problem without violating any rights. As he himself suggests, the four men can device a survival lottery, and throw overboard him who draws the 'winning' ticket. They are not allowed to involve the dog in the lottery, however, since the dog cannot consent. If they do not want to construct a survival lottery, any one among the four men can volunteer and *jump* overboard. Or, finally, if no one is prepared to do so, they may well go under together, without any violation of rights.

So even if the fact that Regan's rights are merely prima facie rights allows for some situations where one right has to yield in the interest of another—where, in order to stop violations of rights we have to violate some rights—the case at hand is not an example of this.

If I am right about this it means that the moral rights theorist of Regan's variety should bite the bullet here and claim that it is the *dog* that possesses a privileged position in the thought experiment. He cannot rightfully be thrown overboard, he cannot give consent

10. Ibid., p. 324.

to any survival lottery, and it is unlikely that he should 'volunteer' and sacrifice his life. If any one among the men survives, so does he.

3.5. Problematic Aspects of the Theory

The moral rights theory may be the last word on animal ethics. However, there are some points that are likely to attract critical comments, in particular for those who would rather favour a utilitarian answer to the practical problems here discussed. The objections would mainly be as follows.

First of all, even though Regan himself believes that all mammals pass his subject-of-a-life test, he may be wrong about this (non-moral, factual matter). And even if he is right, there are non-human sentient animals that do not pass the test (as he admits). They are not protected by his favoured moral theory. This does not mean that we ought to treat them with cruelty, but his theory does not *as such* protect them against cruel treatment. This may seem problematic.

A way of mitigating the problem may be to claim that, in order to err on the safe side, we should treat these individuals *as if* they had passed the test. This is a claim made by Regan. Hence, for example, we should treat frogs as if they were moral patients. It is not quite clear why we should do so, it seems to me, and progress in animal psychology can lead to the conclusion that we may safely leave them out. Is that acceptable?

A problem, many have thought, with the moral rights theory, in Nozick's version of it, has been that it is so complacent with regard to suffering. It allows me to live high while others starve to death, if I am not responsible for their plight. This permits Nozick to contend that rights claims never conflict with one another, which may be an intellectual virtue. However, the complacency in relation to suffering may be seen as a moral vice. Regan's version of the moral rights theory goes some way towards meeting this kind of objection, and he pays the intellectual price of having to admit that rights can come into conflict. Hence, they are only of a prima facie nature. However, it should be noted that perhaps Regan does not go far enough. He claims that we have an obligation to assist those who have their rights violated, but he does not think that we have an obligation to help moral patients who are just in *need* of help. If they suffer from natural disasters, we need not assist them. Could that be correct?

One could, of course, add even more obligations to help, a possibility Regan himself opens for in the preface to the 2004 edition of his book. But then one is in danger of having one's moral rights theory collapsing into utilitarianism, the idea to be examined in the next section.

4. UTILITARIANISM

According to the Sanctity-of-Life Doctrine, you have moral standing if you are a human being, and according to the moral rights theory, you have moral standing if you are a moral agent (or, in Regan's version of it, at least a moral *patient*). Utilitarians rarely use the notion of an individual having moral standing. However, in a manner of speaking, an individual has moral standing, according to utilitarianism, if he is capable of pleasurable or painful experiences. If he is, then what happens to him can affect the moral status of an action causing this to happen. Who has this capacity? Obviously, human beings, but also many animals as well. This is what Jeremy Bentham famously had to say about the moral status of animals:

> The day *may* come when the rest of the animal creation may acquire those rights which never could have been witholden from them but by the hand of tyranny. The French have already discovered that the blackness of the skin is no reason why a human being should be abandoned without redress to the caprice of a tormentor. It may one day come to be recognized, that the number of the legs, the villosity of the skin, or the termination of the *os sacrum*, are reasons equally insufficient for abandoning a sensitive being to the same fate? What else

> is it that should trace the insuperable line? Is it the faculty of reason, or, perhaps, the faculty of discourse? But a full-grown horse or dog, is beyond comparison a more rational, as well as a more conversable animal, than an infant of a day or a week, or even a month, old. But suppose they were otherwise, what would it avail? the question is not, Can they *reason*? nor, Can they *talk*? but, Can they *suffer*?[11]

What is presupposed by utilitarianism, we remember, is that each sentient being, at each time, is at a certain level of happiness. We may speak of this as the hedonic situation of the individual. What matters to the hedonic situation of an individual at a certain time is how the situation at this time is experienced by this individual. Does it feel better than a moment ago? Does it feel roughly the same? Or does it feel worse? An individual for which questions like these are meaningful possesses moral standing according to utilitarianism.

The core claim of utilitarianism is that we ought to maximize the sum total of happiness. As we remember from the chapter on abortion, there are two ways to improve the hedonistic situation in the world: you can make existing individuals happier, or you can make happy (additional) individuals. This is important to keep in mind when we turn to questions about the raising and killing of animals for food.

4.1. The Raising and Slaughtering of Animals for Food

According to deontology we are allowed, if we like, to raise and slaughter non-human animals for food—just because they are non-human or lack rationality. According to the moral rights theory in Tom Regan's form we are not allowed to do so, since the very killing of the animals, to the extent that they are moral patients, is

11. Jeremy Bentham, *Principles of Morals and Legislation*, p. 282b.

wrong. These animals have moral rights. What is the verdict given by utilitarianism?

When we raise animals for food, we don't just raise them and then eat them. In between, we kill them. Now, mammals and birds, at least, have moral standing (they are most likely sentient). Is it a problem, as such, to kill a sentient being? It is not, according to utilitarianism.

A basic claim in utilitarianism is that there is no 'natural' type of action that is wrong as such. This is true, as we remember from a previous chapter, also of murder. An act of killing is right if and only if it maximizes the sum total of happiness in the universe. Hence, Bentham does, as one would have expected, defend the killing of animals for food:

> If the being eaten were all, there is very good reason why we should be suffered to eat such of them as we like to eat: we are the better for it, and they are never the worse. They have none of those long protracted anticipations of future misery which we have. The death they suffer in our hands commonly is, and always may be, a speedier, and by that means a less painful one, than that which would await them in the inevitable course of nature.[12]

It is not crystal clear what Bentham means here, but, to make best sense of him, I take it that his reference to the fact that animals do not anticipate future misery means that, even if we raise them for food, this is not something that will render their lives worse (they will know nothing about their future). Furthermore, when one animal is killed, another one is brought up instead of it, seeing to it that no loss of happiness is caused by its death.

Now, even if we may raise, kill, and eat animals, according to utilitarianism, this is not to say that any *way* of killing animals is acceptable. If we raise them for food and hence kill them, it is

12. Ibid.

crucial that they are provided with a good death, as was alluded to by Bentham. This is of importance to humans as well. Thus, utilitarians, we remember, have typically defended euthanasia and physician-assisted suicide for human beings. They have argued that, while killing in general, if it were allowed, would create fear in society, this is not true of a regulated use of euthanasia and physician-assisted suicide. This is a controversial claim, of course, but one often made by utilitarians. And, as noted by Bentham, the killing of animals causes no similar fear among those to be killed.

Now, if killing is not a problem as such, according to utilitarianism, what are we to say about the living conditions that are provided to animals raised for food? Are they acceptable? In most cases, they are certainly not. What conclusion should we draw from this? Should we draw the conclusion that their conditions ought to be improved? Or, should we draw the conclusion that animals should not be raised for food?

To the total hedonistic utilitarian, accepting the 'repugnant' conclusion discussed in the chapter on abortion, the answer to the question depends first and foremost on the answer to another question: do the animals we raise for food live, on average, above or below the line where life begins to be worth experiencing?

Note that the animals we raise for food are 'additional' sentient beings. They would not exist at all, if it were not for our interest in eating them. So it is crucial to know whether their addition means an addition of happiness or pain.

On the one hand, if we make the pessimistic assumption that their lives are typically below the line, and if we add that so they will remain even if we make all sorts of improvements on their situation, then it seems that vegetarianism follows from utilitarianism. On the other hand, if we make the more optimistic assumption that their lives are above the line, then our utilitarian obligation is to raise, kill, and eat them.

This does not mean that, according to utilitarianism, we should be complacent in relation to their moments of suffering, of course. I suppose the most reasonable tactics for a utilitarian who believes that the lives of the animals we raise for food typically are above the line, but who feels that much improvement of their lot is possible, would be to be picky as consumers and demanding as citizens. The message sent from this kind of picky consumer and demanding citizen is that unless the animals are provided with a good life and a good death, she will not consume them. This kind of utilitarian would also vote for parties promising to legislate in defence of animal well-being.

It is sometimes objected to the utilitarian defence of raising and eating animals that it seems to work just as well for a practice where we raise and eat fellow human beings. The utilitarian answer to this objection is that, indeed, there is no *principled* difference here. So if a utilitarian defends the eating of non-human animals, but not the eating of human beings, it has nothing to do with principles but everything to do with side effects. However, the ban against killing (murder) human beings is based on a very *strong* rationale. If we started to kill one another, for food or any other reason, society would turn into a terrible place where *everyone* would be utterly unhappy.

4.2. The Use of Animals in Experiments

The use of animals in experiments is in some way similar to the use of animals for food. To the utilitarian, the same question as to their conditions of life and death obtain. Typically, their death is not so problematic. They are 'put down', or 'euthanized', we say. Their typical living conditions, however, are worse than the living conditions of animals we raise for food, or at least this seems to be so with a part of their lives. This has to do with the experiments we conduct on them. The magnitude of the problem, if indeed it is a problem, is also enormous. Only in the United States, some ten billion animals are utilized each year for medical experiments.[13]

13. I have the figure from Peter Singer's *Animal Liberation*.

I have, for many years, taught courses in animal ethics for people who do research on animals, and each time I see a new class I ask them for their opinion: do they believe that the animals they experiment on are living, on average, above or below the line where life is worth experiencing? Even in Sweden, where a comparatively strict animal protection legislation exists, they have usually and shockingly responded that their animals live below the line.

Supposing they are right, does that mean, if we assess the matter from the point of view of utilitarianism, that we should opt for the abolition of animal experimentation? We now have a strong utilitarian presumption in favour of abolition, of course, but there is more to be said about the case. For while in the raising of animals for food there is little of value we can put in the *other* scale, as it were, there is much in relation to experimentation on animals. It is not difficult for human beings to become vegetarians or vegans. Some would claim that doing so would mean an improved quality of life, not a genuine sacrifice. The abolition of animal experimentation would mean a loss in terms of both human and non-human happiness, however. I think here of the retarding effects on the development of medicine.

However, if it turns out that the pessimistic assessment of animal welfare in animal experiments is correct, then, of course, it is according to utilitarianism mandatory to abolish all experiments that are not *crucial* to medical development. In many situations it is possible to find other, even better, alternatives to experiments on animals. Moreover, just as there is much room for improvement of the lot of animals we raise for food, this is certainly true of the animals we use for experiments as well.

Even on the pessimistic assessment of the quality of the lives of the animals on which experiments are performed, there may be some room for such experiments, if utilitarianism is true. The gain for others may be so important that they render reasonable the sacrifice of these animals. It should be noted, however, that to the extent that we can find willing human beings who are prepared to undergo the experiments in question, this might be preferable, on the utilitarian view. It is preferable in that they can console themselves, when they suffer, that they have agreed to this, and with the thought that there is meaning in their suffering. Moreover, to the extent that we perform the experiment in order to find out about the effects on humans of certain drugs, it is better to perform the experiments on humans directly, rather than making shaky analogy arguments from how the drugs affect non-human animals.

4.3. Wild Life

The difference between utilitarianism, on the one hand, and all other theories discussed in this book, on the other, is most pronounced in relation to wild life. Neither on the Sanctity-of-Life Doctrine, nor on the moral rights theory of Regan's variety, need we assume responsibility for wildlife. This is how Tom Regan puts the point:

> our ruling obligation with regard to wild animals is to *let them be*, an obligation grounded in a recognition of their general competence to get on with the business of living, a competence that we find among members of both predator and prey species.[14]

The utilitarian must view what happens in wildlife very differently. What happens in wildlife is indeed of moral concern, according to utilitarianism. When there is famine among the antelopes, the utilitarian sees a problem. It is as bad when wild animals suffer from natural causes, as it is when they are treated badly in the food industry. To the moral rights theorist, as we see in the quote above, it is not a moral problem when the wolf kills the lamb. It is a problem from the point of view of utilitarianism, however. If there is anything one can do about it, one should not hesitate to do it.

Is there anything we can do about animal suffering in wildlife? There was a time when many said that nothing should be done to obviate human suffering, since attempts to establish a welfare state

14. *Preface*, p. xxxvi.

would either be in vain, jeopardize what kind of welfare there happens to exist, or produce perverse (even worse) results.[15] We rarely meet with that reaction any more. However, many seem to be ready to argue that wildlife constitutes such a complex system of ecological balances that any attempt to interfere must produce no good results, put into jeopardy whatever ecological 'balances' there happen to exist, or perversely make the situation even worse. This is not the place to settle whether they are right or not, but, certainly, there must exist *some* measures we could take, if we bothered to do so, rendering wildlife at least *slightly* less terrible. If this were so, we should do so, according to utilitarianism.

5. A TENTATIVE CONCLUSION

It seems that people, including them philosophers, have become growingly sceptical with regard to anthropocentrism. So to the extent that people still cling to the Sanctity-of-(Human)-Life Doctrine today, they are prepared to see it, not as the whole of morality, but merely as a part of it. They feel that things other than human beings have moral standing. Hence, there is a tendency to better treatment of at least some animals. The fact that such a move has no rationale in the Sanctity-of-Life Doctrine itself, or in deontology in general, poses a problem for the doctrine (for deontology), it seems to me. The moral rights theory may seem to be the theory that gives the strongest protection possible to nonhuman animals. However, appearances may be deceptive. For the sake of the argument, I granted Regan the assumption that most mammals actually pass his subject-of-a-life test. However, the mere hypothetical fact that, if they did not, they would lack moral standing is problematic for the theory, it seems to me. It is a problem for the theory that there is logical space available for creatures who do not pass the test but who can suffer. This logical space is probably filled in reality, if

15. See Albert O. Hirschman, *The Rhetoric of Reaction*, about this line of thought.

not by mammals, so at least with members of other species. Should their suffering count for nothing?

Utilitarianism gives a more nuanced picture of our obligations towards nonhuman animals. It is a strong intuition on my part that a suffering animal, whom I am capable of helping, puts a heavy moral demand on me. And I see no reason to debunk this intuition.

Many may find some of the implications from utilitarianism absurd, though. In particular, I have noted, many people find the idea that we should reform the living conditions of animals in wild-life ridiculous. However, we should bear in mind that the same used to be said about the ideas of those who, some centuries ago, started to argue in defence of the welfare state.

Chapter 12

What Are We to Believe?

1. TAKING STOCK

Time has come to take stock. As I have insisted, justification begins and ends at home. Hence, I will now give a list of some (of my) considered moral intuitions, gathered from various chapters of this book. The idea is to see if there is anyone among the three theories that is compatible with them (or even implies them). We can then say that this theory explains them. If there is more than one theory fitting the considered intuitions, the one that best explains them gains inductive support from them (by an inference to the best explanation). As I explained in the first chapter of the book, I will tolerate no recalcitrant evidence. One single intuition at variance with a theory is sufficient to refute the theory, unless we can explain away this intuition as somehow mistaken. Or, at the very least, we should be prepared to claim that it *must* be mistaken, even if we cannot (yet) explain why this is so.

In the theory of science we speak of the 'empirical content' of a theory. This is the set of all (possible) observations implied by the theory. In a similar vein, we may speak of the intuitive content of a normative theory. This is the set of all (possible) considered intuitions implied by the theory. In order to be empirically adequate, the theory should not be at variance with any of our actual observations. In a similar vein, in order to be intuitively adequate, a normative theory should not be at variance with any of our actual considered intuitions.

It is sometimes held that two theories can be empirically equivalent (they have the same empirical content), and yet be different.[1] This is in an *obvious* manner the case with normative theories. Even two theories that are intuitively adequate and intuitively equivalent can yield different implications in a field where we hold no intuitions whatever. There we must just *deduce* what to do. It is indeed a problem in normative ethics that this is the case. This partly explains, I believe, why it is so difficult to reach agreement about normative theories. Our evidential base for them is very slim, but their implications are very broad in scope. Still, if we hold a justified belief in a moral theory, it is reasonable to follow its verdicts on unknown cases, even if these verdicts may seem strange to us. Think, for example, about the Footbridge case in a preceding chapter on the trolley cases. If my argument is correct, then we have no considered intuitions about it. Both the intuition that it is wrong to push the big man and the intuition that it is all right to push him have been debunked. This means that, in the case, we must rely on the implication from the theory that has, in the cases where we do have access to considered intuitions, been confirmed. We must act on it in the hope that it gives us the right answer. Or, so I will argue at the end of this chapter.

After having gone through all the examples provided in the book, I will also ponder the possibility that there may exist a combination of elements from the three theories that is superior to any one of them viewed in isolation. This possibility is especially important to consider if each theory faces at least one recalcitrant intuition, inconsistent with it. As we will see, this is the case. Utilitarianism fares best in the competition. And yet, for all that, there seems to exist at least one intuition that does indeed provide recalcitrant evidence even to utilitarianism, at least on a superficial understanding of the matter. So we had better try out the possibility that what

1. See, for example, Lars Bergström, 'Quine, Underdetermination, and Skepticism', on this.

could be called a common sense morality, combining elements from the three theories here under scrutiny, fares any better.

Here are some of my considered intuitions concerning the various different kinds of killing I have discussed. Most of these intuitions are inconsistent with *some* of the three theories; that is part of the explanation of why I present them. I have looked for *crucial* experiments. In some cases I also present intuitions consistent with all three of the theories. Then the problem is, of course, to see which one of them can best explain them.

In each section I start by myself answering the questions I have posed to the Chinese, the Russians, and the Americans. I hold firm and considered intuitions about most of them. That is part of my reason for choosing to include them in my survey. I here present my intuitions, after I have delved into the kind of cognitive psychotherapy I advocate. As we have seen, there are many ways in which it is possible to explain away seemingly recalcitrant evidence. However, as we have also seen, there is a limit to how this can be done.

2. MY CONSIDERED INTUITIONS

2.1. The Trolley Cases

The trolley cases have been thought to avoid some kinds of cultural bias; they are cast in terms that should not trigger any cultural idiosyncrasies. And yet, in my survey, the Chinese differed. The Chinese turned out to be much less utilitarian in their responses than the Russians or the Americans. So perhaps there is need also in relation to these examples to try, not only to avoid cognitive mistakes, but also to transcend one's limited cultural horizon. Here are my considered intuitions in relation to them.

(1) A trolley is running down a track. In its path are five people who have been tied to the track. It is possible for you to flip a switch, which will lead the trolley down a different track. There is a single

person tied to that track. You ought to flip the switch and have one person killed in order to save the five.

This intuition is compatible with deontology, at least in the form of the Sanctity-of-Life Doctrine. When you kill the one you merely foresee his death. You do not intend it. And there is a reasonable proportion between what you merely foresee (his death) and what you intend (to save the five). It is also consistent with Kantianism in that you do not kill intentionally and by flipping the switch you fulfil your imperfect duty of beneficence. It is also of note that you do not use the person on the side-track as a (mere) means. He plays no causal role when you save the five. My considered intuition is also consistent with utilitarianism. It is at variance with the moral rights theory, however. Not only have you a right *not* to interfere, on that theory, it is *wrong* to interfere. If you flip the switch, you actively kill one person. You have no right to do so, not even in order to save the five.

(2) As in (1), you can divert the trolley onto a separate track. On this track is a single big man. However, beyond the big man, this track loops back onto the main line towards the five, and if it weren't for the presence of the big man, turning the switch would not save the five. You ought to flip the switch and have the big man killed in order to save the five.

As we remember, (2) conflicts with the moral rights theory but it is consistent not only with utilitarianism, but also with deontology if it is cast in the form of the Sanctity-of-Life Doctrine, at least if this doctrine is taken to include the principle of double effect in its standard (very liberal) interpretation. However, there is also a Kantian understanding of deontology, prohibiting that we use human beings as mere means, even to very noble causes (such as the saving of lives). In that version, deontology is inconsistent with (2). I haven't been able to debunk my intuition that it is right to flip the switch in the Loop. I here side with the majority.

I explained in the previous chapter that there exist no considered intuitions in relation to the Footbridge. It goes against our gut feelings if we are invited to save the five by pushing a big man onto the track, using him as a means to save the five. However, this reaction to upfront physical killing is most reasonably seen as produced by a kind of heuristic device selected for us by evolution. The device provides us with the right answer in most ordinary situations. That's why it is there and that is also why it, morally speaking, is a good idea to try to keep it. However, in an isolated thought experiment, when we want to know the truth, it is not reliable.

Some people believe that it is right to push the big man onto the tracks in order to save the five. I belong to this group. And yet, I do not count this as a considered intuition. I think I have just *deduced* this conclusion from my favoured moral theory (utilitarianism). There is some evidence for this: I hesitate. I *think* it is right to kill the big man in order to save the five but still, it is my gut *feeling* that this is horrific!

2.2. Murder

Remember how murder was defined. **Murder** is the active, intentional, and not requested for killing, performed not in self-defence, of another human being without legal sanction, not performed under the influence of any serious mental disorder rendering the act unavoidable to the agent. It is of note that, while the killings in the trolley cases did not involve any intention to kill an innocent human (rational) being, this is indeed the case with murder. Here are my considered intuitions with regard to murder.

(4) A woman is stalked by her ex-husband. He does not threaten to kill her, but he never leaves her alone and she thinks that this makes life meaningless for her. She asks the police for help but receives none. She then kills her ex. She comes forward and assumes responsibility for her action, but claims that she had no choice. It *is* possible that she did the right thing.

It is my considered intuition that (4) is true. I see no reason to believe that I have been deceived by any cultural bias; as a matter of fact, many people in the culture where I have been brought up disagree. In the survey, a majority of Chinese, Russians, and Americans disagree. And I think, moreover, that the reason she may have done the right thing has to do with the fact that her life was ruined by her ex, as well as by thoughts to the effect that her ex must have been a nuisance to other people as well. For me that settles the matter. If he ruined her life, if he ruined other lives, and if he himself led a poor life, then it seems likely that it was all right to murder him.

What do I have to say to people who disagree? My conjecture is that they have conflated the question of whether, in general, it is a good thing to act on an intention like the present one (intentionally to kill a fellow human being) with the question of what it is that renders these actions wrong. In general, it is bad to act on this intention. If you do, you will probably act wrongly more often than rightly. However, it is not the bad intention as such that makes these actions wrong, I claim. What *makes* them wrong should refer to what happens to the patient, not to what is present in the mind of the agent! It might even be the case that those who disagree *define* 'wrong action' as an action produced by a motive one should not in general act from (such as an intention to kill a fellow human being). But if this is so, they cannot explain the wrongness of the act with reference to the motive. Our seeming difference of opinion is merely verbal. We speak at cross-purposes.

Here a comment on Nagel's claim about evil intentions is in place. His claim was, we remember, that 'to aim at evil, even as a means, is to have one's action guided by evil . . . But the essence of evil is that it should *repel* . . . so when we aim at evil we are swimming head-on against the normative current'.[2] In some cases, even a murderer may satisfy this requirement. If, as a matter of fact, it is wrong not to save lives, even when this must be done by killing an innocent individual, to kill intentionally is not to be guided by evil. Even a utilitarian can grant this. If the motive is to save as many lives as possible, and if killing an innocent is not wrong *as such*, then this is fine. Moreover, there are of course cases where people act wrongly, without any evil intention. Think of the executioner who kills an

2. *The View from Nowhere*, pp. 181–182.

innocent person in the belief that he is guilty. I have here used the phrase 'blameless wrongdoing' to account for this. The notion has a place both in utilitarian and deontological thought. However, there may also, according to utilitarianism, and in contradistinction to deontology, exist cases where a person kills intentionally, and without any thought of saving lives, such as where someone kills someone else only to inherit his belongings, and where this, according to utilitarianism, is all right. It is not all right to possess such a motive, of course, but the act that flows from it may, in a singular instance, happen to be right (it maximizes the sum total of happiness in the universe).

Is this counterintuitive? If we think so, then it might be helpful to rely on the notion of *blameful rightdoing*. It has a secure place in utilitarian thinking. And once there, it is not difficult, I think, to concede that even a murder, performed from a nasty motive, may in a singular instance be all right.

There are two ways of reading Nagel. He can be seen as making a claim about each particular case where someone acts from an evil intention. I guess that this would be his own favourite reading of the passage. In this case his claim must be rejected by the utilitarian. However, he can also be seen as giving a more general prescription. Then the utilitarian need not disagree with him. At least as a general rule of thumb, one had better not have one's actions guided by nasty motives that are likely to result in wrongdoing more often than not. In that sense, what is evil *should* repel us. In this the utilitarian may concur.

(5) If I can save lives, by committing a singular murder, and if there are no bad side effects, I ought to commit this murder.

Again, this is a considered intuition I hold, and it is unlikely that it should be the result of any cultural bias. I hold it in relation to the example I formulated in an earlier chapter, of the mother who saved the lives of her children by killing one of them. I have the same intuition in relation to Bernard Williams's famous example with Jim and the Indians. And even if the motive of this mother need not be an evil one, it is perhaps an inappropriate one for a mother to have in relation to one of her children. But then the conclusion is not that what she did was wrong, but rather that it was a case of blameful rightdoing.

Have I just deduced the content of this intuition from my favourite moral view, utilitarianism? Remember that if I have done so, it should be discarded. It's not that it must be false, in this case. The problem is that it has no independent evidential value. I think not, however. The intuition is more basic. My belief that it is correct sometimes to murder in order to save lives is *much* stronger than my belief in utilitarianism. It is of note that some non-utilitarian thinkers, such as Bernard Williams himself, also share this intuition. According to Williams, it may well be all right to kill one single innocent individual in order to save many others. His objection is not to (5) as such—as we have seen. His objection is that a utilitarian reaches this conclusion only too swiftly.

What should help those who believe that it was wrong of the mother to kill one of her children to the conclusion that it was right, after all, is mainly the observation that it may be wrong to develop a character allowing for this kind of killing. Once the notions or blameless wrongdoing and blameful rightdoing are in place, (4) and (5) may seem to be true, after all.

While (4) and (5) are implied by utilitarianism, they are inconsistent, in an obvious way, with both deontology and the moral rights theory.

Here is a third example of murder, condoned by deontology and the moral rights theory, but at variance with utilitarianism:

(6) A person is terminally ill, the rest of his life will provide him with much more suffering than pleasure, he realizes this, he is as clever and knowledgeable as I, but he still wants to go on with his life, claiming that he is not a hedonistic utilitarian; he is prepared to endure, he claims. Under the circumstances, it would be wrong to kill him (merely in his own interest), even if this could be done in a manner that is painless and not noticeable to him.

I do indeed hold this intuition, and it is problematic to hold it if you want to be a utilitarian. It is tempting to believe that it is hedonism that is the problem. It is not; it is utilitarianism that is the issue. For each version of utilitarianism, where things other than happiness are taken to matter, one can construct similar (and much worse) examples. For instance, according to utilitarianism of a kind where objective perfectionist values are the only things that count, it would be right to kill a person who wants to go on with his life, and who will be happy in doing so, but who would not excel in any way; this would be the case even if she wants to stay alive (claiming that she is a hedonist)! Some people make living wills with this intent. If I become happily demented, and do not recognize my close ones any more, they stipulate, then kill me. I find *that* horrific.

Is (6) the result of cultural bias? I doubt that. I hold so many other ideas that are at variance with the culture in which I have been brought up. So why should I not be able to give up this one, in the manner I have given up many other ideas into which I was inculcated?

Is it a result of some cognitive mistake? I cannot think of anyone right now. Hence, for the time being, I take it for a fact.

(7) Murder ought to be legally prohibited.

This again is a considered intuition. It is indeed part of the culture in which I have been brought up, but I do not see it as idiosyncratic. It seems to be part and parcel of *all* civilized cultures, and the best explanation for this fact is that, indeed, murder *ought* to be legally prohibited.

Where does this leave our three moral theories? Deontology and utilitarianism agree on one point: (7). The moral rights theory, in contradistinction, can *accept* that murder is rendered criminal, but it does not imply that murder *ought* to be criminal. According to the theory, we may stay in state of nature with regard to murder if, for some reason, we see fit to do so.

Moreover, while deontology and utilitarianism concur in the claim that murder ought to be legally prohibited, they give different reasons for this claim. According to deontology, murder should be universally forbidden because it is universally wrong. The utilitarian rationale behind the prohibition is different. It has to do with the fear we would all feel in a society where murder was (sometimes) legally permitted.

No theory in my competition, as I have set it up, can cater for all four of my considered intuitions with regard to murder. The moral rights theory does not even imply (7). It allows that we render murder illegal but it does not require it. Deontology and the moral rights theory are in conflict with (4) and (5), moreover, while utilitarianism implies (4) and (5). Deontology and the moral rights theory imply (6), while utilitarianism is at variance with (6). So *no* theory is intuitively adequate in its handling of murder, at least not on the superficial treatment I have given them here. I will return to the problem below, however.

2.3. Capital Punishment

Here are my considered intuitions with regard to capital punishment.

(8) If it could be shown beyond reasonable doubt that the death penalty reduces the number of murders, then capital punishment would be morally acceptable.

This is my considered intuition. It is not the result of any cultural bias. I have, in fact, been brought up as a principled *opponent* of capital punishment. The content of this intuition has not been derived from any basic moral belief, either. It has its own credence. I came to believe in it when I pondered seriously the question with fresh eyes. I then came to think of those who would not be murdered if we were to execute some murderers, as well as of those who would not, for the same reason, become murderers. I *sympathize* with them. That's it.

(9) If it could be shown, beyond reasonable doubt, that the death penalty does not reduce the number of murders, then capital punishment would not be morally acceptable.

Here it is more difficult to avoid the suspicion that my intuition has been inculcated in me. However, even if this is the case, it survives my knowledge about its origin. Again, I sympathize with the murderers who are executed, now in vain. I see no point in this practice, under the assumption now made. And the observation that should help people who disagree to an acceptance of (9) is the following. There is no such thing as a *deserved* punishment.

One way of substantiating this claim would be as follows. The deep notion of moral desert, defended by Immanuel Kant, relies on an untenable assumption. We lack the kind of categorical freedom it requires, and which is resorted to by Kant only to save his moral theory. Of course, there are a few philosophers who defend the thesis that we possess a strong categorical kind of free will, roughly of the sort presupposed by Kant. This is true in particular of those who believe in some notion of 'agent-causality'; they pay a high intellectual price when they need to rely on this notion, however. There is no such thing as agent-causality. Others who believe in a categorical notion of free will speak about something that doesn't seem to obtain in the right kind of context. The examples they give are when a person is undecided between two options. This has been described as a 'torn decision';[3] there are pros and cons, and they seem, in her deliberation, to weigh equally heavily. In such situations she can exercise her free will and make an effective decision about what to do. However, this is, according to those who believe in this categorical kind of free will, a rare phenomenon, and it is probably not typical of premeditated murder. In premeditated murder, qualifying for the death penalty, the murder has not confronted a difficult problem with pros and cons. She has typically acted in accordance with her character and her wishes in a manner that made her action next to predicable. Hence, we lack the required form of free will.

However, even if it is tempting to argue in the manner just gestured at, I will keep to my method in the book, and not go into metaphysical and methodological problems with respective theories. I will focus exclusively on the moral implications of the theories and assume that, somehow, the metaphysical and methodological problems can be solved. Nevertheless, it strikes me as overly bloodthirsty

3. See, for example, Peter van Inwagen, 'When Will Is Not Free', and Mark Balaguer, *Free Will as an Open Scientific Problem.*

to believe in punishment, even when an evil act is the result of a free choice. It is *wrong* to punish a person when this has no good consequences whatever.

Let us suppose that human history is over. It is time for God, who assembles us resurrected individuals in order to judge us. Should She send some of us (the sinners) to Hell and others (the good guys) to Heaven? I see no reason in the circumstances for Her to send any one of us to Hell. To send even the sinners to Hell means that unnecessary suffering is inflicted on them. God, have mercy with them!

It might be that I would have reacted differently if I were myself the victim of murder, for example in the following way. One of my close ones had been brutally murdered. The murderer is caught and convicted. I may now feel that she should be killed. However, this does not strike me as a moral intuition, properly speaking. What I would now express would be a primitive and bloodthirsty *desire* for revenge. Such a desire for revenge cannot be properly articulated as a moral *judgement* at all. Hence, it cannot be the content of any moral intuition, let alone a considered one.

(8) is implied by both deontology in its retributivist (Kantian) version and utilitarianism, while (9) is at variance with deontology in the same retributive version. On the non-retributivist version of the Sanctity-of-Life Doctrine (upheld by the present pope, for example), it is consistent with (9) but inconsistent with (8). All this spells problems for deontology. It is either, in its Kantian retributivist version, much too bloodthirsty—it wants murderers to be executed, even if there is no deterrent effect of the practice—or it is too squeamish cast in the present non-retributivist version of the Sanctity-of-Life Doctrine, in that it wants to spare the murderers, even if the price is more murders (and more murderers).

If taken at face value the moral rights theory is in conflict with (8); there is no room whatever for either desert or deterrence in this theory. However, as we saw in the chapter on capital punishment, there are indirect routes to an acceptance of capital punishment, if the moral rights theory is taken as our point of departure. People may contract and arrange with a legal system where capital punishment forms a part. This means that the moral rights theory is at variance with the following considered intuition of mine:

(10) It is wrong to execute murderers, even if we have all agreed on a system where capital punishment is practiced, if the system being in place doesn't reduce the number of murders in society.

2.4. Suicide

Remember how we defined suicide. To commit **suicide**, then, is intentionally to kill oneself (for whatever reason) when one could have abstained from doing so; one's killing of oneself was either active or passive; the killing happened in a situation where one could have gone on with one's life for an indefinite time.

Here are my considered intuitions with regard to suicide.

(11) There are situations where it is morally permissible to commit suicide.

This is at variance with deontology but consistent with the moral rights theory and utilitarianism.

(12) If it would mean very bad consequences for your close ones if you commit suicide, you should abstain, unless your own life is truly terrible.

This is at variance with the moral rights theory but consistent with utilitarianism.

(13) If Schopenhauer is right and life is always terrible, then we ought all to commit suicide.

This is at variance with both deontology (prohibiting suicide) and the moral rights theory (allowing that we go on with our lives even if they are terrible). It is implied by utilitarianism.

(14) Suicide is a morally acceptable method, if no other method works, to draw attention to political oppression and to instigate resistance to tyranny.

In this both the moral rights theory and utilitarianism concur. This intuition is at variance with deontology, however.

Utilitarianism, and utilitarianism only, can cater for *all* my considered intuitions regarding suicide.

2.5. Assisted Death

Assisted death, in the form where a physician kills a terminal patient at request (euthanasia), is legally allowed only in three countries, the Netherlands, Belgium, and Luxemburg. And yet there is a majority supporting assisted death in all the examined countries, China, Russia, and the United States. I concur in this majority view:

(15) A person who suffers from an incurable fatal disease and who doesn't want to live any more should have the right to request and receive a lethal injection that terminates his or her life.

In this the moral rights theory concurs. The intuition is at variance with deontology, however. It is consistent with utilitarianism.

(16) If the legalization of euthanasia would bring with it very bad side effects, it should not take place.

This is consistent with deontology and utilitarianism, but inconsistent with the moral rights theory. If indeed legislation has bad side effects, then utilitarians and deontologists both agree that the suffering people who are denied euthanasia have to undergo is of a 'morally necessary' kind. Moral rights theory advocates legislation *regardless* of such bad side effects and sides with the individual patient. This means, however, that the moral rights theory is far too liberal in its assessment of euthanasia, just as it is in its assessment of suicide. It pays no respect to negative external effects of such actions and practices. But these negative external effects, if they were to surface, even if they would not constitute any boundary-crossings, would be morally relevant. Deontology is too conservative, however, when it condemns all kinds of assisted death. This is so even if it, in the form of the Sanctity-of-Life Doctrine, leaves room for some cases of not intended but merely foreseen hastening of death.

2.6. Survival Lotteries

Survival lotteries play a considerable role in philosophers' thinking on the ethics of killing. They have also entered the popular culture. They are not popular, however. Yet they seem to be reasonable, if only we can set some of our taboos to one side. Here are some of my considered intuitions with regard to them:

(17) Some people are stranded on a desert island. They have no food. In order to survive they arrange a lottery. Everyone agrees to take part in the lottery. The person who draws the winning ticket is killed and eaten by the rest. Half of the group survives because of the lottery. It would be morally permissible to arrange and take part in the lottery.

Similarly, we should welcome John Harris's organ lottery, if we had the guts to put it into place:

(18) If there are no bad side effects, then it is right to arrange with a lottery where organs for transplant purposes are distributed in a manner guaranteeing better survival expectancy for all who take part in it.

I suppose that Gilbert Harman designed *his* thought experiment in order to tease out something other than my considered intuition to it, but here it is:

(19) You have five patients in the hospital who are dying, each in need of a separate organ. One needs a kidney, another a lung, a third a heart, and so forth. You can save all five if you take a single healthy person and remove his heart, lungs, kidneys, and so forth, to distribute to these five patients. Just such a healthy person is in room 306. He is in hospital for routine tests. Having seen his test results, you know that he is perfectly healthy and of the right tissue compatibility. If you do nothing he will survive without incident; the other patients will die, however. The other five patients can be saved only if the person in Room 306 is cut up and his organs distributed. In that case, there would be one dead but five saved. If there are no bad side effects, you ought to kill the patient in Room 306 and save the other five.

This is close to Harman's thought experiment discussed earlier in the book. I have made one addition to it, however, needed in order to allow me to reach the conclusion that the doctor ought to kill the patient and save the other five. There should be no bad side effects. For some reason, Harman did not add that clause himself. And it is a big if, of course, when *I* assume in the example that there are no bad side effects. In real life we must assume that there are such bad side effects. What should help those who disagree to agree with me is the usual observation made over and over in the book: it might be a good idea to not allow yourself to become a person who is capable of doing what the doctor does in the example. His action is an example of blameful rightdoing. Medical doctors should be trained not to do the right thing in circumstances such as the one described by Harman. Yet what he does *is* the right thing.

It should furthermore be noted that Harman, when he designs his thought experiment, violates what I have called a requirement of impartiality. He invites the reader to think what he would be prepared to do, were he in the *doctor's* position. Why not instead ask what you would think the doctor should do, if you had been one of the patients in need of an organ? But even better would have been to cast the case in impartial terms. And it should of course be added to the description of the case that there are no bad side effects.[4] Otherwise we let the utilitarian off the hook only too easily.

Anyway, *my* considered intuition is that the doctor did the right thing, provided there were no bad side effects (other than the death of the patient whose organs were removed). And my conjecture is that those who disagree fail to take seriously the claim that there are no bad side effects (since it is hard to imagine that, in a health-care setting, such bad side effects are indeed not present; if the case became known, this would surely put an end to transplant surgery for a long time).

I commented in the chapter on survival lotteries that Harman's case is similar to the Footbridge one discussed in the chapter on the trolley cases. One should expect that the same heuristic device is

4. Should we expect different effects where examples are cast in the second person and in the third person? There is some evidence to the effect that, at least among non-philosophers, this makes a difference. See Thomas Nadelhoffer and Adam Feltz, 'The actor-observer bias and moral intuitions: Adding fuel to Sinnott-Armstrong's fire' about this.

operative here. And this should give pause to those who place a heavy burden on the example in their argument against utilitarianism.

It is also of note that, here as in the Footbridge case, we need not impute any intention to *kill* to the person who performs the life-saving action. The death of the anaesthetized patient, when his vital organs are removed, is a merely foreseen but not wanted side effect of the surgery. Hence, if one should search for a principled opposition to what the doctor did, it would be of no avail to rely on the deontological prohibition against intentional killing of innocent people (rational beings). The Kantian doctrine, that one should not treat anyone as a mere means, implies, however, that the doctor did the wrong thing. The same is true, of course, of the moral rights theory.

(20) It should be legally prohibited to kill healthy patients in order to save patients who need organs in order to survive; if such an action would be found out, it should be punished.

Clearly, as was noted above, (19) is at variance with deontology in its Kantian version with its insistence that one should never treat a human being as a mere means, and the moral rights theory. It is consistent with, and explained, by utilitarianism and the Sanctity-of-Life Doctrine, however. All three theories are consistent with (20) but give different explanations of it. It is of note that, in a legal context, this kind of killing would probably be punished as murder; yet, on my narrow definition of murder, where murder presupposes an *intention* to kill the victim, it is not, strictly speaking, murder. From the point of view of utilitarianism this is of little importance. An act that is not an act of murder, may well be *considered* an act of murder when it comes to legal issues. It all boils down in the final analysis to the value of the consequences of the legal view taken up on the action.

(21) If I can either save one person or five persons it would be wrong to toss a coin when deciding what to do; I ought to save the five, all other things being equal.

This is consistent with deontology and utilitarianism. The moral rights theory implies that I may do as I see fit. This strikes me as absurd.

2.7. Abortion

I asked people in my survey the following question: *If a woman feels that she doesn't want to take care of her expected child, is it then morally permissible for her to have an abortion?* While the Russians were sympathetic to this idea, the Chinese and the Americans disagreed. I am not myself prepared to agree. My intuition goes some way to meet the idea that it might be right to have an abortion if you do not want to take care of the expected child, but not all the way. This is *my* considered intuition:

(22) Abortion is sometimes right, sometimes wrong, depending on the consequences for the aborted foetus (what kind of life would it have lived?), the family, and society.

I also have the considered intuition that:

(23) Abortion should be legally permitted.

As we saw in the chapter on abortion, (22) and (23) are consistent with utilitarianism. They are inconsistent with the Sanctity-of-Life Doctrine. It is consistent with deontology in its Kantian version, however. It is not straightforward how the moral rights theory would assess them. However, on one interpretation of the theory, it is consistent with it (foetuses are then denied moral standing). On another interpretation of it, only early abortions are morally unproblematic (before the foetus has acquired moral standing).

Abortion cannot be assessed unless we form considered beliefs also in population ethics. Here are some of my considered intuitions in population ethics:

(24) If you could improve the hedonic situation of an already very happy population by adding happy people to it, this is something you should do (even if the added people are not as happy as the original ones). We may speak here of benign addition.

(25) If you can level out happiness between very happy people and less happy people in a way that means that, everyone among those who are less happy gains more than everyone among those who are happier loses, and if the sum total of happiness is increased, then you should do so; if it can only be done if some happy people

(but not so happy as the existing ones after the transformation) are at the same time added to the population, then these people should indeed be added. We may once again speak of this as benign addition.

(26) If Adam and Eve have a choice to have children or not to have children, and if their choice not to have children would mean the end of sentient life while their decision to have children would mean that many generations of happy people would come to live, then it would be wrong of them not to have children.

These considered intuitions prepare the ground for an argument in defence of the 'repugnant' conclusion that, for any large and very happy population, there exists a much larger population of people living lives barely worth living, which is better. As I pointed out, I hold no considered intuition at all with regard to this comparison. And I have tried to debunk the intuition that the world with many very happy people is better. Here we are, I have claimed, in the area where we have to project our moral theory unto unknown territory.

(22)–(26) are consistent with utilitarianism and the Kantian version of deontology.

All this means that utilitarianism and Kantianism explain all my considered intuitions with regard to abortion.

2.8. Killing in War

There should be no war. This is my considered intuition:

(27) If my country would be offered guarantees for its safety and sovereignty by the United Nations, now equipped with military forces of its own, it would be in order if my government decided to disarm completely, only offering some restricted military resources to the United Nations, to keep the peace in the world.

Many people believe that a world with eternal peace is extremely utopian. They reject (27), or perhaps just the realism in the claim made in the antecedent. It is remarkable, though, that some people accept (27). Perhaps they share my optimism, as I explain it in my book on *Global Democracy. The Case for a World Government*. However, we have not yet been able to obviate war in this manner. Thus, we need to regulate war. Therefore, this is also a considered intuition I hold:

(28) Until we can create a global democracy and obviate war, we should regulate war in international law.

Furthermore, it is my belief that:

(29) Existing international law on war is *roughly* as it should be.

As we have seen, deontology has a problem with (29). Deontologists seem to need the idea that just and unjust combatants are on equal moral terms, in order to defend (29). But, according to deontology, just and unjust combatants are *not* on equal terms. They are not on equal moral terms either according to utilitarianism or the moral rights theory, but utilitarianism can yet, for all that, explain (29) with reference to the consequences of having such legislation in place. The moral rights theory has typically been thought to be in need of the moral symmetry assumption in its defence of legal regulation of jus in bello. However, this is strictly speaking not so. The moral rights theorist may well stick to the judgment that unjust combatants violate the rights of just combatants when they kill them; and yet, for all that, there is no need to legislate here. It is perfectly possible, as it were, to stay in a state of nature with regard to this kind of killing. So the moral rights theory occupies (if understood in this original manner) a middle place here. Utilitarianism explains (29), the moral rights theory is consistent with (29), but deontology is inconsistent with (29).

I also hold the moral intuition that

(30) It might be all right to take part in an unjust war, provided this means that the war ends earlier, easier, and on better terms than if it had gone on for a long time.

This intuition squares poorly with deontology and with the moral rights theory, but it is nicely explained by utilitarianism.

2.9. The Killing of Animals

I share the majority view among Chinese, Russians, and Americans that:

(31) It is morally permissible for us human beings to raise animals for food and clothing.

However, I also believe that:

(32) It is no better as such to inflict pain on non-human animals than on humans.

I also have the considered intuition that:

(33) If we humans could 'civilize' wildlife, and provide better living and dying conditions to non-human animals, then we ought to do so. We ought to side with the lamb against the wolf.

All these intuitions are in line with, and can be explained with reference to, utilitarianism. Or, so I have at least argued in the chapter on the killing of animals. We have seen that deontology has nothing to say in this area, and that the moral rights theory would at least have serious problems with (32); on a standard interpretation of it, it implies that at least most humans have moral standing while very few, if any, non-human animals have moral standing. We saw that there is one exception from this rule, to wit, Tom Regan's theory on animal rights, but we found severe internal problems with this theory. If we cast it in a consistent form, it implies that it is wrong to kill a dog in order to save a human life. This strikes me as just plain incorrect, if for no other reason than that the average life of a human being is much longer than the average life of a dog. It is of note that Tom Regan seems to concur in my intuition here, which is inconsistent with his theory when stated in a consistent manner.

This concludes my review of my considered intuitions with regard to killing. The idea is now to use (1) through (32) as premises in an inductive (or abductive) argument to the best explanation of them. We have seen that both deontology and the moral rights theory are widely off the mark, however. Utilitarianism is close to the mark. But none of these theories is intuitively adequate. In particular, there is one intuition at variance with utilitarianism:

(6) A person is terminally ill, the rest of his life will provide him with much more suffering than pleasure, he realizes this, he is as clever and knowledgeable as I, but he still wants to go on with his life, claiming that he is not a hedonistic utilitarian; he is prepared

to endure, he claims. Under the circumstances, it would be wrong to kill him (merely in his own interest), even if this could be done in a manner that is painless and not noticeable for him.

Confronted with this result, there seem to be three options available.

(A) We could accept that no theory can explain all our considered intuitions and suspend judgement; we become moral sceptics, at least with regard to moral explanation.
(B) We find some other theory, which is, after all, consistent with our consistent intuitions. The most promising candidate would be some kind of combination of the theories into a common sense morality.
(C) We find some way, after all, to debunk intuition (6).

I see (A) as a last resort. Of course, if particularism is correct—if there are *no* true moral principles, as Jonathan Dancy and others have argued[5]—then (A) is what we *must* resort to. But we should not vest any belief in particularism until we have done our best to find a true moral principle, and failed. We are not yet there.

I will first try out (B). There are different ways in which we may conceive of (B), however. One way would be to take up the stand that *all three* principles here discussed are true—but only if conceived of as principles stating *prima facie* obligations. This again, is too defensive a move, however. The problem with this idea, famously defended by W. D. Ross, is that such a system of principles is utterly lacking in intuitive content. Such a system of principles yields no definite implications in the kind of cases I have discussed in this book. The reason is that when the principles conflict, as they typically do in real life, they are silenced. It is now up to a moral judge to decide what should be done in an *absolute* sense. This is how Ross put the point:

5. See, for example, his *Moral Reasons* and *Morals Without Principles*.

> When I am in a situation, as perhaps I always am, in which more than one of these *prima facie* duties is incumbent on me, what I have to do is to study the situation as fully as I can until I form the considered opinion (it is never more) that in the circumstances one of them is more incumbent than any other; then I am bound to think that to do this *prima facie* duty is my duty *sans phrase* in the situation.[6]

This lack of implications from the set of principles in the cases I have discussed, which in most cases constitute abstract thought experiments, is more of a problem for the theory advocated by Ross than for this book. The more content a theory has, empirical (as in the sciences) or intuitive (as in moral philosophy), the better. So, again, if we should resort to particularism as a very last alternative, we should resort to intuitionism of Ross's variety only as next to this very last alternative. Before we do any such thing, however, we should try to see whether we can find a theory with definite implications about the cases we have discussed, when we see all three approaches here examined as providing us with intellectual resources. The idea is to combine *elements* from utilitarianism, deontology (in its both main versions), and the moral rights theory into something one could speak of as common sense morality. Such a combined theory would be very complex, but if it turned out that it had intuitive content, and was intuitively adequate, then the intellectual price in terms of its complexity might be worth paying.

3. COMMON SENSE MORALITY

It is doubtful whether there exists any morality that deserves to be called a 'common sense' morality. We have seen in the survey that the moral opinions people hold depend on cultural differences. So if a common sense morality should be a morality people hold in

6. W. D. Ross, *The Right and the Good*, p. 19.

common, we may have to speak of different moralities for different communities. Moreover, it is likely that there are also individual idiosyncrasies. Perhaps there are certain basic intuitions that people would agree about, if they were to submit them to cognitive psychotherapy, but ordinary people, just like moral philosophers, hold moral theories as well, and these theories help them to project their moral views unto unknown cases in bewilderingly different ways.

However, be all this as it may, it still seems as though we could construct a morality, with the resources given by the three theories I have examined in this book, which is close to what has sometimes been *called* common sense morality. I think of the kind of morality *criticized* by Shelly Kagan,[7] to wit, a morality with both options (or prerogatives[8]) allowing that there are limits to the sacrifices you must make in order to maximize the sum total of happiness in the world, as well as constraints on what you are allowed to do in order to maximize the sum total of happiness in the world. Perhaps some morality of this kind, for all the problems with it pointed out by Kagan, could be designed in such a way as to render it intuitively adequate in the field here examined, to wit, within the ethics of killing.

3.1. Some Options and Relaxed Constraints

Irrespective of whether it is a misnomer or not, let us speak of this kind of morality as common sense morality. It takes as its point of departure utilitarianism. We ought to maximize the sum total of happiness.

The requirement that we should maximize the sum total of happiness in the world is not strict, however. From the moral rights theory we borrow the idea that sometimes we may do as we see fit. In particular, we are not required to help people in distress, if this would take too much of an effort from us. We depart from the moral

7. Shelly Kagan, *The Limits of Morality*.

8. This is a term used by Samuel Scheffler in *The Rejection of Consequentialism*.

rights theory, however, in that we insist that, if we can *easily* maximize happiness, this is what we ought to do. We have *some* obligation to help people in distress, then.

From deontology as well as the moral rights theory we borrow the idea that some actions are wrong, period. We are not allowed to murder in order to improve the situation in the world. And we are not allowed to commit murder even if it is very *hard* for us not to do so. The restrictions trump the options. However, this idea of restrictions or side-constraints may have been put too strictly in both deontology and the moral rights theory. When I presented the ideas, I left it open whether they should include an escape clause for cases where disaster would ensue unless the restrictions were violated. Let us here make such a disaster clause part of common sense morality. If we can only save the entire world, or even very *many* lives, if we murder, this may be permitted, after all. However, we are not allowed to commit murder for trifle things. In particular, we are not allowed to murder only because the prize to us ourselves of not committing murder is high.

It may also be that deontology went wrong when it insisted that suicide (and assisted suicide, or euthanasia) was morally just as bad as murder. We remember that this was also Wittgenstein's view. If anything is strictly forbidden, he claimed, it is suicide. He, too, may have been mistaken. Perhaps murder is forbidden, but not suicide. This is how I will understand common sense morality. We borrow here the idea from the moral rights theory that we own ourselves.

Moreover, when deontology, in the form of the Sanctity-of-Life Doctrine, insists that abortion is just as bad as murder, it may again have gone astray. On the Kantian version of deontology, we remember, deontology is extensionally equivalent to utilitarianism in its dealing with abortion. We could side with Kant here in our understanding of common sense morality. It is only the intentional killing of *rational* beings that is prohibited. Some abortions, then, are right. No similar rationale can be constructed behind the killing (murder) of a grownup person.

It might be a good idea to allow common sense morality to operate with the principle of double effect, borrowed from the Sanctity-of-Life Doctrine, as well as the distinction between active and passive killing, borrowed from the moral rights theory. Furthermore, when common sense morality borrows from deontology, it should avoid incorporating Kant's prohibition against using people as mere means. At least when this happens for a noble end, it should be allowed. Then common sense morality can concur in the verdicts on the trolley cases delivered by utilitarianism and the Sanctity-of-Life Doctrine. Here much more would be needed to say if we wanted to make sense of common sense morality, of course. What has now been said is sufficient for my present purposes, however.

Once again, my claim is not that what I have now adumbrated *can* be worked out as a consistent and compelling moral theory. Perhaps it cannot. My quest is different. *If* it could be worked out as a consistent moral theory, *would* it be intuitively adequate? It seems to me that it wouldn't. But if this is correct, we can set it to one side even before we have tried to find out if it could be given a form where it has answers to Shelly Kagan's and other philosophers' complaints.

3.2. Common Sense and My Considered Intuitions

The common sense morality here adumbrated can handle our intuitions about the trolley cases. It allows for a flip of the switch in order to save the five, even in the Loop. We saw that even the Sanctity-of-Life Doctrine could handle that case, unless we understood it to incorporate the Kantian idea that we are not allowed to use human beings as mere means. I have not included this obscure idea in my characterization of common sense morality, however. Common sense morality can cater for our intuitions about killing in war (when we decide about the international laws, we rely on utilitarianism); it needs to be elaborated further in order to cater for our intuitions about non-human animals—which might be possible to do; and it can cater for our intuitions about abortion, euthanasia, and suicide (and has actually been devised to do that). I suppose it can side with utilitarianism in its assessment of capital punishment, and hence cater to our intuitions about capital punishment as well. But in that case we must also jettison Kant's retributivism. This seems to be a wise move to make anyway. It does cater to the intuition at variance with utilitarianism as well. It is obvious that it implies:

(6) A person is terminally ill, the rest of his life will provide him with much more suffering than pleasure, he realizes this, he is as clever and knowledgeable as I, but he still wants to go on with his life, claiming that he is not a hedonistic utilitarian; he is prepared to endure, he claims. Under the circumstances, it would be wrong to kill him (merely in his own interest), even if this could be done in a manner that is painless and not noticeable for him.

However, there seems to be no way that we can revise it without giving it up, in order to make it cater to the rest of the intuitions with regard to murder. It is clearly at variance with:

(4) A woman is stalked by her ex-husband. He does not threaten to kill her, but he never leaves her alone and she thinks that this makes life meaningless for her. She asks the police for help but receives none. She then kills her ex. She comes forward and assumes responsibility for her action, but claims that she had no choice. It *is* possible that she did the right thing.

And it is also at variance with:

(5) If I can save lives, by committing a singular murder, and if there are no bad side effects, then I ought to commit this murder.

Or, it is at variance with (5) unless, by a singular murder, I can save very *many* lives. But that is not assumed in (5). According to (5), it is right to murder one individual in order to save two lives.

4. ARE WE AT AN IMPASSE?

We have seen that no theory examined so far is intuitively adequate within the field of killing. There seem to be two possible reactions to this finding that remain, to accept that we cannot find any deep understanding of our considered intuitions (with reference to intuitively adequate moral principles), and turn either to particularism or intuitionism as defended by Jonathan Dancy and by W. D. Ross, respectively, or we can, after all, find a way of debunking our intuition (6) and accepting utilitarianism. I will now try out that possibility by once again turning to cognitive psychotherapy. Let us once again consider:

(6) A person is terminally ill, the rest of his life will provide him with much more suffering than pleasure, he realizes this, he is as clever and knowledgeable as I, but he still wants to go on with his life, claiming that he is not a hedonistic utilitarian; he is prepared to endure, he claims. Under the circumstances, it would be wrong to kill him (merely in his own interest), even if this could be done in a manner that is painless and not noticeable for him.

If it is right to kill one in order to save two (where there are no bad side effects), why is it not right to kill this person, in order to spare *him* terrible and unnecessary suffering?

Could this intuition be the result of the use of some heuristic device of the kind discussed in relation to the Footbridge case? Evolution has made us reluctant to kill upfront in a manner that involves personal force. This device leads us right most of the time, hence it is there, and hence it is a good thing to keep it. Yet, in a particular abstract thought experiment, it may have led us astray. Can something similar be plausibly said about (6)?

As already noted, this does not strike me as convincing in the case under consideration. There is nothing said about how I would kill him. However, since he is in hospital, I suppose I could just give him some kind of injection (adding poison to an infusion that has already been provided for him). Technically speaking, even if it means murder, this is no different from euthanasia.

Perhaps this is rather the mechanism working. When he makes his choice, which is the wrong one, no one but he himself has to suffer the consequences. But then he is also himself to blame, I tend to think. I need not cater for his needs. It would have been different had he hurt someone else with his unwise choice. Then I would have had to interfere.

This may be *part* of the explanation as to why (6) strikes me as correct. And to the extent that it is, this must be seen as something that could be part of a debunking explanation of (6). For, certainly, this is a kind of very primitive thinking, which I am capable of, in some circumstances, but which I cannot seriously endorse. It is no better than my lust for revenge when a child of mine has been murdered. He does in no way *deserve* to suffer.

There may exist another explanation as to why (6) strikes me as correct, however. If I act on my favoured moral theory in this case, to wit, hedonistic utilitarianism, then this may be seen as terribly *arrogant*. After all, my colleague, who is not a hedonistic utilitarian, has thought just as hard about moral theory as I have. Should not this give me pause?

It should—in our seminar room. There we have often met and discussed the matter. He has not been able to convince me that hedonistic utilitarianism is wrong, but I realize that my belief to the effect that it is correct is not a very strong one. I am much more certain that there is a table in front of me in the seminar room, that several people are there, engaged in a discussion, than I am that hedonistic utilitarianism is true. Hedonistic utilitarianism is not self-evidently true. It is possible that there exists evidence (considered intuitions) such that, would I come by it, would make me reject hedonistic utilitarianism. It is likely that this will always be the case with our moral views, irrespective of how much effort we devote to the testing of them. All this means that it would indeed be arrogant of me to just claim that I am right and he is wrong—in the seminar room. However, when I realize this, my intuition that it would be wrong to kill him withers. My killing him doesn't represent any rude manners in the seminar room. It just means that I try honestly to make the world a better place. And I act on the best understanding available to me.

Note that this humble thought of mine, that I might be wrong, does not reflect any hesitation between hedonism and any other view in particular on what matters in life. It is not an example of what has been called moral uncertainty. It is not that my credence in hedonistic utilitarianism is something like 75 per cent while my credence in the view of my colleague is 25 per cent. I have no credence at all in his view. And yet, I realize that I *might* be wrong.

However, the seminar room is one thing. There we need not act on our beliefs. That's why we call our seminar room, at the department of philosophy in Stockholm, our metaphysical laboratory. In the seminar room the only experiments we perform are thought experiments. Our actual lives are quite another thing. Are we not *bound* to act on our moral beliefs, once we leave the seminar room and lead our lives? So what would represent arrogance in the seminar room may well represent an honest and conscientious attempt to do what we ought to do, outside the seminar room. Would it not be irrational to make exceptions in cases like these from our justified moral beliefs? Must we not follow their directions, even when we project our justified moral beliefs onto unknown territory, where we (now) hold no firm intuitions (any more)?

Frank Jackson may seem to disagree. I suppose he holds that we should act on our best empirical beliefs. However, when it comes to moral beliefs, he seems to hesitate. Or at least this is one way of understanding him when he writes:

> Most of us take a very different attitude to abortion as opposed to infanticide: we allow that the first is permissible in many circumstances, but that the second is hardly ever permissible, and yet it is hard to justify this disparity in moral judgement in the sense of finding a relevant difference. Some think that we should abandon the disparity—by changing our attitude to infanticide, or our attitude to abortion. Most of us think that we should look harder for the relevant difference.[9]

9. Frank Jackson, *From Metaphysics to Ethics. A Defence of Conceptual Analysis*, p. 134.

Of course, a way of understanding this is as follows. Intuitively we see a difference between abortion and infanticide. So unless we find a moral theory that can cater for the difference, we must remain moral sceptics. However, on a different reading Jackson wants us to stick to our traditional way of making a distinction between abortion and infanticide, even if we see no principled difference, and even if we hold no considered intuition about this. We just want to go with the majority opinion. But that strikes *me* as unreasonable.

Tentatively I conclude, then, that my intuition (6) has to go. It was mistaken. It was based both on the primitive idea that my colleague was himself to blame for his plight, and the idea that it would somehow be arrogant of me to act on my otherwise favoured moral theory (as if I had not listened to his arguments in the seminar room). And, together with this intuition, my colleague has to go as well. The 'intuition' expressed in (6) has been given a debunking explanation. When I believe (6), I do so because I conflate how I should think in the seminar room with how I should think when leading my life. Utilitarianism is intuitively adequate, after all. But then, being morally conscientious, being eager to make the world a better place, if I can, I act on it.

What if I *cannot* do this? After all, if I perform this action, I act from a character that one should probably not have. In relation to a friend, one should, as a rule of thumb, rather be prepared to do for him what he likes to be done to him, than what I would have liked him to do to me, were I in his position. What if my inhibition, created by my having adopted that kind of character trait, is so strong that I do not act? *Tant pis*, then, not for me, but for my colleague! I can comfort myself with the thought that this is blameless wrongdoing on my part. The colleague is the one who has to suffer the consequences of my acting in rather than out of my good character.

5. CONCLUSION

Utilitarianism is intuitively adequate in the field here examined, the ethics of killing. It is uniquely adequate, so there is no way in which either deontology or the moral rights theory can explain our (my) considered intuitions in any superior way. They cannot explain them at all.

This does not mean that I have shown that utilitarianism is true. In particular, I have not shown that hedonistic utilitarianism is true. I have glanced over the problem of what it is that should be maximized, according to utilitarianism. I do believe that hedonistic utilitarianism is the most promising version of utilitarianism, but this is not something I have even attempted to show in the present context.

Moreover, and more importantly, I have just discussed one narrow field, the ethics of killing. This is a field where crucial experiments have been possible to set up for a test of utilitarianism in a competition with deontology (in both its versions, as Kantianism and as the Sanctity-of-Life Doctrine) and the moral rights theory. And this seems to be the field where deontology and the moral rights theory are as plausible as possible. If anything is absolutely prohibited, it should be murder. If there is anything an individual can own, it should be himself! Moreover, this is a field where many would have expected utilitarianism, with its insistence that the end justifies the means, to be in troubled water. So it is of no small consequence when it has been shown that utilitarianism does indeed gain the upper hand in this competition.

However, there are many other fields where utilitarianism could and should be confronted with other theories as well. For example, in problems to do with the *distribution* of happiness (or whatever currency you refer to in your favoured moral theory), utilitarianism must compete with egalitarian and prioritarian theories.

To arrange such a competition must be the task for some other occasion, however.

REFERENCES

Ahlenius, Henrik, and Torbjörn Tännsjö, 'Chinese and Westerners Respond Differently to the Trolley Dilemmas', *Journal of Cognition and Culture*, Vol. 12, 2012, pp. 195–201.

Allen, Woody, *Without Feathers* (New York: Random House, 1972).

Allmark, Peter et al., 'Is the Doctrine of Double Effect Irrelevant in End-of-Life Decision Making?', *Nursing Philosophy*, Vol. 11, 2010.

Andersson, Anna-Karin, *Libertarianism and Potential Agents* (Stockholm: Stockholm Studies in Philosophy, 2007).

Aquinas, Thomas, '*Summa Theologica*', in Anton C. Pegis (ed.), *Basic Writings of Saint Thomas Aquinas*, Vol. 1 (New York: Random House, 1945).

Arrhenius, Gustaf, *Population Ethics* (Oxford: Oxford UP, 2016).

Balaguer, Mark, *Free Will as an Open Scientific Problem* (Cambridge, MA: MIT Press, 2010).

Bales, R. Eugene, 'Act-Utilitarianism; Account of Right-Making Characteristics or Decision-Making Procedure?', *American Philosophical Quarterly*, Vol. 8, 1971, pp. 257–265.

Beccaria, Cesare, *Dei delitti e delle pene* (Leghorn, false imprint Haarlem, 1764). First English edition: *An Essay on Crimes and Punishments*, translated from the Italian; with a commentary, attributed to Mons. de Voltaire, translated from the French (London, 1767).

Bennett, Jonathan, *Morality and Consequences*, The Tanner Lectures on Human Values II (Salt Lake City: University of Utah Press, 1981), pp. 110–111.

——— *The Act Itself* (Oxford: Oxford University Press, 1995).

Bentham, Jeremy, *An Introduction to the Principles of Morals and Legislation*, ed. by J. H. Burns and H. L. A. Hart (London: Methuen, 1970).

Bentham, Jeremy, *A Plan for a Universal and Perpetual Peace*, http://www.laits.utexas.edu/poltheory/bentham/pil/pil.e04.html.

Bergström, Lars, 'Quine, Underdetermination, and Skepticism', *Journal of Philosophy*, Vol. 90, 1993.

Berker, Selim, 'The Normative Insignificance of Neuroscience', *Philosophy and Public Affairs*, Vol. 37, 2009, pp. 293–329.

Berndt-Rasmussen, Katharina, 'Should the Probabilities Count?', *Philosophical Studies*, Vol. 59, 2012, pp. 205–218.

Bernheim, J. I., and A. Mullie, 'Euthanasia and Palliative Care in Belgium: Legitimate Concerns and Unsubstantial Grievances', *Journal of Palliative Medicine*, Vol. 13, 2010, pp. 798–799.

Bloom, Paul, *Just Babies: The Origins of Good and Evil* (New York: Crown Publishers, 2013).

Brandt, Richard B., *Ethical Theory: The Problems of Normative and Critical Ethics* (Englewood Cliffs, NJ: Prentice Hall, 1959).

——— 'Utilitarianism and the Rules of War', *Philosophy and Public Affairs*, Vol. 1, 1972, pp. 145–165.

——— *A Theory of the Good and the Right* (Oxford: Clarendon Press, 1979).

Brock, Dan W., 'From the Moral Rights' Perspective', in Torbjörn Tännsjö (ed.), *Terminal Sedation: Euthanasia in Disguise?* (Dordrecht: Kluwer, 2004).

Cappelen, Herman, *Philosophy Without Intuitions* (Oxford: Oxford University Press, 2012).

Cholbi, Michael, Entry on 'Suicide', in *Stanford Encyclopedia of Philosophy*, 2008, http://plato.stanford.edu/entries/suicide/.

Cohen, G. A., *Self-Ownership, Freedom, and Equality* (Cambridge: Cambridge University Press, 1995).

Conell, F. J., 'Double Effect, Principle of', in *The New Catholic Encyclopedia*, Vol. 4 (New York: McGraw-Hill, 1967), pp. 1020–1022.

Christiano, Tom, Entry on 'Democracy' in the *Stanford Encylopedia of Philosophy*, accessible at http://plato.stanford.edu/entries/democracy/.

Cosculluela, Victor, *The Ethics of Suicide* (New York: Garland, 1995).

Dancy, Jonathan, *Moral Reasons* (Oxford: Blackwell, 1993).

——— *Morals Without Principles* (Oxford: Clarendon, 2003).

Descartes, René, *Discourse on Method*; comments on animals, reprinted in Tom Regan and Peter Singer (eds.), *Animal Rights and Human Obligations*, Second edition (Englewood Cliffs, NJ: Prentice Hall, 1989).

Donagan, Alan, *The Theory of Morality* (Chicago: The University of Chicago Press, 1977).

Dworkin, Ronald, *Life's Dominion. An Argument About Abortion, Euthanasia, and Individual Freedom* (New York: Random House, 1994).

Estlund, David, 'On Following Orders in an Unjust War', *Journal of Political Philosophy*, Vol. 15, 2007, pp. 213–234.

Feigl, Herbert, 'Validation and Vindication', reprinted in *Readings in Ethical Theory*, selected and edited by Wilfrid Sellars and John Hospers (New York: Appleton-Century-Crofts, 1952).

Feldman, Fred, 'Actual Utility, the Objection from Impracticality, and the Move from Expected Utility', *Philosophical Studies*, Vol. 101, 2006, pp. 49–79.

——— 'Death and the Disintegration of Personality', in Ben Bradley, Fred Feldman, and Jens Johansson (eds.), *Oxford Handbook of Philosophy and Death* (Oxford: Oxford University Press, 2012).

Finnis, John, *Fundamentals of Ethics* (Washington: Georgetown University Press, 1983).

Fohr, Susan Andersson, 'The Double Effect in Pain Medication: Separating Myth from Reality', *Journal of Palliative Medicine*, Vol. 1, 1998, p. 319.

Foot, Philippa, 'The Problem of Abortion and the Doctrine of the Double Effect', in *Virtues and Vices* (Oxford: Basil Blackwell, 1978).

——— 'Morality, Action and Outcome', in Ted Hondrich (ed.), *Morality and Objectivity* (London: Routledge and Kegan Paul, 1985), pp. 23–38.

Gauthier, David, *Morals by Agreement* (Oxford: Clarendon Press, 1986).

Geddes, L., 'On the Intrinsic Wrongness of Killing Innocent People', *Analysis*, Vol. 34, 1973.

Glover, Jonathan, *Causing Death and Saving Lives* (London: Penguin, 1977).

Greene, Joshua D. et al., 'The Neural Bases of Cognitive Conflict and Control in Moral Judgment', *Neuron*, 44(2), 2004, pp. 389–400.

——— *Moral Tribes: Emotion, Reason, and the Gap Between Us and Them* (New York: Penguin, 2013).

Greene, Joshua D., Fiery A. Cushman, Lisa E. Stewart, Kelly Lowenberg, Leight E. Nystrom, and Jonathan D. Cohen, 'Pushing Moral Buttons: The Interaction Between Personal Force and Intention in Moral Judgement', *Cognition*, Vol. 30, 2009.

Grubb, Andrew et al., 'Survey of British Clinicians' Views on Management of Patients in Persistent Vegetative State', *Lancet*, Vol. 348, 1996, pp. 35–40.

Hampton, Jean, 'An Expressive Theory of Retribution', in W. Cragg (ed.), *Retributivism and Its Critics* (Stuttgart: Fritz Steiner Verlag, 1992), pp. 1–25.

Harman, Gilbert, *The Nature of Morality* (Oxford: Oxford University Press, 1977).

Harris, John, 'The Survival Lottery', *Philosophy*, Vol. 50, 1975, pp. 81–87, reprinted in Helga Kuhse and Peter Singer, *Bioethics. An Anthology* (Oxford: Blackwell, 1999), pp. 399–403. Quoted from Kuhse's and Singer's anthology.

Hauser, Marc, Fiery Cushman et al., 'A Dissociation Between Moral Judgments and Justifications', *Mind & Language*, Vol. 22, 2007, pp. 1–21.

Hawton, Keith, and Kees van Heeringen, 'Suicide', *Lancet*, Vol. 379, 2009, pp. 1372–1381.

Hirschman, Albert O., *The Rhetoric of Reaction: Perversity, Futility, Jeopardy* (Cambridge, MA: The Belknap Press of Harvard University Press, 1991).

Hooker, Brad, *Ideal Code, Real World: A Rule-Consequentialist Theory of Morality* (Oxford: Oxford University Press, 2000).

Huemer, Michael, 'In Defence of Repugnance', *Mind*, Vol. 117, 2008, pp. 899–933.

Hurka, Thomas, 'Liability and Just Cause', *Ethics and International Affairs*, Vol. 20, 2007, 199–218.

Inwagen, Peter van, 'When the Will Is Not Free', *Philosophical Studies*, Vol. 75, 1994, pp. 95–113.

Jackson, Frank, *From Metaphysics to Ethics. A Defence of Conceptual Analysis* (Oxford: Clarendon Press, 1998).

Johansson, Jens, 'What Is Animalism?', *Ratio*, Vol. 20, 2007, pp. 194–205.

Kamm, Frances, *Intricate Ethics: Rights, Responsibilities, and Responsible Harm* (Oxford: Oxford University Press, 2007).

——— 'The Morality of Killing in War', in Ben Bradley, Fred Feldman, and Jens Johansson (eds.), *Oxford Handbook of Philosophy and Death* (Oxford: Oxford University Press, 2012), pp. 432–464.

Kagan, Shelly, 'The Additive Fallacy', *Ethics*, Vol. 99, 1988, pp. 5–31.

——— *The Limits of Morality* (Oxford: Clarendon, 1989).

Kahane, Guy, 'On the Wrong Track: Process and Content in Moral Psychology', *Mind and Language*, Vol. 25, 2012, pp. 519–545.

Kahane, G., Everett, J. A. C., Earp, B., Farias, M., and Savulescu, J., '"Utilitarian" Judgments in Sacrificial Moral Dilemmas Do Not Reflect Impartial Concern for the Greater Good', *Cognition*, Vol. 134, 2015, 193–209.

Kain, Patrick, 'Kant's Defense of Human Moral Status', *Journal of the History of Philosophy*, Vol. 47, 2009, pp. 59–102.

Kant, Immanuel, *On the Old Saw: That May Be Right in Theory But It Won't Work in Practice*, translated by E. B. Ashton (Philadelphia: University of Pennsylvania Press, 1974).

——— *Perpetual Peace and Other Essays*, translated with introduction by Ted Humphrey (Cambridge: Hackett Publishing Company, 1983).

——— *Groundwork of the Metaphysics of Morals*, edited by Mary Gregor and with an introduction by Christine M. Korsgaard (Cambridge: Cambridge University Press, 1997).

——— *Lectures on Ethics*, in P. Heath and J. Schneewind (eds.), *Lectures on Ethics* (Cambridge: Cambridge University Press, 1997).

——— *Metaphysical Elements of Justice*, 2nd edition translated with introduction and notes by John Ladd (Indianapolis: Hacket, 1999).

Kennedy, Randall L., 'McCleskey v. Kemp: Race, Capital Punishment, and the Supreme Court', *Harvard Law Review*, Vol. 101, 1988, pp. 1388–1443.

Keown, John, *Euthanasia, Ethics and Public Policy* (Cambridge: Cambridge University Press, 2002).

Koenig, Michael et al., 'Damage to the Prefrontal Cortex Increases Utilitarian Moral Judgements', *Nature*, Vol. 446, 2007, pp. 908–911.

Korsgaard, Christine M., *The Sources of Normativity* (New York: Cambridge University Press, 1996).

Lazari-Radek, Katarzyna de, and Peter Singer, 'The Objectivity of Ethics and the Unity of Practical Reason', *Ethics*, Vol. 123, 2012, pp. 9–31.

Liao, Mathew, 'The Loop Case and Kamm's Doctrine of Triple Effect', *Philosophical Studies*, Vol. 146, 2009, pp. 223–231.

Lillehammer, Hallvard, 'Voluntary Euthanasia and the Logical Slippery Slope Argument', *Cambridge Law Journal*, Vol. 61, 2002, pp. 545–550.

Lippert Rasmussen, Kasper, *Deontology, Responsibility, and Equality* (Copenhagen: University of Copenhagen, 2005).

——— 'Why Killing Some People Is More Seriously Wrong than Killing Others', *Ethics*, Vol. 117, 2007, pp. 716–738.

——— 'Against Self-Ownership: There Are No Fact-Insensitive Ownership Rights over One's Body', *Philosophy and Public Affairs*, Vol. 36, 2008, pp. 86–118.

Locke, John, *The Second Treatise of Government* (New York: Cambridge University Press, 1993).

McMahan, Jeff, 'Killing, Letting Die, and Withdrawing Aid', *Ethics*, Vol. 103, 1993, pp. 250–279.

——— *The Ethics of Killing. Problems at the Margins of Life* (Oxford: Oxford University Press, 2002).

——— *Killing in War* (Oxford: Oxford University Press, 2009).

Marquis, Don, 'Why Abortion Is Immoral', *Journal of Philosophy*, Vol. 86, 1989, pp. 183–220.

Marquis, Don, 'Abortion and Death', in Ben Bradley, Fred Feldman, and Jens Johansson (eds.), *Oxford Handbook of Philosophy and Death* (Oxford: Oxford University Press, 2012), pp. 409–431.

Mill, John Stuart, Speech before the British Parliament on 21 April 1868, in opposition to a bill banning capital punishment. http://web.mnstate.edu/gracyk/courses/web%20publishing/Mill_supports_death_penalty.htm.

Miller, Greg, 'The Roots of Morality', *Science*, Vol. 320, 2008, pp. 734–737.

Monk, Ray, *Ludwig Wittgenstein: The Duty of Genius* (London: Vintage, 1991).

Montgomery, Henry, and Torbjörn Tännsjö, 'Why Are People Reluctant to Push the Big Man off the Footbridge?' (unpublished manuscript).

Nadelhoffer, Thomas, and Adam Feltz, 'The Actor-Observer Bias and Moral Intuitions: Adding Fuel to Sinnott-Armstrong's Fire', *Neuroethics*, Vol. 1, 2008, pp. 133–144.

Nagel, Thomas, *The View from Nowhere* (Oxford: Oxford University Press, 1986).

Nozick, Robert, *Anarchy, State, and Utopia* (Oxford: Basil Blackwell, 1974).

——— *Philosophical Explanations* (Cambridge, MA: Belknap Press, 1981).

——— *The Examined Life: Philosophical Meditations* (New York: Simon and Schuster, 1989).

Okin, Susan Moller, *Justice, Gender, and the Family* (New York: Basic Books, 1989).

Olson, Erik, *The Human Animal* (New York and Oxford: Oxford University Press, 1997).

Parfit, Derek, *Reasons and Persons* (Oxford: Clarendon, Oxford, 1984).

——— 'Postscript', in Jesper Ryberg and Torbjörn Tännsjö (eds.), *The Repugnant Conclusion* (Dordrecht: Kluwer, 2004), p. 257.

——— *On What Matters* (Oxford: Oxford University Press, 2011).

Petersson, Björn, 'Collective Responsibility and Omissions', *Philosophical Papers*, Vol. 37, 2008, pp. 243–261.

Popper, Karl, *Objective Knowledge* (Oxford: Clarendon Press, 1972).

Quinn, Warren S., 'Actions, Intentions, and Consequences: The Doctrine of Double Effect,' *Philosophy and Public Affairs*, Vol. 18, 1989, pp. 334–351.

——— *Morality and Action* (Cambridge: Cambridge University Press, 1993).

Rachels, James, in 'Active and Passive Euthanasia', *New England Journal of Medicine*, Vol. 292, No. 2, 1975, pp. 78–80.

Rawls, John, 'Two Concepts of Rules', *Philosophical Review*, Vol. 64, 1955, pp. 3–32.

——— *A Theory of Justice* (Cambridge, MA: Harvard University Press, 1971).

Regan, Tom, *The Case for Animal Rights*, updated and with a new preface (Berkeley: University of California Press, 1983/2004).

Reichberg, Gregory M., 'Just War and Regular War: Competing Paradigms', in David Rodin and Henry Shue (eds.), *Just and Unjust Warriors. The Moral and Legal Status of Soldiers* (Oxford: Oxford University Press, 2008), pp. 193–213.

Rietjens, Judith A. C., Paul J. van der Maas, Bregje D. Onwuteaka-Philipsen, Johannes J. M. van Delden, och Agnes van der Heide, 'Two Decades of Research on Euthanasia from the Netherlands. What Have We Learnt and What Questions Remain?', *Journal of Bioethical Inquiry*, Vol. 6, 2009, pp. 271–283.

Ross, W. D., *The Right and the Good* (Oxford: Clarendon, 1930/1973).

Ryberg, Jesper, *The Ethics of Proportionate Punishment: A Critical Investigation* (Dordrecht: Kluwer, 2005).

Ryder, Richard D., *Victims of Science: The Use of Animals in Research* (Davis-Poynter, 1975).

Scanlon, Thomas, *What We Owe to Each Other* (Cambridge, MA: The Belknap Press of Harvard University Press, 1998).

Scheffler, Samuel, *The Rejection of Consequentialism*, revised edition (Oxford: Clarendon, 1994).

Sidgwick, Henry, *The Methods of Ethics*, Seventh Edition (London: Macmillan, 1907), pp. 428–429.

Singer, Peter, *Practical Ethics*, Third Edition (Cambridge: Cambridge University Press, 1979/2011).

——— *Rethinking Life and Death. The Collapse of Our Traditional Ethics* (New York: St. Martin's Griffin, 1994).

——— 'Ethics and Intuitions', *Journal of Ethics*, Vol. 9, 2005, pp. 331–352.

Smart, J. J. C., and Bernard Williams, *Utilitarianism. For and Against* (Cambridge: Cambridge University Press, 1973).

Steiner, Hillel, *An Essay on Rights* (Cambridge, MA: Blackwell Publisher, 1994).

Stephen, James Fitzjames, 'On Capital Punishment', *Fraser's Magazine*, 1864.

Sumner, L. W., *Assisted Death. A Study in Ethics and Law* (Oxford: Oxford University Press, 2011).

Sunstein, Cass R., and Adrian Vermeule, 'Is Capital Punishment Morally Required? Acts, Omissions, and Life-Life Tradeoffs', *Stanford Law Review*, Vol. 58, 2006.

Tännsjö, Torbjörn, 'Blameless Wrongdoing', *Ethics*, Vol. 106, 1995, pp. 120–127, reprinted in *Writing Social Justice in the Arts and Humanities* (Roosevelt University: Prentice, 2003).

——— *Hedonistic Utilitarianism. A Defence* (Edinburgh: Edinburgh University Press, 1998).

——— *Du skall understundom dräpa* (Stockholm: Prisma, 2001).

Tännsjö, Torbjörn, 'Why We Ought to Accept the Repugnant Conclusion', *Utilitas*, Vol. 14, 2002, pp. 339–59, reprinted in Jesper Ryberg and Torbjörn Tännsjö (eds.), *The Repugnant Conclusion. Essays on Population Ethics* (Dordrecht: Kluwer, 2004).

——— *Terminal Sedation: Euthanasia in Disguise* (Dordrecht: Kluwer, 2004).

——— *Zur Ethik des Tötens. Neue Anstösse zur Reflexion eines umstrittenen Problems* (Berlin: LIT Verlag, 2006).

——— 'The Myth of Innocence. On Collective Responsibility and Collective Punishment', *Philosophical Papers*, Vol. 36, 2007, pp. 295–314.

Tännsjö, Torbjörn, *Noen ganger skal man drepe* (Oslo: Pax, 2007).

——— 'Why No Compromise is Possible', *Metaphilosophy*, Vol. 38, pp. 330–343, reprinted in Lori Gruen, Laura Grabel, and Peter Singer (eds), *Stem Cell Research: The Ethical Issues* (Oxford: Blackwell, 2007).

——— *Global Democracy. The Case for a World Government*, 2nd edition (Edinburgh: Edinburgh University Press, 2014).

———*Animal Ethics* (Stockholm: Thales, 2010).

——— *From Reasons to Norms. On the Basic Question in Ethics* (Dordrecht: Springer, 2010).

——— 'Sophie's Choice', Ward Jones and Samantha Wise, *Ethics in Film* (Oxford: Oxford University Press, 2010).

———'Applied Ethics. A Defence', *Ethical Theory and Moral Practice*, Vol. 14, 2011, pp. 397–406.

——— 'The Ethics of Killing. An Example: Abortion', in Rysiek Sliwinski and Frans Svensson (eds.), *Neither/Nor. Philosophical Papers Dedicated to Erik Carlson on the Occasion of His Fiftieth Birthday* (Uppsala: Uppsala Philosophical Studies 28, 2011).

——— 'Capital Punishment', in Ben Bradley, Fred Feldman, and Jens Johansson (eds.), *Oxford Handbook of Philosophy and Death* (Oxford: Oxford University Press, 2012).

——— 'Hedonism', entry in James E. Crimmins (ed.), *The Bloomsbury Encyclopedia of Utilitarianism* (London and New York: Bloomsbury Academic, 2013).

——— *Understanding Ethics*, 3rd revised edition (Edinburgh: Edinburgh University Press, 2013).

———"Morality and Personal Identity", in *Festschrift to Peter Gärdenfors*, http://www.lucs.lu.se/spinning/categories/moral/Tannsjo/index.html.

——— 'Moral Epistemilogy and the Survival Lottery', in John Coggon, Sarah Chan, Soren Holm, and Thomasine Kushner (eds.), *From Reason to Practice in Bioethics: An anthology dedicated to the works of John Harris*, (Manchester: Manchester University Press, 2015).

Taurek, John, 'Should the Numbers Count?', *Philosophy and Public Affairs*, Vol. 6, 1977, pp. 293–316.

Tersman, Folke, 'Should We Worry about Opposing Intuitions?' (in review).

Thomson, Judith Jarvis, 'A Defense of Abortion', *Philosophy and Public Affairs*, Vol. 1, 1971, pp. 47–66, reprinted in Helga Kuhse and Peter Singer (eds.), *Bioethics. An Anthology* (Oxford: Blackwell, 1999), pp. 36–45. Quoted from the anthology.

——— 'The Right to Privacy', *Philosophy and Public Affairs*, Vol. 4, 1975, 295–314.

———'Killing, Letting Die, and the Trolley Problem', 59 *The Monist*, Vol. 59, 1976, pp. 204–217.

———'Physician Assisted Suicide: Two Moral Arguments', *Ethics*, Vol. 109, 1999, pp. 497–518.

———'Turning the Trolley', *Philosophy and Public Affairs*, Vol. 36, 2008, pp. 359–374.

Tooley, Michael, 'Abortion and Infanticide', *Philosophy and Public Affairs*, Vol. 2, 1972, pp. 37–65, reprinted in Helga Kuhse and Peter Singer (eds.), *Bioethics. An Anthology* (Oxford: Blackwell, 1999), pp. 21–35. Quoted from the anthology.

Uniacke, Suzanne, *Permissible Killing* (Cambridge: Cambridge University Press, 1994).

——— 'Self-Defence, Just War and a Reasonable Prospect of Success', in Helen Frowe and Gerald Lang (eds.), *How We Fight: Ethics in War* (Oxford: Oxford University Press, 2014).

Vallentyne, Peter, Hillel Steiner, and Michael Otsuka', `Why Left-Libertarianism Is Not Incoherent, Indeterminate, or Irrelevant: A Reply to Fried', *Philosophy & Public Affairs*, Vol. 36, 2005, pp. 201–222.

Velleman, David J., 'A Right to Self-Determination', *Ethics*, Vol. 109, 1999. pp. 606–628.

Walzer, Michael, *Just and Unjust Wars. A Moral Argument with Historical Illustrations* (New York: Basic Books, 1977).

Wellman, Christopher Heath, 'The Rights Forfeiture Theory of Punishment', *Ethics*, Vol. 122, 2012, pp. 371–393.

WHO *World Report on Violence and Health*, World Health Organization, Geneva (2002).

Williams, Bernard, 'Consequentialism and Integrity', in J. J. C. Smart and Bernard Williams (eds.), *Utilitarianism. For and Against* (Cambridge: Cambridge University Press, 1973).

———*Ethics and the Limits of Philosophy* (London: Fontana, 1985).

Wittgenstein, Ludwig, *Notebooks 1914–1916*, trans. G. E. M. Anscombe (New York: Harper, 1961).

INDEX